# HOUSE OF LORDS

# Companion to the Standing Orders and Guide to the Proceedings of the House of Lords

D1428613

Laid before the House by the Clerk of the Parliaments
2013

# PREFACE

This is the 23rd edition of the Companion to the Standing Orders of the House of Lords since Sir John Shaw-Lefevre, then Clerk of the Parliaments, compiled his first edition for private circulation in 1862. It is issued with the authority of the Procedure Committee.

The Companion is the authoritative guide to procedure, but it is by no means the only source of information for members. A summary of key elements of procedure is given in the Brief Guide on *Procedure and Practice in the House and Grand Committee*, while general services are covered in the *Handbook on facilities and services for Members*. Members may also consult the *Guide to the Code of Conduct*, the *Guide to Financial Support for Members* (from the Finance Department) and the booklets on participation in legislative business issued by the Legislation Office. All such guidance is available online. The Table Clerks and procedural offices are always available to advise members.


DAVID BEAMISH
Clerk of the Parliaments

# TABLE OF CONTENTS

## CHAPTER 4: CONDUCT IN THE HOUSE ..................................... 61

6

# ABBREVIATIONS

| | |
|---|---|
| *Erskine May* | *Erskine May's Treatise on The Law, Privileges and Usage of Parliament*, 24th edition, 2011 |
| GO | General Order (see paragraph 9.94) |
| HL Deb. | House of Lords Official Report (Hansard) |
| LJ | House of Lords Journals |
| PBSO | Private Business Standing Order |
| SO | Public Business Standing Order |

# REFERENCES TO HOUSE OF LORDS COMMITTEE REPORTS

| | |
|---|---|
| Leave of Absence | House of Lords (Leave of Absence) Select Committee |
| Offices | Select Committee on the House of Lords' Offices |
| Procedure | Select Committee on Procedure of the House |

# CHAPTER 1
# THE HOUSE AND ITS MEMBERSHIP

## Composition of the House

1.01    The following are members of the House of Lords:

- Lords Spiritual:
    - the Archbishops of Canterbury and York;
    - the Bishops of London, Durham and Winchester;
    - twenty-one other diocesan bishops of the Church of England according to seniority of appointment to diocesan sees;
- Lords Temporal:
    - Lords created for life under the Appellate Jurisdiction Act 1876 (as amended) to serve as Lords of Appeal in Ordinary;[1]
    - Life Peers created under the Life Peerages Act 1958;
    - 90 Hereditary Peers elected under SO 9[2] or 10 pursuant to the House of Lords Act 1999;
    - The Earl Marshal;[3]
    - The Lord Great Chamberlain.[4]

## Disqualification for membership

1.02    The following are disqualified for membership of the House of Lords:

- those under the age of twenty-one;[5]

---

[1]  The Appellate Jurisdiction Act 1876 was repealed by Schedule 7 of the Constitutional Reform Act 2005, but Lords previously created under the Act remain members of the House.

[2]  SO followed by a number refers to the standing orders relating to public business. PBSO followed by a number refers to the standing orders governing private business.

[3]  House of Lords Act 1999, s. 2(2).

[4]  House of Lords Act 1999, s. 2(2).

[5]  SO 2.

- aliens

    By the Act of Settlement 1701[1] "no person born out of the Kingdoms of England, Scotland or Ireland, or the Dominions thereunto belonging ... (except such as are born of English parents)" may be a member of the House of Lords. By virtue of a modification contained in the British Nationality Act 1981,[2] this provision does not apply to Commonwealth citizens or citizens of the Republic of Ireland. Under the 1981 Act,[3] "Commonwealth citizen" means a British citizen, a British Overseas Territories citizen, a British subject under that Act, or a citizen of an independent Commonwealth country;

- those convicted of treason

    The Forfeiture Act 1870 provides that anyone convicted of treason shall be disqualified for sitting or voting as a member of the House of Lords until he has either suffered his term of imprisonment or received a pardon;

- bankrupts

    Under the Insolvency Act 1986,[4] a member of the House (a) who, in England and Wales or Northern Ireland, is subject to a bankruptcy restrictions order (including an interim order) or a bankruptcy restrictions undertaking; (b) who, in England and Wales, is subject to a debt relief restrictions order (including an interim order) or a debt relief restrictions undertaking; or (c) in Scotland, whose estate is sequestered, is disqualified for sitting and voting in the House of Lords or in any committee of the House. A writ is not issued to any person who would otherwise be entitled to one while he is so disqualified. The court or, in the case of a bankruptcy restrictions undertaking or debt relief restrictions undertaking, the government, notifies

---

[1] s. 3.

[2] Schedule 7. See also s. 47 of the Constitutional Reform and Governance Act 2010.

[3] s. 37.

[4] s. 426A and s. 427 as amended by the Enterprise Act 2002, the Tribunals, Courts and Enforcement Act 2008 and the Insolvency Act 1986 (Disqualification from Parliament) Order 2012.

the restriction or sequestration to the Lord Speaker and it is recorded in the Journals;

- Members of the European Parliament (MEPs)

  The European Parliament (House of Lords Disqualification) Regulations 2008 provide that any Life Peer who is elected to the European Parliament is disqualified for sitting and voting in the House of Lords or in any committee of the House or joint committee. A writ is not issued to a Life Peer who is disqualified under this regulation;

- Holders of disqualifying judicial office

  Under the Constitutional Reform Act 2005,[1] a member of the House who holds a disqualifying judicial office[2] is disqualified for sitting and voting in the House of Lords or in any committee of the House or joint committee. Such members are not however disqualified for receiving a writ of summons.

## Membership of the House under SOs 9 and 10

1.03   Section 1 of the House of Lords Act 1999 provides that "No-one shall be a member of the House of Lords by virtue of a hereditary peerage".[3] However, section 2 of the Act provides that 90 hereditary peers, and also the holders of the offices of Earl Marshal and Lord Great Chamberlain, shall be excepted from this general exclusion and shall remain as members for their lifetime or until a subsequent Act otherwise provides.

1.04   In accordance with SO 9, 75 of the 90 excepted hereditary peers were elected by the hereditary peers in their political party or Crossbench grouping.[4] The remaining 15 were elected by the whole House to act as Deputy Chairmen and other office-holders.[5]

---

[1]   s. 137.

[2]   Defined in the House of Commons Disqualification Act 1975, as amended, and the Northern Ireland Assembly Disqualification Act 1975, as amended.

[3]   Certain members of the House who sat formerly by virtue of a hereditary peerage now sit by virtue of a life peerage. Under SO 7 they use their higher title.

[4]   Under SO 9(2)(i), 2 peers were elected by the Labour hereditary peers, 42 by the Conservative hereditary peers, 3 by the Liberal Democrat hereditary peers, and 28 by the Crossbench hereditary peers.

[5]   The elections were held on 27–28 October 1999 and 3–4 November 1999. SO 9(2)(ii).

1.05   Under SO 10, any vacancy due to the death of one of the 90 is filled by holding a by-election. By-elections are conducted in accordance with arrangements made by the Clerk of the Parliaments and take place within three months of a vacancy occurring. If the vacancy is among the 75, only the excepted hereditary peers (including those elected among the 15) in the relevant party or Crossbench grouping are entitled to vote. If the vacancy is among the 15, the whole House is entitled to vote.

1.06   The Clerk of the Parliaments maintains a register of hereditary peers who wish to stand in any by-election under SO 10. Any hereditary peer other than a peer of Ireland is entitled to be included in the register. Under SO 11, any hereditary peer not previously in receipt of a writ of summons who wishes to be included in the register petitions the House and any such petition is referred to the Lord Chancellor to consider and report upon whether such peer has established the right to be included in the register.

## Retirement

1.07   There is no retirement age for members of the House of Lords, except that bishops retire from their sees on reaching the age of seventy, and cease to be members of the House.[1]

## Writ of summons

1.08   Members of the House may not take their seat until they have obtained a writ of summons. Writs of summons are issued by direction of the Lord Chancellor from the office of the Clerk of the Crown in Chancery.

1.09   New writs are issued before the meeting of each Parliament to all Lords Spiritual and Temporal who have established their right to them and who are not statutorily disqualified from receiving them.

1.10   An archbishop, on appointment or translation to another see, and a bishop who has become entitled to sit or who already has a seat and is translated to another see, applies for a writ to the Lord Chancellor with evidence to support his claim.

1.11   Writs, called writs of assistance or writs of attendance, are also sent to the following, unless they are members of the House: the

---

[1]   Ecclesiastical Offices (Age Limit) Measure 1975.

Attorney General, the Solicitor General, the Lord Chief Justice, the Master of the Rolls, the President of the Family Division, the Vice-Chancellor, Justices of the Supreme Court, the Lords Justices of Appeal and the Justices of the High Court.[1] The attendance of such judges is normally now confined to the State Opening of Parliament.

### Introduction and sitting first in Parliament

1.12 The following are ceremonially introduced before taking their seats in the House:

- newly created Life Peers;
- archbishops, on appointment or on translation;
- bishops, on first receiving a writ of summons or, if already a member of the House, on translation to another see.

1.13 When a writ has been issued to any such person, the Lord Speaker fixes a day for the introduction. The following rules apply:

- introductions may not take place on the first day of a new Parliament;[2]
- the House has agreed that, save in exceptional circumstances, no more than two new members should be introduced on any one day.[3] This rule does not apply to introductions on swearing-in days at the beginning of a new Parliament;
- introductions normally take place on Mondays, Tuesdays and Thursdays[4];
- new Lords are normally supported on introduction by two others of the same degree in the House. However, archbishops may act as

---

[1] Holders of disqualifying judicial office who are members of the House receive a writ of summons at the start of each Parliament, notwithstanding their disqualification from taking part in proceedings of the House.

[2] Procedure 1st Rpt 1970–71.

[3] LJ (1997–98) 775. In the 2010–12 session the House twice agreed, exceptionally and temporarily, to allow three introductions on Mondays, Tuesdays and Thursdays (Procedure 1st and 3rd Rpts 2010–12).

[4] Procedure 3rd Rpt 2005–06.

supporters at the introductions of bishops, and bishops may so act at the introductions of archbishops;[1]

- no member of the House may act as supporter without having first taken the oath.

1.14    Appendix K (page 268) describes the ceremony of introduction.

1.15    Hereditary peers elected under SO 10 require no introduction and, on receiving a writ, can take their seat and the oath of allegiance without any ceremony.

1.16    New members of the House may not use the facilities of the House, other than the right to sit on the steps of the Throne, before taking their seat for the first time.[2] However, they may use the dining facilities on the day of introduction.

## Oath of allegiance and affirmation

1.17    The oath of allegiance must be taken or solemn affirmation made by all members before they can sit and vote in the House:

- on introduction;
- in every new Parliament;[3]
- after a demise of the Crown.

1.18    The oath is usually taken after prayers, but may be taken at the end of business before the adjournment.[4]

1.19    The form of the oath, prescribed by s. 2 of the Promissory Oaths Act 1868 and s. 1 of the Oaths Act 1978, is:

*"I (giving name and title) do swear by Almighty God that I will be faithful and bear true allegiance to Her Majesty Queen Elizabeth, Her heirs and successors, according to law. So help me God."*

---

[1]  Members of the House holding offices which give them special precedence under the House of Lords Precedence Act 1539, such as the Lord Chancellor, the Lord President and the Lord Privy Seal, may act as supporters for new Lords of the same degree; their precedence as office holders determines their seniority as supporters: Procedure 2nd Rpt 1992–93.

[2]  Offices 2nd Rpt 1975–76. The issue of Letters Patent entitles a newly created Lord to use his title and sit on the steps of the Throne.

[3]  SO 75(1).

[4]  SO 41(5).

1.20    Under the Oaths Act 1978, members of the House who object to being sworn may affirm:

> "*I (giving name and title) do solemnly, sincerely, and truly declare and affirm that I will be faithful and bear true allegiance to Her Majesty Queen Elizabeth, Her heirs and successors, according to law.*"

1.21    The oath or affirmation must be taken in English but may be repeated in Welsh[1] or in Gaelic.[2]

1.22    Before taking the oath members go to the Table, bringing their writ of summons (except on a demise of the Crown, when new writs are not issued). They then recite aloud the words of the oath, reading them from a card kept at the Table, and holding a New Testament in the right hand. The oath may also be taken in the Scottish form with uplifted hand. In the case of members of the House who are of the Jewish faith, the Old Testament is used; in the case of other faiths, the appropriate sacred text is used.

1.23    In cases of disability or infirmity the oath may be taken seated.

1.24    After taking the oath, members must sign the Test Roll at the head of which the oath and affirmation are written. They then sign an undertaking to abide by the House of Lords Code of Conduct. Finally they go to the Woolsack, shake hands with the Lord Speaker and leave the Chamber.

1.25    Members who sit by virtue of one peerage but are known by another title take the oath and sign the Roll using the title by virtue of which they sit.

1.26    Any member of the House who sits or votes without having taken the oath is subject to a penalty of £500.[3] However, a member may attend prayers or an introduction before taking the oath. On a swearing-in day (see paragraph 2.01) it is convenient for members to occupy their seats while they are waiting to take the oath. Members who attend the House without taking the oath are not recorded in the attendance lists in the Journals, and votes cast by such members in divisions are invalid.[4] A

---

[1]  Procedure 1st Rpt 1982–83.

[2]  Procedure 1st Rpt 2001–02.

[3]  Parliamentary Oaths Act 1866, s. 5.

[4]  Procedure 2nd Rpt 1993–94.

member of the House may not attend the State Opening of Parliament without having taken the oath.[1]

## Leave of absence

1.27   Members of the House are to attend the sittings of the House. If they cannot attend, they should obtain leave of absence.[2] At any time during a Parliament, a member of the House may obtain leave of absence for the rest of the Parliament by applying in writing to the Clerk of the Parliaments.

1.28   Before the beginning of every Parliament the Clerk of the Parliaments writes to those members who were on leave of absence at the end of the preceding Parliament to ask whether they wish to renew that leave of absence for the new Parliament. In addition, at the start of each session of Parliament the Clerk of the Parliaments writes to those members (other than bishops) who attended very infrequently in the previous session, inviting them to apply for Leave of Absence.

1.29   The House grants leave of absence to those who apply. The House also grants leave to all members to whom the Clerk of the Parliaments has written as described in the preceding paragraph who fail to reply within three months of the Clerk of the Parliaments' letter being sent.

1.30   Directions relating to those on leave of absence are as follows:

(a) members of the House who have been granted leave of absence should not attend sittings of the House or of any committee of the House until their leave has expired or been terminated, except to take the oath of allegiance;

(b) members of the House on leave of absence who wish to attend during the period for which leave was granted should give notice in writing to the Clerk of the Parliaments at least three months before the day on which they wish to attend; and their leave is terminated three months from the date of this notice, or sooner if the House so directs;

---

[1]   Procedure 1st Rpt 1970–71. This restriction does not apply to those members who, while in receipt of a writ of summons, are disqualified from attending under s. 137 of the Constitutional Reform Act 2005. See above, paragraph 1.02.

[2]   SO 22.

(c) a member of the House on leave of absence may not act as a supporter in the ceremony of introduction;[1]

(d) a member of the House on leave of absence may not vote in the election of the Lord Speaker or in by-elections for hereditary peers.

1.31   In applying the provisions on leave of absence the Clerk of the Parliaments may seek the advice of the Leave of Absence Sub-Committee of the Procedure Committee (see paragraph 11.73).

## The voluntary retirement scheme

1.32   Any member of the House of Lords may, at any time, write to the Clerk of the Parliaments indicating his or her wish permanently to retire from the service of the House.[2]

1.33   By retiring from the service of the House a member indicates his or her wish permanently to cease taking any part in the work of the House; and the House, in return, recognises the member's completed service to the House.

1.34   Having received an application to retire, the Clerk of the Parliaments consults the Lord Speaker and the member's party or group, who in turn consult the member and seek confirmation that it is his or her intention to retire permanently from the service of the House. Not less than two weeks is allowed for this informal consultation to be completed.

1.35   The Lord Speaker notifies the House on the day the retirement takes effect.

1.36   Members who have retired from the service of the House should not attend sittings of the House or of any committee of the House. They may not vote in any election of the Lord Speaker or by-elections for hereditary peers. Retired members may sit on the steps of the Throne, and are afforded the same access to other facilities as members on Leave of Absence, with the exception that they are not entitled to receive parliamentary papers. Retired members are not subject to the Code of Conduct.

---

[1]   Leave of Absence 1st Rpt 1957–58.

[2]   Procedure 5th Rpt 2010–12.

1.37 Retired members remain peers, and retirement does not affect the use of their title. Retired members also continue to be treated for the purposes of general law as members of the House.

## Access to the facilities of the House

1.38 Members of the House who are on leave of absence, or who are disqualified from participation in the proceedings of the House as Members of the European Parliament or as judges,[1] enjoy access to the following facilities:

    (a) they may apply for places for their spouses at the State Opening of Parliament, and the usual number of places at such functions as The Queen's Birthday Parade (Trooping the Colour);

    (b) they may use the Library, the Dining Room, and other facilities of the House outside the Chamber, and may obtain tickets for the Public Gallery. Their spouses enjoy the same facilities as the spouses of other members of the House;

    (c) they may sit on the steps of the Throne during a sitting of the House;

    (d) they may receive parliamentary papers.

1.39 Retired bishops who have sat in the House are entitled to sit on the steps of the Throne and use the facilities of the House outside the Chamber.[2]

1.40 Rights of access enjoyed by members who are suspended from the service of the House are cancelled for the duration of the suspension. Members who are suspended may not enter the parliamentary estate, including as guests of other members.[3]

---

[1] House Committee 2nd Rpt 2008–09.

[2] Offices 4th Rpt 1970–71.

[3] House Committee minutes, 19 May 2009.

## Tax status

1.41 All members of the House who are entitled to receive writs of summons to attend the House are treated as resident, ordinarily resident and domiciled in the United Kingdom for the purposes of certain taxes.[1]

## Notification of death of member

1.42 The Lord Speaker informs the House of the death of a member of the House, before the first oral question or, on a Friday, at the start of the sitting.[2] The Lord Speaker's announcement takes a standard form and is distinct from tributes, which are a matter for the Leader of the House and the usual channels. It is not debatable.

## The Lord Speaker[3]

### Election of the Lord Speaker

1.43 The House resolved on 12 July 2005 to "elect its own presiding officer".[4] The first election was held on 28 June 2006, and a further election on 13 July 2011.

1.44 The process of election is governed by Standing Order 19. A new election is to be held in the fifth calendar year after the previous election, on a day no later than 15 July in that year, or within three months of the Lord Speaker dying, giving written notice of her resignation to the Leader of the House, or being deemed to have resigned (see below), if sooner.[5]

1.45 The result of the election is subject to the approval of the Queen. If the House passes a motion for an Address to Her Majesty seeking the Lord Speaker's removal from office, the Lord Speaker shall be deemed to have resigned with effect from the date on which the motion is passed.

---

[1] s. 41 of the Constitutional Reform and Governance Act 2010.

[2] Procedure 1st Rpt 2006–07.

[3] The decisions of the House with regard to the office of Lord Speaker are found in various sources, including Standing Orders; Report of the Select Committee on the Speakership of the House of Lords, HL Paper 92, 2005–06; resolutions of the House on 12 July 2005 and 31 January 2006; Procedure 3rd and 4th Rpts 2005–06 and 4th Rpt 2010–12; and House Committee 1st Rpt 2005–06.

[4] LJ (2005–06) 152.

[5] An election held in such circumstances would then be treated as the "previous election" for the purpose of calculating the date of the next election.

1.46   All members of the House who have taken the oath and are not disqualified, suspended, retired, or on Leave of Absence are entitled to stand and vote.[1] However, a member who has been successful in two previous elections is not entitled to stand.

1.47   The election itself is conducted in accordance with arrangements made by the Clerk of the Parliaments. The Alternative Vote system is used,[2] according to which candidates are numbered in order of preference, and the first-preference votes for the least successful candidates are successively reallocated until one candidate has at least half the total number of valid votes.

## Role of the Lord Speaker

1.48   The primary role of the Lord Speaker is to preside over proceedings in the Chamber, including Committees of the whole House.[3] She takes the oath first at the opening of a new Parliament; her role in the ceremonies accompanying oath-taking, the State Opening of Parliament, and royal commissions, are described in the appendices.[4] The Lord Speaker seeks the leave of the House for any necessary absence of a full sitting day or more.

1.49   The Lord Speaker has no power to act in the House without the consent of the House. She observes the same formalities as any other member of the House, addressing the House as a whole, and not an individual member, and not intervening when a member is on his feet. The Speaker's function is to assist, and not to rule. The House does not recognise points of order.

1.50   Any advice or assistance given by the Lord Speaker is subject to the view of the House as a whole.[5] The Lord Speaker has specific responsibilities with regard to Private Notice Questions and the application of the *sub judice* rule; these are described below (paragraphs 6.36 and 4.63).

---

[1] Procedure Committee 2nd Rpt 2009–10.

[2] Report of the Select Committee on the Speakership of the House of Lords, HL Paper 92, 2005–06.

[3] SO 62.

[4] Appendices C–G.

[5] Procedure 3rd Rpt 2005–06.

1.51 Outside the Chamber, the Lord Speaker chairs the House Committee, which oversees the administration of the House (see paragraph 11.65). She is a member of the Procedure Committee; has formal responsibility for the security of the Lords part of the parliamentary estate; is one of the three "keyholders" of Westminster Hall; and has a wide role representing the House at home and overseas.[1]

1.52 The Lord Speaker may, after consultation with the government, recall the House whenever it stands adjourned.[2]

1.53 The Lord Speaker is a salaried office-holder, and is required to lay aside outside financial interests falling into specific categories, including remunerated directorships and other employment.[3] The Lord Speaker is also expected to lay aside any party or group affiliation on appointment, and to refrain from political activity, including voting in the House.[4]

## Chairman of Committees

1.54 At the beginning of every session, and whenever a vacancy occurs, a member is appointed by the House to fill the salaried office of Chairman of Committees.[5] As a salaried office-holder, he is required to lay aside outside financial interests falling into specific categories, including remunerated directorships and other employment.[6] He is also expected to lay aside any party or group affiliation on appointment and for the duration of his time in office.

1.55 He is chairman *ex officio* of all committees unless the House otherwise directs. In practice this means that he chairs the following "domestic" committees:

(a) Administration and Works Committee

(b) Liaison Committee

(c) Committee for Privileges and Conduct

(d) Procedure Committee

---

[1] Report of the Select Committee on the Speakership of the House of Lords, HL Paper 92, 2005–06.

[2] SO 17(1). See also paragraph 2.21.

[3] Privileges 2nd Rpt 2009–10.

[4] Procedure 4th Rpt 2005–06.

[5] SO 61.

[6] Privileges 2nd Rpt 2009–10.

(e) Refreshment Committee

(f) Committee of Selection.

1.56   The Chairman speaks and answers questions in the House on matters relating to the internal administration of the House, to the work of the House Committee (of which he is a member), or to the work of any of the committees chaired by him.

1.57   The Chairman also exercises general supervision and control over private bills and hybrid instruments. His duties in this respect are described in more detail in chapter 9.

1.58   The Chairman is *ex officio* the first of the Deputy Speakers appointed by Commission (see paragraph 1.60 below). He is empowered, in the absence of the Lord Speaker, to recall the House during a period of adjournment.[1]

## Principal Deputy Chairman of Committees

1.59   The Principal Deputy Chairman of Committees is a salaried office-holder appointed in the same manner as the Chairman of Committees. As a salaried office-holder, he is required to lay aside outside financial interests falling into specific categories, including remunerated directorships and other employment.[2] He is also expected to lay aside any party or group affiliation on appointment and for the duration of his time in office. In addition to assisting the Chairman in his duties, he is appointed to act as chairman of the European Union Committee.[3]

## Deputy Speakers and Deputy Chairmen

1.60   Certain members of the House are appointed by the Crown by Commission under the Great Seal to act as Deputy Speakers of the House of Lords in the absence of the Lord Speaker.[4] In addition, at the beginning of every session the House on motion appoints a number of members, proposed by the Committee of Selection, to serve as Deputy Chairmen of Committees for the remainder of that session.[5] Deputy

---

[1]   SO 17(2).

[2]   Privileges 2nd Rpt 2009–10.

[3]   Procedure 1st Rpt 1973–74, 3rd Rpt 1974–75.

[4]   SO 18.

[5]   SO 63(5).

Chairmen exercise all the functions of Deputy Speakers, and it is the practice that they are appointed Deputy Speakers at a convenient opportunity after their appointment as Deputy Chairmen.

1.61 In practice the duties of Deputy Chairmen and Deputy Speakers are indistinguishable. In the absence of the Lord Speaker or Chairman of Committees, one of the panel of Deputy Chairmen officiates in their place. If no Deputy Chairman is present, the House appoints some other member, on motion, to perform his duties on that occasion.

1.62 Deputy Chairmen or Deputy Speakers may not recall the House under SO 17 in an emergency.

### Seating in the Chamber

1.63 The side of the House on the Sovereign's right hand when she is seated on the Throne is called the spiritual side, and that on the left the temporal side.

1.64 By convention the government and their supporters occupy the benches on the spiritual side, with the exception of the first two benches nearest to the Throne, which are taken by the bishops. Lords Spiritual must speak from the bishops' benches. Only the two Archbishops and the Bishops of London, Durham and Winchester may speak from the front one of these benches, and they also have priority in relation to seating on this bench. Lords Temporal may sit on the bishops' benches, when space allows, but may not speak from them.

1.65 The benches on the temporal side are, by convention, occupied by the opposition party or parties. The diagram at the end of chapter 1 shows the usual seating arrangements.

1.66 The Cross Benches are for those who are not members of any of the main political parties in the House[1]. Crossbench members also sit on the benches nearest the Bar on the temporal side.

1.67 On both sides of the Chamber the front benches closest to the Bar are customarily occupied by Privy Counsellors.

### Steps of the Throne

1.68 The following may sit on the steps of the Throne:

---

[1] The Crossbench Group is made up of members who are not affiliated to any political party. Members who belong to smaller parties may also sit on the Cross Benches.

- members of the House of Lords in receipt of a writ of summons, including those who have not taken their seat or the oath and those who have leave of absence or who have taken voluntary retirement;

- members of the House of Lords who are disqualified from sitting or voting in the House as Members of the European Parliament or as holders of disqualifying judicial office;[1]

- hereditary peers who were formerly members of the House and who were excluded from the House by the House of Lords Act 1999;[2]

- the eldest child (which includes an adopted child)[3] of a member of the House (or the eldest son where the right was exercised before 27 March 2000);[4]

- peers of Ireland;

- diocesan bishops of the Church of England who do not yet have seats in the House of Lords;

- retired bishops who have had seats in the House of Lords;

- Privy Counsellors;

- Clerk of the Crown in Chancery;

- Black Rod and his Deputy;

- the Dean of Westminster.

---

[1] House Committee 2nd Rpt 2008–09.

[2] Offices 1st Rpt 1999–2000.

[3] House Committee, decision by correspondence, November 2004.

[4] Offices 4th Rpt 1999–2000.

1. Throne
2. Cloth of Estate
3. Chairs of State
4. Steps of the Throne
5. Clerks' box
6. Officials' box
7. Woolsack
8. Judges' Woolsacks
9. Upper end of Earls' Bench
10. Spiritual side of the House
11. Temporal side of the House
12. Lower end of Barons' bench
13. Bishops' benches
14. Table of the House
15. Clerks at the Table
16. Chairman of Committees' Chair at the Table
17. Wheelchairs
18. Cross benches
19. Government front bench
20. Opposition front bench
21. Bar of the House
22. Black Rod's box
23. Seats for members' spouses
24. Hansard reporters
25. Brass Gates

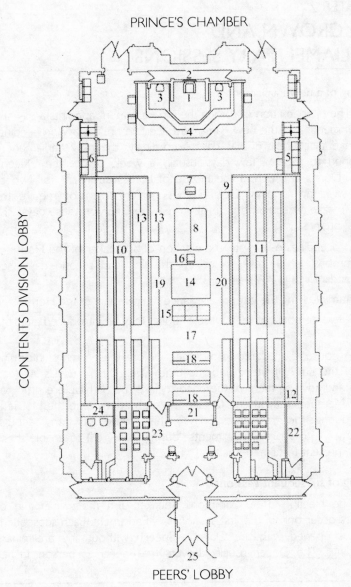

CONTENTS DIVISION LOBBY

NOT CONTENTS DIVISION LOBBY

# CHAPTER 2
# THE CROWN AND PARLIAMENTARY SESSIONS

## Opening of a new Parliament

2.01   The proclamation dissolving the old Parliament appoints a day and place of meeting of the new Parliament. Certain preliminary proceedings must take place before that day. Accordingly, the new Parliament is summoned to meet a few days, usually a week, before the Queen's Speech. During this period the House of Lords usually sits for two or three "swearing-in" days. Only business which does not require the House to take a decision on a motion may be taken on these days. The principal business is:

- proceedings relating to the election of a Speaker of the House of Commons, which takes place on the first and second days (see appendix D page 252), and

- administering the oath of allegiance to members of the House.[1]

2.02   New members of the House of Lords may be introduced after the first day.

2.03   A notice is circulated to members before these sittings, informing them of the time of sitting and the time when the House is likely to adjourn and advising them of the need to take the oath before sitting or voting.[2] Members may attend to take the oath at any time the House is sitting during the swearing-in days. The House sits long enough (sometimes with short adjournments "during pleasure") to enable those who are present to take the oath.

## Opening of subsequent sessions

2.04   The election of a Commons Speaker and the swearing-in of members occur only in the first session of a Parliament. Each subsequent session is opened with the Queen's Speech without any preliminary proceedings. The Queen usually delivers the Speech in person. In her

---

[1] SO 75(1).

[2] Procedure 1st Rpt 1970–71.

absence the presiding Commissioner delivers it. The procedure for delivery of the Queen's Speech is described in appendix E (page 256).

## First meeting after State Opening

2.05   At the time appointed for the sitting of the House the Lord Speaker takes her seat on the Woolsack. Prayers are read and members of the House may take the oath. A bill, for the better regulating of Select Vestries, is then read a first time pro forma on the motion of the Leader of the House, in order to assert the right of the House to deliberate independently of the Crown.[1] Until this has taken place, no other business is done.

2.06   Immediately after the Select Vestries Bill has been read a first time, the Lord Speaker informs the House that the Queen delivered The Gracious Speech earlier in the day to the two Houses of Parliament. She says:

*"My Lords,*
*I have to acquaint the House that Her Majesty was pleased this morning to make a Most Gracious Speech from the Throne to both Houses of Parliament assembled in the House of Lords. Copies of the Gracious Speech are available in the Printed Paper Office. I have for the convenience of the House arranged for the terms of the Gracious Speech to be published in the Official Report."*

2.07   A government backbencher chosen by the Leader of the House then moves:

*"That an humble Address be presented to Her Majesty as follows:*
*Most Gracious Sovereign,*
*We, Your Majesty's most dutiful and loyal subjects, the Lords Spiritual and Temporal in Parliament assembled, beg leave to thank Your Majesty for the most gracious Speech which Your Majesty has addressed to both Houses of Parliament."*

2.08   The mover then makes a speech and at the end says *"I beg to move that an humble Address be presented to Her Majesty."* He or she then proceeds to the Woolsack with the Address and bows to the Lord Speaker, who rises and bows in return and receives the Address. When

---

[1] SO 75(2).

the mover has returned to his or her seat, the Lord Speaker rises and says:

> "The Question is that an humble Address be presented to Her Majesty as follows"

and reads the text of the Address.

2.09    A government backbencher also chosen by the Leader then seconds the motion for an Address. It is customary for the speeches of the mover and seconder to be uncontroversial. After the speech of the seconder the Leader of the Opposition moves the adjournment of the debate. On this motion the Leader of the Opposition and the other party leaders congratulate the mover and seconder and comment generally on the Queen's Speech. After the Leader of the House has responded, the debate on the Address is adjourned.

2.10    Certain formal business is then taken. The Chairman and Principal Deputy Chairman of Committees are nominated on the motion of the Leader of the House. Formal entries in the Minutes of Proceedings record the laying before the House by the Clerk of the Parliaments of a list of members of the House, a list of hereditary peers who wish to stand for election as members of the House of Lords under Standing Order 10 (Hereditary peers: by-elections), and the sessional order for preventing stoppages in the streets.

2.11    The general debate on the Address is resumed on the next sitting day. The principal topics for debate (e.g. foreign affairs, home affairs, economic affairs, agriculture, transport) are taken on different days. Amendments, of which notice must be given, may be moved to the Address at any time in the debate, and are disposed of at the end of the day on which they are debated or at the end of the whole debate. If no amendment has been moved to the Address, the Lord Speaker declares the Question decided "*nemine dissentiente*". The House then orders the Address to be presented to Her Majesty. This is usually done by the Lord Chamberlain.

## Prorogation

2.12    The prorogation of Parliament, which brings a session to an end, is a prerogative act of the Crown. By current practice Parliament is prorogued by Commissioners acting in the Sovereign's name.[1]

---

[1]    Parliament was last prorogued by the monarch in person in 1854.

2.13　On the day appointed for prorogation, prayers are read and any necessary business is transacted. The procedure followed at prorogation, with or without Royal Assent, is given at appendix G (page 261). Parliament is always prorogued to a definite day. Prorogation for further periods may be effected by proclamation.[1] Parliament, while prorogued, can be summoned by proclamation pursuant to the Meeting of Parliament Acts 1797 and 1870[2] and the Civil Contingencies Act 2004.

## Dissolution

2.14　No Parliament may continue to sit for more than five years from the day on which, by writ of summons, it was appointed to meet.[3] Under the Fixed-term Parliaments Act 2011, a general election will be held on 7 May 2015; future general elections will be held on the first Thursday in May in the fifth calendar year following the previous general election, and Parliament will be dissolved at the beginning of the 17th working day before polling day.[4] Parliament is nowadays dissolved by Royal Proclamation under the Great Seal.

## Effect of termination of session

2.15　Prorogation has the effect of putting an end to all business before the House, except:

- private bills, personal bills, provisional order confirmation bills and hybrid bills which may be "carried over" from one session to another (including dissolution);[5]

---

[1]　Prorogation Act 1867 s. 1, amended by the Statute Law Revision Act 1893.

[2]　As amended by the Parliament (Elections and Meeting) Act 1943.

[3]　Septennial Act 1715, as amended by s. 7 of the Parliament Act 1911. A bill containing any provision to extend the maximum duration of Parliament beyond five years is exempted from the restrictions imposed on the powers of the House of Lords by the Parliament Acts 1911 and 1949.

[4]　Fixed-term Parliaments Act 2011, s. 1 and s. 3. Section 1 of the Act enables the Prime Minister to postpone the set polling day, by means of an affirmative instrument, for up to two months; s. 2 of the Act sets out the circumstances in which an early general election may be held, following the passing of motions to that effect by the House of Commons.

[5]　The procedure by which this is done provides for the waiving of certain Standing Orders by agreement between the two Houses in order that the bills may be taken *pro forma* up to the stage that they had reached in the previous session.

- proceedings on Measures, statutory instruments and special procedure orders laid in one session, which may be continued in the next, notwithstanding prorogation or dissolution. Prorogation and dissolution are disregarded in calculating "praying time";[1]

- certain sessional committees which remain in existence notwithstanding the prorogation of Parliament until the House makes further orders of appointment in the next session (but this does not apply to a dissolution, when all select committee activity must cease);[2]

- impeachments by the Commons which may be carried on from one session to another and from one Parliament to another. The jurisdiction of the Lords in such impeachments has fallen into disuse.[3]

2.16 Government public bills may also be "carried over" from one session to the next, but not over a dissolution. See paragraph 8.10.

## Demise of the Crown

2.17 The Succession to the Crown Act 1707[4] provides that in the event of the demise of the Crown, Parliament, if adjourned or prorogued, must meet as soon as possible[5] and if sitting must immediately proceed to act without any summons in the usual form.

2.18 The Representation of the People Act 1985[6] provides that, in the case of the demise of the Crown after the dissolution of one Parliament and the proclamation summoning the next, but before the election, the election and the meeting of Parliament are postponed by fourteen days. If the demise occurs on or after the date of the election, Parliament meets in accordance with the proclamation summoning the next Parliament.

2.19 When Parliament meets under either of these Acts, there is no speech from the Throne. Members take the oath of allegiance to the new Sovereign. In the course of a few days a message under the Sign Manual is sent formally acquainting the House with the death of the Sovereign, and stating such other matters as may be necessary. The House votes an

---

[1] See paragraph 10.09.

[2] SO 64.

[3] See *Erskine May*, p. 182.

[4] s. 5.

[5] Notice of the time of meeting is given by any means available.

[6] s. 20.

Address to the new Sovereign in answer to the message, expressing condolences upon the death of his predecessor and loyalty to him upon his accession.

2.20   If the demise of the Crown has taken place during the session, business is resumed and proceeds as usual; but if it has occurred during an adjournment or prorogation, both Houses again adjourn as soon as the Addresses have been presented.

## Emergency recall of the House

2.21   The Lord Speaker, or, in her absence, the Chairman of Committees, may, after consultation with the government, recall the House whenever it stands adjourned, if satisfied that the public interest requires it[1] or in pursuance of section 28(3) of the Civil Contingencies Act 2004.

## Addresses to the Crown

2.22   The ordinary method by which the Houses communicate with the Sovereign is by Address. Addresses may be agreed by both Houses and jointly presented, or agreed separately but presented together, but are more commonly agreed and presented separately. From the House of Lords, they may be presented by certain designated members, by members who are members of the Royal Household or Privy Counsellors, or by the whole House. The most common form of Address occurs at the beginning of every session in reply to the Queen's Speech. Other forms of Address are those requesting the Queen to make an Order in Council in the form of a draft laid before the House or praying the Queen to annul a negative instrument. There has been an Address for the exercise of the prerogative of mercy.[2] There are also Addresses of condolence or congratulation to the Sovereign on family or public occasions. An Address may also be presented in response to a Royal Message, concerning for example the Civil List or the declaration of a State of Emergency.

2.23   The Sovereign's reply is communicated to the House on the first convenient occasion. The member reporting the reply to the House

---

[1]  SO 17(1), (2).

[2]  The case of Guardsmen Fisher and Wright, HL Deb. 20 July 1998, cols 653–72.

(usually the Lord Chamberlain or another member of the Royal Household) does so at the beginning of business.

### Messages to members of the Royal Family

2.24 The congratulations or condolences of the House are communicated to a member of the Royal Family other than the Sovereign by a message, and not by an Address. In such a case certain members of the House are ordered to present the message, and one of them reports the answer or answers.[1]

### Address presented by the whole House

2.25 On occasions of particular importance an Address may be presented by the whole House. Until 1897 (the diamond jubilee of Queen Victoria's accession) such Addresses were presented at Buckingham Palace or another royal residence. Since then Addresses by the whole House have been presented, together with Addresses from the House of Commons, within the Palace of Westminster. Thus Addresses were presented in Westminster Hall to mark the 50th Anniversary of the end of World War II (1995) and the Queen's Diamond Jubilee (2012).[2]

2.26 After prayers on the day appointed for the presentation of the Address, the House proceeds to the designated place. The motion that the House do now proceed to the designated place also provides that the House do thereafter adjourn during pleasure and meet again in the Chamber at an appointed time. The Lord Speaker and the Commons Speaker either lead their respective Houses or arrive with their processions after the members of both Houses are seated. The Commons Speaker usually arrives last. Both Houses sit facing the Queen, the Commons on Her left and the Lords on Her right. As soon as the Queen has arrived, the Lord Speaker reads the Lords' Address and then presents it to the Sovereign. The Commons Speaker likewise reads and presents the Commons' Address. The Queen delivers Her reply to the Addresses and withdraws. The Lords withdraw followed by the Commons. By virtue of the terms of the motion moved earlier in the

---

[1]  For example HL Deb. 8 June 2011 col. 255, 13 June 2011 col. 541 and 30 June 2012 col. 1855 (90th birthday of His Royal Highness the Duke of Edinburgh).

[2]  LJ (1994–95) 387, Minutes of Proceedings, 20 March 2012.

Chamber, the House then adjourns during pleasure and resumes its sitting at the appointed time.

## Messages from the Crown

2.27 Messages from the Crown are rare. They are formal communications relating to important public events that require the attention of Parliament, for example, the declaration of a State of Emergency. A message from the Crown is usually in writing under the Queen's Sign Manual. It is brought by a member of the House who is either a minister, for example the Leader of the House, or one of the Queen's Household. A message from the Crown has precedence over other business, except for introductions, oaths and the Lord Speaker's leave of absence.

2.28 The member bearing a message announces to the House that he has a message under the Queen's Sign Manual that the Queen has commanded him to deliver to the House. He reads it at the Table, and then gives it to the Lord Speaker at the Woolsack, who hands it to the Clerk of the Parliaments. When the message has been read, it is either considered immediately on motion or, more usually, a later day is appointed.[1] An Address is then moved in reply, usually by the Leader of the House. However, the House takes no further action on messages from the Crown in reply to an Address from the House.[2]

---

[1] SO 41(1).

[2] Such as those received following the end of the debate on the Queen's Speech or replying to an Address to annul a statutory instrument.

# CHAPTER 3
# SITTINGS AND DOCUMENTS OF THE HOUSE

3.01  The House usually sits for public business on Mondays and Tuesdays at 2.30 p.m., on Wednesdays at 3 p.m. and on Thursdays at 11 a.m. The House also sits on Fridays at 10 a.m. when pressure of business makes it necessary. It is a firm convention that the House normally rises by about 10 p.m. on Mondays to Wednesdays, [1] by about 7 p.m. on Thursdays, and by about 3 p.m. on Fridays. The time of meeting of the House can be varied to meet the convenience of the House. In exceptional circumstances the House has met on Saturday and on Sunday. [2]

3.02  The length of a session within a Parliament is at the discretion of the Government. Since 2010 sessions have started and ended in the late spring.

3.03  The House breaks for recesses as follows:

- over Christmas and New Year (usually two weeks);
- sometimes in late February (up to one week);
- at Easter (one or two weeks);
- over the Spring Bank Holiday (one week); and
- in the summer (usually between late July and early October).

### Lord Speaker's procession and the Mace

3.04  Before each day's sitting the Lord Speaker walks in procession from her room to the Chamber, preceded by the Mace. [3] During the procession, doorkeepers and security staff ensure that the route is

---

[1]  Procedure 5th Rpt 2001–02.

[2]  e.g. the House sat on a Saturday and a Sunday at the outbreak of the Second World War and in 1982 met on a Saturday to discuss the situation in the Falkland Islands: LJ (1938–39) 383–4, (1981–82) 216. The House attended the State Funeral for Sir Winston Churchill in St Paul's Cathedral on Saturday 30 January 1965.

[3]  The procession consists of a Doorkeeper, followed by the Deputy Serjeant-at-Arms (the Yeoman Usher) or Principal Doorkeeper bearing the Mace, followed by the Lord Speaker. In the Prince's Chamber, Black Rod joins the end of the procession. Procedure 4th Rpt 2005–06.

unobstructed. The procession crosses the Prince's Chamber and moves down the Not-content Lobby, entering the Chamber from below Bar on the temporal side. The Lord Speaker continues up the temporal side of the House to the Woolsack. After the Bishop has read the Psalm, the Lord Speaker and other members present kneel or stand for prayers. When these have been read, the Lord Speaker takes her seat on the Woolsack.

3.05   If the Lord Speaker is absent at the beginning of the sitting, the Deputy Serjeant-at-Arms (the Yeoman Usher), alone, takes the Mace by way of the Library Corridor to meet the Deputy Speaker and Black Rod in the Peers' Lobby.

## Prayers

3.06   Prayers are read at the beginning of each sitting. Ordinarily prayers are read by one of the Bishops, who take a week each in turn.[1] In the absence of a Bishop, a member of the House who is an ordained minister of the Church of England may read prayers. If no such member is present, the Lord on the Woolsack reads prayers. The prayers are printed in appendix J (page 265). During prayers the doors and galleries of the House are closed and visitors are excluded.

## Quorum

3.07   The quorum of the House is three, including the Lord Speaker or Deputy Speaker. There is however a quorum of 30 for divisions on bills and on any motion to approve or disapprove delegated legislation.[2]

## Change of Speaker

3.08   During the course of business the Lord Speaker may be replaced on the Woolsack by a Deputy Speaker. When one Lord takes the place of another on the Woolsack, there is no interruption of business. The Lord who is to preside stands at the side of the Woolsack, on the spiritual side. The Lord on the Woolsack rises and moves to the temporal side. They bow to each other. The Lord previously on the Woolsack withdraws and the replacement sits down on the Woolsack.

---

[1]  The two Archbishops and the Bishops of London, Durham and Winchester do not take part in this rota.

[2]  SO 57.

## Adjournment

3.09   At the end of business a member of the government moves *"That the House do now adjourn."* The Lord Speaker puts the Question, but does not collect the voices because this Question is not usually debated. If any member of the House wishes to debate it, the Lord Speaker should be informed beforehand.

3.10   As soon as the Lord Speaker has put the Question for the adjournment she leaves the Chamber by the temporal side and the Bar, preceded by the Mace, and returns in procession to her room via the Law Lords' and Library Corridors.

3.11   If a Deputy Speaker is on the Woolsack when the House adjourns, the above ceremony is observed, but the Deputy Speaker leaves the procession in the Peers' Lobby.

## Secret sittings

3.12   If the House wishes to meet in secret, a motion of which notice is not required is made to that effect.[1] When an order for a secret sitting is made, the Chamber is cleared of everyone except members of the House, the Clerks at the Table and Black Rod. Members of the House of Commons are not required to withdraw.

## Grand Committee

3.13   Certain types of business may take place in Grand Committee. The procedure in a Grand Committee is the same for each type of business as the procedure would have been in the House when such business is considered, except that divisions may not take place in Grand Committee.[2]

3.14   A Grand Committee is a committee of unlimited membership. Any member of the House may participate in it. Only one Grand Committee sits on any one day. The place of meeting is usually the Moses Room.

3.15   The following types of business may take place in Grand Committee:

---

[1]  SO 15.

[2]  Report to the Leader from the Group on sittings of the House: HL Paper (1993–94) 83, paragraph 20; Procedure 1st Rpt 2005–06.

(a) Committee stages of public bills (only one bill per day—see paragraph 8.101)

(b) Motions to consider affirmative instruments (see paragraph 10.17)

(c) Motions to consider negative instruments (see paragraph 10.10)

(d) Motions to take note of reports of select committees (see paragraph 11.37), or of the Intelligence and Security Committee (see paragraph 11.79)

(e) General motions for debate (see paragraph 6.57)

(f) Questions for short debate (see paragraph 6.46)

(g) Debates on proposals for National Policy Statements, laid before Parliament under the Planning Act 2008 (see paragraph 10.58).[1]

3.16   In addition, second reading debates on Law Commission bills may take place in a "Second Reading Committee" in the Moses Room, though this is not formally a Grand Committee (see paragraph 8.43).

3.17   Grand Committees sit for times agreed in advance, irrespective of the rising of the House.[2] Notice of the proceedings is given in *House of Lords Business*. The normal sitting times[3] of Grand Committee are:

- Monday, Tuesday 3.30–7.30 p.m.
- Wednesday 3.45–7.45 p.m.
- Thursday 2–6 p.m.

3.18   Committee proceedings begin at the appointed time without any preliminary motion. Members speak standing and, so far as they can, observe the same degree of formality as in the Chamber. Forms of words used in Grand Committee are the same as in Committee of the whole House. The committee adjourns for 10 minutes for a division in the House. If the committee is to break (e.g. for a division or a statement in the Chamber), and when it adjourns at the end of the day's proceedings, the committee is simply adjourned without Question put. The verbatim

---

[1]   Procedure 2nd Rpt 2008–09.

[2]   Procedure 3rd Rpt 2003–04.

[3]   Procedure 2nd Rpt 2005–06.

report of the Grand Committee's proceedings is published, and the minutes are published as an appendix to the Minutes of Proceedings.

## Leave of the House

3.19   The leave of the House is required before certain procedures or items of business can proceed. Similar rules apply in Committees of the whole House.

3.20   In certain cases where leave is sought, it is granted by majority and the objection of a single member of the House is not sufficient to withhold leave. Leave is granted by majority:

(a) to ask questions;

(b) to make ministerial or personal statements;

(c) to take business not on the order paper of which notice is not required;

(d) to speak more than once to a motion.

3.21   In other cases leave must be unanimous, notably in those cases where, if leave were granted, the House or committee would be deprived of having a Question put.[1] Leave is withheld if a single member of the House objects to:

(a) withdrawal of an amendment or a motion which is before the House;

(b) moving motions, amendments and clauses *en bloc* (see paragraph 3.49);

(c) moving a motion that the order of commitment or recommitment of a bill be discharged;

(d) moving a motion or asking a question when the mover or questioner is absent, unless the authority of the member named on the order paper has been given;

(e) postponing business without notice till later the same day.[2]

3.22   Leave is usually obtained without putting the Question; but if necessary, the Question *"that leave be given"* could be divided upon in a case where leave may be granted by a majority decision. However, this would be exceptional, as a member who requests leave usually tests the

---

[1] SO 31.

[2] SO 42(3).

feeling of the House and, if there is opposition to leave being granted, the request is generally withdrawn.

## Suspension of standing orders

3.23 SO 86 provides that no motion shall be agreed to for making a new standing order, or for dispensing with a standing order, unless notice has been given on the order paper. Consequently, when it is desired that a standing order should be suspended for a specific period, or dispensed with for a particular purpose, notice of a motion, customarily in the name of the Leader of the House, is inserted on the order paper under the heading "Business of the House". Such motions are taken before other notices relating to public business. SOs 40 (arrangement of the order paper) and 46 (no two stages of a bill to be taken on one day) are sometimes suspended when pressure of business increases before a recess or prorogation, to enable the government to arrange the order of business and to take more than one stage of a bill at a sitting.

## House documents

3.24 The House publishes three core documents giving information about the business that the House has done and the business it expects to do:

- *House of Lords Business*, a single document containing future business and the Minutes of Proceedings, the daily record of business transacted;
- the white order paper (the agenda for the day);
- Hansard (the official report of what is said in debate).

3.25 On sitting days, copies of the order paper are available from the Printed Paper Office, from the desks in the Peers' Entrance, and from the desks adjacent to the Chamber in the Prince's Chamber and Peers' Lobby.

## House of Lords Business

3.26 *House of Lords Business* is printed after each sitting day and is also published on the Internet. It shows future business to be taken in the House, so far as it has been tabled or definitely arranged.[1] It also includes:

(a) business of which notice has been given but for which no day has been named. This business is grouped under five headings:

(i) Motions for balloted debates;

(ii) Select committee reports for debate (with the date on which the report was published);

(iii) Other motions for debate;

(iv) Motions relating to delegated legislation;

(v) Questions for short debate;

(b) a list of questions for written answer tabled that day, together with a table showing any written questions which remain unanswered after 10 working days. A cumulative list of all unanswered written questions is published on the parliamentary website[2] after each sitting day;

(c) lists of bills, Measures and various types of delegated legislation in progress, showing the stage reached by each and the next date on which they will be taken, if known;

(d) notices of committee sittings.

3.27 The Minutes of Proceedings of the House are also contained in *House of Lords Business*. They are issued under the authority and signature of the Clerk of the Parliaments. The Minutes record actions or decisions of the House rather than what is said in the Chamber. For this reason some "silent" entries are included which happen off the floor.

3.28 The Minutes of Proceedings are compiled in the following order:

(a) preliminary matters, such as prayers, introductions, members taking the oath, messages from the Queen and matters relating to leave of absence;

(b) select committee report printing orders;

---

[1] Each week the Government Whips' Office publishes a separate document entitled 'Forthcoming Business', which informally advertises business for the following week and that provisionally proposed for subsequent weeks.

[2] The list is published at http://www.publications.parliament.uk/pa/ld/ldcumlst.htm.

(c) private business (except where such business is taken part-way through public business);

(d) public business, in the order in which it is taken in the House;

(e) minutes of proceedings of Grand Committees, Second Reading Committees and public bill committees;

(f) papers laid before the House.

## Arrangement of business

### The usual channels

3.29    The Government Chief Whip is responsible for the detailed arrangement of government business and the business of individual sittings. The smooth running of the House depends largely on the Whips of the main political parties.   They agree the arrangement of business through the "usual channels". The usual channels consist of the Leaders and Whips of the three main political parties. For certain purposes the usual channels include the Convenor of the Crossbench Peers.

### Notices

3.30    Motions or questions may be handed in to the House of Lords Table Office on sitting days between 10 a.m. and House Up; the Table Office may also be contacted during these hours by telephone (020 7219 3036). Motions or questions may also be sent at any time by post, email or fax to the House of Lords Table Office (fax 020 7219 3887; email holtableoffice@parliament.uk). In addition, while the House is sitting they may be handed in at the Table. At other times (e.g. non-sitting Fridays or recesses) business may be handed in between 10 a.m. and 5 p.m., either to the Table Office or to the Duty Clerk, using the same contact details.

3.31    Whenever any new notice is put down in House of Lords Business, or any material alteration is made to the text of an existing motion or question, it is marked with a dagger (†) to draw attention to it.[1]

3.32    Business may be tabled any length of time in advance, up to the end of the session, except:

---

[1]  Procedure 1st Rpt 1969–70.

- oral questions, which may be tabled up to four weeks in advance including recesses;[1]

- motions and questions for short debate, which may be tabled up to four weeks in advance excluding recesses.[2]

3.33 A member of the House who wishes a notice to appear in *House of Lords Business* before a specific date has been fixed for it may enter it under either "Motions for Debate", "Questions for Short Debate" or "Motions relating to Delegated Legislation". There is no strictly formulated rule against anticipation; but:

(a) a member should not put down for a specific date a question or subject for debate which already appears in the name of another member under any of the undated headings without first consulting that member; and

(b) it is not in the interests of good order and courtesy that a member should table for an earlier day a question or motion similar to one that has already been tabled for a particular day.

3.34 Italic notes are often used to give the House advance notice of business that is not yet in a position to be tabled.[3]

3.35 Notices may be withdrawn or put down for a later date by the member of the House in whose name they stand.[4] Oral questions and questions for short debate may be brought forward to an earlier day without leave, at the request of the member asking the question. Other notices can only be brought forward by leave of the House obtained on a motion, of which notice must be given. Such a motion is generally moved by the Leader of the House.[5]

3.36 Business of which notice is required (see paragraph 3.38) must first be called before it can proceed. Questions and motions are called by the Clerk, in the order in which they appear on the order paper.[6] Amendments to bills are called by the Lord on the Woolsack or in the

---

[1] See paragraph 6.26 for a full explanation of the times at which oral questions may be tabled.

[2] SO 43.

[3] Procedure 5th Rpt 1966–67.

[4] SO 42(1).

[5] Procedure 5th Rpt 1966–67, 1st Rpt 1975–76.

[6] SO 39.

Chair, in the order of the marshalled list. Amendments to motions are called by the Lord on the Woolsack.

3.37   If a member of the House is absent when a motion or question standing in his or her name is called and has authorised another member to act on his or her behalf, that member may do so, explaining the situation. Otherwise, the motion or question cannot be proceeded with on that day unless unanimous leave is granted by the House.[1] In that case, when the Clerk has called the motion or question, a member may ask for leave to move the motion or ask the question standing in the name of the absent member. If there is a single dissenting voice, the House passes on to the next business. Notice must be given before business not proceeded with can be taken on a subsequent date. This paragraph does not apply to government motions, which may be moved by any member of the government without leave, or to amendments to bills (see paragraph 8.64).

*Business of which notice is required or not required*

3.38   Business of which notice is required must appear at least on the white order paper of the day on which it is to be taken, and wherever possible also in *House of Lords Business*.[2] Notice must be given of oral questions, questions for short debate and all motions except those which the House customarily allows to be moved without notice. The following list, which is not exhaustive, shows what business the House in practice allows to be taken without notice:[3]

    (a) business which does not involve a decision of the House:

        (i) Royal Assent;

        (ii) obituary tributes and personal statements;

        (iii) ministerial statements and private notice questions;

        (iv) statements or questions on business, procedure and privilege;

        (v) oaths of allegiance;

        (vi) presentation of public petitions;

    (b) manuscript amendments to bills and motions;

---

[1]   Procedure 2nd Rpt 1992–93.

[2]   SO 36, Procedure 5th Rpt 1970–71.

[3]   Procedure 5th Rpt 1970–71.

(c) business expressly exempted from the need to give notice,[1] namely:

(i) messages from the Crown;

(ii) introduction of bills;

(iii) messages from the Commons and first reading of Commons bills;

(iv) consideration of Commons amendments and reasons, though reasonable notice should be given when possible;[2]

(d) motions relating to the way in which the House conducts its business, for example:

(i) motions for the adjournment of a debate, or of the House;

(ii) the motion to go into Committee of the whole House for more freedom of debate on a motion;[3]

(iii) in Committee of the whole House, motions to adjourn debate on an amendment, or to resume the House;

(iv) the motion that leave be not given to ask a question;

(v) the motion that the noble Lord be no longer heard (see paragraph 4.54);

(vi) the Closure (see paragraph 4.60);

(vii) the Next Business motion (see paragraph 4.56);

(viii) the motion that the Lord X be appointed Lord Speaker *pro tempore*;

(ix) the motion that the House should meet in secret (see paragraph 3.12).

*Order of business*

3.39　The House proceeds with the business of each day in the order in which it stands on the order paper.[4] Business is entered on the order paper in the order in which it is received at the Table, subject to the following main conditions laid down in SO 40:

---

[1] SO 41.

[2] Procedure 1st Rpt 1987–88.

[3] SO 62, HL Deb. 16 June 1958 col. 892.

[4] SOs 39, 40.

(a) oral questions are placed first;

(b) private business is, subject to the Chairman of Committees' discretion, placed before public business;

(c) business of the House motions and, if he so desires, the Chairman of Committees' business (for example, consideration of reports from domestic committees) are placed before other public business;

(d) on all days except Thursdays,[1] public bills, Measures, affirmative instruments and reports from select committees of the House have precedence over other public business. On Thursdays, the general debate day,[2] motions have precedence over public bills, Measures and delegated legislation;

(e) any motion relating to a report from the Delegated Powers and Regulatory Reform Committee on a draft order laid under the Legislative and Regulatory Reform Act 2006, or a subordinate provisions order made or proposed to be made under the Regulatory Reform Act 2001, is placed before a motion to approve that order;[3]

(f) any motion relating to a report from the Joint Committee on Human Rights on a remedial order or draft remedial order laid under Schedule 2 to the Human Rights Act 1998 is placed before a motion to approve that order or draft order;[4]

(g) questions for short debate are placed last, even when it is known that they will be taken in the lunch or dinner break.

3.40   Royal Assent is frequently notified before oral questions, but may be notified between any two items of business or at the end of business, if necessary after an adjournment.

3.41   Private bills are entered on the order paper after oral questions.[5] But if a private bill is likely to be debated on second or third reading it may be entered at a later point on the order paper. Similarly, if a debate unexpectedly arises upon a private bill, the Chairman of Committees may

---

[1] Procedure 6th Rpt 2005–06.

[2] See paragraph 6.49.

[3] SO 40(6).

[4] SO 40(7).

[5] Procedure 2nd Rpt 1958–59.

propose the postponement or adjournment of that stage of the bill either to a time later in the same day, or to another day. Members intending to debate any stage of a private bill should accordingly give notice of their intention to the Chairman of Committees. Private bills may also be entered at a later point on the order paper at the discretion of the Chairman of Committees.

3.42    The order in which business is usually taken is as follows:

(a)    prayers;

(b)    introductions;

(c)    oaths of allegiance (or at the end of business);

(d)    the Lord Speaker's leave of absence;

(e)    messages and answers from the Crown;

(f)    Royal Assent (or at any convenient time during the sitting);

(g)    Addresses of congratulation or sympathy to the Crown;[1]

(h)    notification of death and obituary tributes;

(i)    personal statements;

(j)    oral questions;

(k)    private notice questions;

(l)    presentation of public petitions;

(m)    questions of privilege;

(n)    statements on business;

(o)    ministerial statements (or at the first convenient moment);

(p)    presentation of new Lords bills (or at the end of business);[2]

(q)    messages from the Commons (or at any convenient time during the sitting);

(r)    private bills, at the discretion of the Chairman of Committees;

(s)    business of the House motions;

(t)    motions to amend Standing Orders;

(u)    motions relating to the Chairman of Committees' business, if he so desires;

(v)    motions for the appointment of select committees;

---

[1] Procedure 4th Rpt 1964–65.

[2] SO 41(3).

(w)  public business;

(x)  questions for short debate.

## Variation of order of business

3.43  Under SO 40(8) the order of notices relating to public bills, Measures, affirmative instruments and reports from select committees can be varied by agreement of the members in whose names the notices stand. Such variations are subject to SO 40(4) and (5) so that on Thursdays notices relating to public bills, Measures and delegated legislation may not be advanced before notices relating to motions, even with the consent of those affected. In such cases a formal motion is required to vary the order of business.

3.44  Where it is wished to vary the order of business beyond the terms of SO 40(4) and (5), a "business of the House" motion may be put down to suspend or dispense with SO 40. The Standing Order is sometimes suspended so far as is necessary to give the government power to arrange the order of business.

3.45  Business may be postponed until later the same day without notice, with the unanimous leave of the House.[1] When the Clerk has called the business, the Lord in charge of the business says, *"Unless any noble Lord objects, I beg to move that X be postponed until after Y".* If this is agreed to, the House proceeds to the next business on the order paper.

3.46  If business is adjourned, the House may without notice make an order for the adjourned business to be taken later on the same day or taken first on some specified future day,[2] subject to the rules governing the order in which categories of business may be taken.

## Lunch and dinner breaks

3.47  The main business of the day is often interrupted, usually around 7.30 p.m., for other business to be taken during the dinner break. On days when the House sits in the morning there may be a lunch break at around 1.30 p.m. Lunch or dinner break business is marked as such in *House of Lords Business*. Interruptions of this sort may also be

---

[1]  SO 42(3).

[2]  SO 45.

announced after oral questions by means of a business statement. At the desired time a motion is moved that the proceedings be adjourned or, if the House is in committee, that the House be resumed. It is usual at this point for an indication to be given that the main business will not be resumed before a certain time. The House then proceeds to consider the next business on the order paper. If this is disposed of before the time indicated for the resumption of business, the House adjourns "during pleasure"[1] until that time.

3.48   If the intention is simply to interrupt the proceedings for a period without taking any other business, a motion is moved that the House do adjourn during pleasure until a stated time. If the House is in committee, however, the proceedings may, with the consent of the committee, be interrupted without any Question being put. If such an interruption is proposed, and no member of the House objects, the Lord in the Chair announces:

*"The committee stands adjourned until –".*

## Motions en bloc

3.49   Certain categories of motion may be moved *en bloc* when they are not expected to be debated. This means that a single Question is put and decided. The categories are as follows:

(a) Motions to approve affirmative instruments (see paragraph 10.16);

(b) Motions to reappoint or to fill casual vacancies on select committees (see paragraphs 11.06 and 11.10);

(c) Stages of consolidation bills (see paragraph 8.211);

(d) Motions to carry over private bills[2].

3.50   Moving other categories of motion *en bloc* may be authorised by business of the House motion.

3.51   The following rules apply:

- Notice must be given, by means of an italic note in *House of Lords Business.*

---

[1]  Adjournments "during pleasure" are breaks in a sitting for specified or unspecified periods.

[2]  Procedure 2nd Rpt 2006–07.

- If a single member objects, the motions must be moved separately to the extent desired.

3.52 For moving amendments and clauses *en bloc*, see paragraphs, 8.72, 8.134 and 8.167.

## Official Report

3.53 The Official Report, or Hansard, is the substantially verbatim record of debates and proceedings in the House and Grand Committee. It also comprises:

(a) the text of written statements and of replies to questions for written answer.[1] Statements or answers that are excessively lengthy are normally placed in the Library rather than being printed (see paragraph 6.42);

(b) proceedings in public bill committees;

(c) certain items not spoken in the Chamber that are the subject of formal minute entries, relating to the progress of Bills;

(d) a hyperlink (in the online version) to the electronic texts of various relevant documents, including reports from domestic or select committees, copies of Bills or Statutory Instruments, and other official documents of direct relevance to the debate;

(e) texts of amendments moved;

(f) division lists.

3.54 Hansard is produced by an Editor and staff who are accountable to the Clerk of the Parliaments. It is published online in draft form throughout the day, approximately three hours behind real time. This is replaced the following morning by the completed online daily transcripts, at the same time as the printed version is produced. If the House sits after 2.30 a.m., a cut-off time on material printed may be imposed, with the remaining business from that sitting appearing in the next daily part and a draft copy of the text to be printed being made available in the Library. Corrections are made to the online text once published to ensure that it remains accurate and authoritative. A small number of bound volumes are also printed some months after the period covered.

---

[1] SO 44.

*Correction of speeches*

3.55   When correcting their speeches, members should not attempt to alter the sense of words spoken by them in debate. Corrections are accepted only when the words that were actually spoken have been incorrectly reported. The procedure for suggesting corrections to be included in the bound volumes is printed on the inside cover of each daily part.[1]

## Journals

3.56   The Journals are the permanent official record of the proceedings of the House, compiled from the Minutes of Proceedings. The Journals differ from the Minutes in that they include a daily record of members present, most reports of the domestic committees of the House, the letters patent of peers on introduction, and an index. All copies of the Journals of either House are admitted as evidence by the courts and others.[2] If required in evidence, a copy or extract of the Journals, authenticated by the Clerk of the Parliaments, may be supplied on payment of a fee.

## Parliamentary papers

*Papers laid before the House*

3.57   The Minutes of Proceedings record each day the titles of various documents, or "papers", presented or laid in the House on that day and also those laid since the last sitting. These papers fall into two main categories:

(a) papers presented by command of Her Majesty on the initiative of a minister of the Crown. These are known as "Command papers". The majority are published in a numbered series currently labelled "Cm". Command papers may be presented at any time during the existence of a Parliament, including non-sitting days, recesses and prorogation;

(b) papers laid before the House pursuant to an Act, statutory instrument or Measure. These are known as "Act papers".

---

[1]   Procedure 1st Rpt 1969–70.

[2]   Evidence Act 1845, s. 3. The Act does not extend to Scotland.

They may be of either a legislative or an executive character, and they may be either subject to a degree of parliamentary control (depending on the provisions of the parent statute) or purely informative.

3.58 Papers may also be laid as Returns to an Order of the House, for example in response to a motion for papers, though this is now rare.

3.59 Certain statutory instruments can be laid when the House is not sitting for public business, namely those instruments (apart from special procedure orders) which are required to be laid before Parliament after being made, but which do not require to be approved by resolution or lie before Parliament for any period before they come into operation.[1] The times when such instruments may be deposited are those shown in the table.

3.60 No papers of any type may be laid during a dissolution of Parliament.

3.61 If it is necessary to bring a statutory instrument into operation before it has been laid before Parliament, the responsible department must submit a notification and explanation to the Lord Speaker.[2] Their receipt is recorded in the minutes of the next sitting day's proceedings.

*Days when papers may be laid*

3.62 Papers may be laid on the days and times set out in the table.

| Days when papers may be laid | Time at which papers may be deposited in Printed Paper Office | |
| --- | --- | --- |
| | Earliest | Latest |
| House sitting for public business | 9.30 a.m. (or start of business if earlier) | 5 p.m. (or rising of the House if later) |
| Non-sitting day (Monday to Friday) | 11 a.m. | 3 p.m.[3] |

[1] SO 70.

[2] Statutory Instruments Act 1946, s. 4, as amended by Sch. 6 to the Constitutional Reform Act 2005; SO 71.

[3] Procedure 2nd Rpt 2006–07.

| Prorogation | 11 a.m. | 3 p.m. |
|---|---|---|
| Dissolution | Papers may not be laid | |

3.63 Departments wishing to lay Command papers or statutory instruments outside these hours must make special arrangements for their receipt with the Printed Paper Office.

## Entitlement

3.64 Members of the House are entitled to obtain free of charge from the Printed Paper Office such current parliamentary papers and other publications as they clearly require to discharge their current parliamentary duties.[1] These include:

- Command papers;
- Act papers;
- statutory instruments;
- Acts and Measures;
- any document printed pursuant to an order of either House;
- other working papers of the House, including bills, explanatory notes on bills, amendments, *House of Lords Business* and Hansard (Lords and Commons);
- papers relating to the work of the European Union.

3.65 Members are entitled to one copy of these papers. If they have spoken in a debate, they are entitled to collect up to six copies of the Lords Hansard in which their speech is reported.

3.66 Members of the House may also obtain, free of charge, government publications up to a price limit.[2] Papers above the price limit are available for consultation in the Library of the House. Any publication referred to in a motion or question for short debate which has been set down for a named day in *House of Lords Business* will be supplied free to any member on request. Other publications will also be supplied free of charge, provided that they are required for the discharge of the member's current parliamentary duties. Historical, technical, scientific or

---

[1] Offices 4th Rpt 1966–67.

[2] Currently £50: see the *Handbook on facilities and services for Members* (May 2010).

reference and similar classes of publications will not generally be supplied to members free of charge, unless specially authorised by the Clerk of the Parliaments. Further details can be found in the *Handbook on facilities and services for Members.*

3.67   Members of the House may order through the Printed Paper Office any government publications which are not available to them free of charge, and also extra copies of papers above their basic entitlement. These papers are sent to members together with an invoice.

3.68   In order to enable the Printed Paper Office to provide a prompt service to all members of the House, members should first consult the Library when the identification of a paper is in doubt, or when they wish to find answers to specific questions from published sources.

## Public petitions

3.69   Members of the public may petition the House of Lords, but only a member of the House may present a petition. Members of the House should give the following guidance to members of the public who ask them to present petitions on their behalf.

3.70   Petitions to the House of Lords begin:

*"To the Right Honourable the Lords Spiritual and Temporal in Parliament assembled, The humble Petition of [names or designation of petitioners] sheweth".*

3.71   The general allegations of the petition follow. The petition ends with what is called a "prayer", setting out what the petitioners desire the House to do. After the prayer are added the words *"And your Petitioners will ever pray &c."* followed by the signatures. The petition may be written, printed or typed on paper. At least one signature must be on the same sheet as the petition. The signatures must not be stuck on to the paper. The petition of a corporation should be under its common seal, which must be affixed to the first sheet.

3.72   Members of the House presenting petitions should sign them, and either send them to the Clerk of the Parliaments or hand them in at the Table.[1] In either case, having notified the Table in advance, they rise in their place after oral questions and say:

---

[1]   SO 74.

*"My Lords, I beg to present a petition from [names or designation], which prays that this House will [the prayer is read out]."*

3.73   They may add:

*"The petition bears X signatures."*

but no speech may be made and no debate follows.

3.74   Petitions relating to a public bill may be presented at any time during its passage through the House. A petition relating to a bill which has not been before the House, or which has already been rejected by it, cannot be presented.

3.75   The presentation of a petition is recorded in the Minutes of Proceedings, and the petition is retained in the Parliamentary Archives for one year. However, no order is made for the petition to be printed unless a member of the House puts down a motion to debate it for a designated day; otherwise no action follows.

3.76   A member proposing to present a petition should consult the Journal Office at an early stage.

## Messages between the two Houses

3.77   A message is the means of formal communication between the two Houses. It is used for sending bills from one House to the other, for informing one House of the agreement or disagreement of the other to bills or amendments, for requesting the attendance of staff of either House as witnesses, for the exchange of documents, for the setting up of joint committees, to obtain agreement to the suspension of proceedings on legislation from one session to the next, and for other matters on which the two Houses wish to communicate.

3.78   Messages to the Commons are taken by a Lords Clerk and handed to the Serjeant at Arms. Messages from the Commons are brought by a Commons Clerk to the Bar of the House and presented to the Clerk at the Table. There is no special ceremony for the arrival of a message, and the business of the House proceeds without interruption.

# CHAPTER 4
# CONDUCT IN THE HOUSE

## Self-regulation

4.01 The House is self-regulating: the Lord Speaker has no power to rule on matters of order. In practice this means that the preservation of order and the maintenance of the rules of debate are the responsibility of the House itself, that is, of all the members who are present, and any member may draw attention to breaches of order or failures to observe customs.

4.02 The word "undesirable" may be used in the House of Lords as an equivalent of the expression "out of order". If any member is in doubt about a point of procedure, the Clerk of the Parliaments and other Clerks are available to give advice, and members of the House are recommended to consult them.[1]

## Role of the Leader of the House, Whips and Lord Speaker

4.03 The Leader of the House is appointed by the Prime Minister, is a member of the Cabinet, and is responsible for the conduct of government business in the Lords.[2] Because the Lord Speaker has no powers to rule on matters of procedure, the Leader also advises the House on procedure and order, and has the responsibility of drawing attention to violations or abuse. The Leader also expresses the sense of the House on formal occasions, such as motions of thanks or congratulation. However, like the Lord Speaker, the Leader is endowed with no formal authority.

4.04 The Leader, the Government Chief Whip and their offices are available to assist and advise all members of the House. Members greatly assist the effective conduct of the House's business if they give as much notice as possible to the Leader and the Government Whips' Office whenever they propose to raise any matter on which the Leader's guidance might be required.

---

[1] Procedure 2nd Rpt 1981–82.
[2] Procedure 2nd Rpt 1981–82, 1st Rpt 1987–88.

4.05   It is usual for another minister to be appointed Deputy Leader of the House. In the Leader's absence the Deputy Leader takes responsibility for advising the House on matters of procedure and order. In the absence of both of them, this responsibility falls to the senior government Whip present. The Opposition front benches, and the Convenor of the Crossbench Peers (if present), also have a responsibility to draw attention to transgressions of order.

4.06   The role of assisting the House at question time rests with the Leader of the House, not the Lord Speaker.

4.07   At other times of day the Lord on the Woolsack or in the Chair may assist the House by reminding members of the relevant parts of the Companion. Such assistance is limited to procedural advice and is usually given at the start of the business in hand, for example how time is to be divided between the front and back benches in response to a statement, the correct procedure at Report stage, the handling of grouped amendments, and the procedure to be followed in the case of amendments to amendments. Assistance may be helpful at other stages when procedural problems arise.[1]

4.08   The Government Chief Whip advises the House on speaking times in debates. Reinforcing such time limits is handled by the front benches rather than the Lord Speaker, and any member can draw such advice to the attention of the House. Timed debates are brought to an end (if necessary) by the Lord Speaker on an indication from the Table.

4.09   Interventions, in particular those calling attention to the failure of an individual member to comply with the practice of the House, for example when arguments deployed in committee are repeated at length on report, may come from the front benches or other members. . Such interventions would not normally come from the Lord Speaker.

4.10   As indicated above (paragraphs 1.48–50), the Lord Speaker's function in the House is to assist, and not to rule. She observes the same formalities as any other member of the House, addressing the House as a whole, and not an individual member, and not intervening when a member is on his feet. The House does not recognise points of order.

---

[1]   Report of the Select Committee on the Speakership of the House, 2005–06, paragraph 17.

Any advice or assistance given by the Lord Speaker is subject to the view of the House as a whole.[1]

## Conduct in the House

4.11 When the House is sitting, all members should on entering the Chamber bow to the Cloth of Estate behind the Throne.[2] It is not the practice to do so on leaving. Members also bow to the Mace in procession, as a symbol of the authority of the Sovereign. All bows are made with the head and not the body.

4.12 SO 20(1) declares that members of the House "are to keep dignity and order, and not to remove out of their places without just cause, to the hindrance of others that sit near them, and the disorder of the House". In practice, this means that members:

- must not move about the Chamber while a Question is being put from the Woolsack or the Chair;
- must not pass between the Woolsack (or the Chair) and any member who is speaking;
- must not pass between the Woolsack and the Table;[3]
- must leave the Chamber quietly at the end of question time.

4.13 If members wish to speak to other members while the House is sitting, they should go to the Prince's Chamber. Members should not hold conversations in the space behind the Woolsack.[4]

4.14 Unless they are disabled, members of the House must speak standing, except by permission of the House.[5]

4.15 Male members of the House must speak "uncovered" (without a hat), except by permission of the House. Women members may wear hats without seeking permission.[6]

---

[1] Procedure 3rd Rpt 2005–06.

[2] SO 20(2).

[3] Procedure 3rd Rpt 1995–96.

[4] SO 21.

[5] SO 26.

[6] Procedure 1st Rpt 1965–66, SO 26.

4.16   Lords Spiritual wear robes of rochet and chimere in the Chamber. They are expected to wear robes whenever possible in the division lobby.[1]

4.17   Lords Spiritual must speak from the Bishops' benches, and no Lord Temporal may speak from there.[2]

4.18   No-one may speak from the gangways in the House.

4.19   Members address their speech to the House in general and not to any individual.[3] Thus the expressions used are: "Your Lordships", "Your Lordships' House" and "the noble Lord", and not "you".

4.20   Members should not bring into the Chamber:

- books and newspapers (except for papers specifically related to the debate);
- unopened correspondence;
- briefcases and ministerial boxes.[4]

4.21   Exhibits should not be taken into the Chamber or produced in debate, whether to illustrate a speech or for any other purpose.

## Use of electronic devices

4.22   Members and officials may use hand-held electronic devices (not laptops) in the Chamber and Grand Committee for any purpose, provided that they are silent and are used with discretion. Members making speeches may refer to electronic devices in place of paper speaking notes, subject to the existing rule against reading speeches (see paragraph 4.40).

4.23   Members may use hand-held electronic devices to send or receive messages for use in proceedings. They may be used to access documents and information for use in debate.

4.24   Electronic devices may be used silently in select committee meetings, subject to the discretion of the Chairman of the committee on a meeting-by-meeting basis.[1]

---

[1] Procedure 3rd Rpt 1990–91.

[2] See paragraph 1.64.

[3] SO 27.

[4] Procedure 1st Rpt 1969–70.

## Relevance

4.25   Debate must be relevant to the Question before the House; and where more than one Question has been put, for example on an amendment, the debate must be relevant to the last Question proposed until it has been disposed of.[2]

## Order of speaking

4.26   When two or more members rise to speak, the House determines who is to speak. This may, if necessary, be decided upon a motion that one of the members "be now heard". It is customary for speakers from different parties or parts of the House to take turns.

### Speakers' lists

4.27   For most debates a list of speakers is issued by the Government Whips' Office[3] and is available from that Office, and also from the Printed Paper Office, the Prince's Chamber and Peers' Lobby. This list is drawn up after consultation through the usual channels. Members wishing to speak should put their names on the speakers' list at any time before 12 noon on the day of the debate, or 6 p.m. on the previous day if the House is sitting in the morning. Members should remove their names from the list if they become aware in advance that they are unlikely to be able to stay until the end of a debate (see paragraph 4.34).

4.28   Any member whose name is not on the published list may still take part, if time allows, by speaking "in the gap", that is, before the winding-up speeches. They should inform the Table of their wish to do so, and have their name added in manuscript to the list. Any such speaker is expected to be brief (not longer than 4 minutes),[4] and should not take up time allotted to the winding up speeches (for which see paragraph 6.63). Members speaking in the gap are subject to the same rules on attendance at debate as members whose names are included in the speakers list.

---

[1]   Administration and Works 2nd Rpt 2010–12.

[2]   SO 28.

[3]   Procedure 2nd Rpt 1966–67, 2nd Rpt 1971–72.

[4]   Procedure 3rd Rpt 1995–96.

4.29   It is not in order for a member to speak after the mover of a motion or an amendment has exercised his or her right of reply, except when the House is in committee.[1] It is not in order for members to continue the debate on a motion or a question for short debate after the government's reply has been given, save for questions to the minister "before the minister sits down".[2]

4.30   When at the end of a debate the Question has been put, no member may speak save on a point of order.[3]

## Interruption of speeches

4.31   A member of the House who is speaking may be interrupted with a brief question for clarification. Giving way accords with the traditions and customary courtesy of the House. It is, however, recognised that a member may justifiably refuse to give way, for instance, in the middle of an argument, or to repeated interruption, or in time-limited proceedings when time is short. Lengthy or frequent interventions should not be made, even with the consent of the member speaking.

## Speaking more than once

4.32   In the case of motions, no member may speak more than once, except the mover in reply, or a member who has obtained the leave of the House. Such leave may be granted only to:

- a member to explain a material point of their speech, without introducing any new subject matter;

- the Chairman of Committees, or in his absence a Deputy Chairman, and the chairman of a select committee on the report of such a committee;

- a minister of the Crown.

4.33   When the House is in committee there is no restriction on the number of times a member may speak.[4]

---

[1] Procedure 1st Rpt 1978–79.

[2] Procedure 1st Rpt 1977–78.

[3] SO 29.

[4] SO 30.

## Attendance at debate

4.34   A member of the House who is taking part in a debate (including general debates and debates on amendments or motions) should attend the start, end and greater part of that debate.[1] In addition, it is considered discourteous for members not to be present for at least the opening speeches, the speeches before and after their own, and for the winding-up speeches. Ministers may decide not to answer, orally or in writing, points made by a speaker who does not stay to hear the minister's closing speech. Members who believe that they are unlikely to be able to stay to the end of a debate should not seek to participate in it (and if the debate has a speakers' list, should remove their names from the list).

4.35   There are reasons for these customs. Members who have missed the speeches before their own will not know what has already been said and so points may be repeated or missed. Members who leave soon after speaking are lacking in courtesy to others, who may wish to question, or reply to, points they have raised. Debate may degenerate into a series of set speeches if speakers do not attend throughout.

4.36   It is, however, recognised that some members may have commitments related to the committee work of the House which may prevent them from being able to attend as much of the debate as might otherwise be expected.

## Length of speeches

4.37   The House has resolved "That speeches in this House should be shorter".[2] Long speeches can create boredom and tend to kill debate.

4.38   In debates where there are no formal time limits, members opening or winding up, from either side, are expected to keep within 20 minutes. Other speakers are expected to keep within 15 minutes. These are only guidelines and, on occasion, a speech of outstanding importance, or a ministerial speech winding up an exceptionally long debate, may exceed these limits.[3] For length of speeches in time-limited proceedings see paragraph 6.63; in questions for short debate see paragraph 6.47.

---

[1]   Procedure 1st Rpt 1969–70; 1st Rpt 1987–88; 3rd Rpt 1995–96; 1st Rpt 1998–99; 1st Rpt 2002–03.

[2]   LJ (1964–65) 386.

[3]   Procedure 1st Rpt 1987–88.

4.39 Clocks are installed under the galleries to time the length of speeches. The clocks are used principally to record:

- the length of speeches in all debates except debates on amendments and in Committee of the whole House;

- the time taken on amendments at all stages and, in Committee of the whole House, on debates on the Question that a clause or Schedule stand part of the bill;

- the total time taken for oral questions and debates on delegated legislation;

- for ministerial statements, the length of the statement itself, the frontbench exchanges and the backbench exchanges.[1]

## Reading of speeches

4.40 The House has resolved that the reading of speeches is "alien to the custom of this House, and injurious to the traditional conduct of its debates".[2] It is acknowledged, however, that on some occasions, for example ministerial statements, it is necessary to read from a prepared text. In practice, some speakers may wish to have "extended notes" from which to speak, but it is not in the interests of good debate that they should follow them closely.[3]

## Languages other than English

4.41 Languages other than English should not be used in debate, except where necessary. The use of the Welsh language is permitted for the purpose of committee proceedings held in Wales.[4]

## Reference to visitors

4.42 Visitors should not be referred to, whether in the public gallery or in any other part of the Chamber, except for the purpose of a motion for the withdrawal of all visitors.[5]

---

[1] Procedure 6th Rpt 1971–72, 1st Rpt 1982–83.

[2] LJ (1935–36) 241.

[3] Procedure 1st Rpt 1969–70, 4th Rpt 1992–93.

[4] Procedure 2nd Rpt 2008–09.

[5] Procedure 1st Rpt 1980–81.

## Speaking on behalf of outside interests

4.43   When speaking in the House, members speak for themselves and not on behalf of outside interests. They may indicate that an outside body agrees with the substance of their views but they should not read out extended briefing material from such bodies.[1]

## References in debate to the House of Commons

### References to the House of Commons and its members

4.44   The House of Commons may be referred to by name, rather than as "the other place" or "another place".

4.45   Members of the House of Commons are referred to by their names, and not by reference to their constituencies.[2] Ministers may be referred to by their ministerial titles. Additional descriptions such as "Right Honourable", "Honourable" and "Learned" are not used, except when referring to ministerial or party colleagues in the House of Commons as "Right Honourable" or "Honourable" friends.

### Personal criticism of members of the House of Commons

4.46   No member of the House of Commons should be mentioned by name, or otherwise identified, for the purpose of criticism of a personal, rather than a political, nature. Public activities by members of the House of Commons outside their parliamentary duties may be referred to.

### Criticism of Commons proceedings

4.47   Criticism of proceedings in the House of Commons or of Commons Speaker's rulings is out of order, but criticism may be made of the institutional structure of Parliament or the role and function of the House of Commons (see also paragraphs 6.20 and 6.22, in relation to the wording of questions).

---

[1]   Procedure 1st Rpt 1969–70, 4th Rpt 1992–93.

[2]   Procedure 2nd Rpt 1991–92, 1st Rpt 1992–93.

## Maiden speeches[1]

4.48   It is usual for a member making a maiden speech not to be interrupted and to be congratulated by the next speaker only, on behalf of the whole House, plus the front benches if they wish.[2] It is therefore expected that a member making a maiden speech will do so in a debate with a speakers' list, so that the House may know that the conventional courtesies apply. In return the maiden speaker is expected to be short (less than 10 minutes) and uncontroversial. The maiden speaker should not take advantage of the indulgence of the House to express views in terms that would ordinarily provoke interruption.

4.49   Members of the House who have not yet made their maiden speeches may not table oral questions or questions for short debate, but may table questions for written answer.

### Conduct in the House during maiden speeches

4.50   When a maiden speech is being made, and during the following speaker's congratulations, members of the House are expected to remain in their seats and not leave the Chamber. Those entering the Chamber are expected to remain by the steps of the Throne or below the Bar.

## Appellations[3]

4.51   The proper ways of referring to other members of the House in debate are given in the table on pages 71–72.

4.52   When any Peer who has a higher title than that by virtue of which he or she sits in Parliament is named in any record of proceedings of the House or of a committee, the higher title alone is used. When such a Peer takes the oath of allegiance, the title or dignity by which he or she sits in Parliament is added in brackets.[4]

---

[1]  Procedure 1st Rpt 1969–70.

[2]  Procedure 2nd Rpt 2006–07.

[3]  Procedure 1st Rpt 1969–70.

[4]  SO 7.

| | |
|---|---|
| Archbishop of the Church of England | "the most reverend Primate, the Archbishop of ..." |
| Bishop of the Church of England | "the right reverend Prelate, the Bishop of ..." |
| Duke | "the noble Duke, the Duke of ..." |
| Marquess | "the noble Marquess, Lord ..." |
| Earl | "the noble Earl, Lord ..." |
| Countess | "the noble Countess, Lady ..." |
| Viscount | "the noble Viscount, Lord ..." |
| Baron | "the noble Lord, Lord ..." |
| Baroness or Lady | "the noble Baroness, Lady ..." or "the noble Lady, Lady ..." |
| Members with rank of Admiral of the Fleet, Field Marshal or Marshal of the Royal Air Force, members who have held the office of Chief of the Defence Staff, and holders of the Victoria or George Cross | "the noble and gallant ..." (service rank is not referred to)[1] |
| Law Officers of the Crown, Judges of superior courts in the United Kingdom (High Court and above)[2], former holders of these offices or former Lords of Appeal[3] | "the noble and learned ..." |
| Archbishops of other Churches who are members of the House | "the noble and most reverend Lord..." |

---

[1] Procedure 1st Rpt 1969-70, 2nd Rpt 1988–89.

[2] Procedure 1st Rpt 1964–65, 1st Rpt 1969–70.

[3] As defined in the Appellate Jurisdiction Act 1876. The Act was repealed with effect from 1 October 2009, but Members who formerly fell within the definition of "Lord of Appeal" under that Act remain entitled to the appellation "noble and learned".

| Bishops of other Churches who are members of the House | "the noble and right reverend Lord ..." |
|---|---|
| Former Archbishops or Bishops who are members of the House | "the noble and right reverend Lord..."[1] |
| Fellow member of a political party | "my noble friend" (instead of one of the above descriptions) |
| Relatives | "my noble kinsman ..." or "my noble relative ..." (precise relationship is not mentioned) |

## Asperity of speech (SO 32)

4.53   When debate becomes heated, it is open to any member of the House to move "that the Standing Order on Asperity of Speech be read by the Clerk". Standing Order 32 can be read only on a motion agreed to by the House, and this motion is debatable.

## "That the noble Lord be no longer heard"

4.54   If in a speech a member is thought to be seriously transgressing the practice of the House, it is open to another member to move "that the noble Lord be no longer heard". This motion however is very rare; it is debatable and seldom needs to be decided on Question since members generally conform to the sense of the House as soon as this sense becomes clear.

4.55   The effect of agreeing to this motion is to prohibit the member in question from speaking further on the substantive motion, but not on any subsequent motion.

## The Next Business motion

4.56   A member who does not wish the House to record an opinion on a motion that has been moved may, at any time during the course of the debate, move "That the House do proceed to the next business".[2] It is helpful if a member who intends to move this motion gives notice.

---

[1]   Procedure 1st Rpt 1974–75.

[2]   Procedure 5th Rpt 1971–72.

4.57   A Next Business motion supersedes the original motion before the House and, if it is agreed to, the Question on the original motion is not put, and the debate ends. If it is disagreed to, the debate on the original motion is resumed and the Question is put in the usual way.

4.58   The Next Business motion is debatable and, since it cannot be debated without reference to the original motion, the subject matter of both motions may be debated together.

4.59   The Next Business motion is not allowed on an amendment; although, after an amendment has been agreed to, it may be moved on the original motion as amended. It may not be moved in any committee of the House.

## Closure[1]

4.60   The Closure, that is, the motion "that the Question be now put", is not debatable and so requires an immediate conclusion. If carried, it compels the House at once to come to a decision on the original motion. It is a most exceptional procedure, so when a member seeks to move the Closure, the Lord on the Woolsack or in the Chair draws attention to its exceptional nature, and gives the member concerned the opportunity to reconsider, by reading the following paragraph to the House before the Question is put:

> [To be read slowly] *"I am instructed by order of the House to say that the motion "That the Question be now put" is considered to be a most exceptional procedure and the House will not accept it save in circumstances where it is felt to be the only means of ensuring the proper conduct of the business of the House; further, if a member who seeks to move it persists in his intention, the practice of the House is that the Question on the motion is put without debate."*

4.61   If the member of the House who is seeking to move the Closure persists, the Lord on the Woolsack or in the Chair must put and complete the Question forthwith without debate, in the following terms: "The Question is that the Question be now put."

4.62   If the Closure is carried:

---

[1]  Procedure 1st Rpt 1960–61, 6th Rpt 1970–71.

(a) the Lord on the Woolsack or in the Chair remains standing after announcing the result and immediately puts and completes the original Question without further debate;

(b) the original Question cannot be withdrawn because the House has decided that the Question be now put; and

(c) the Lord on the Woolsack or in the Chair may not put any other Question until the original Question has been disposed of.

## SUB JUDICE

4.63 The privilege of freedom of speech in Parliament places a corresponding duty on members to use the freedom responsibly. This is the basis of the *sub judice* rule. Under the rule both Houses abstain from discussing the merits of disputes about to be tried and decided in the courts of law.

4.64 The House of Lords adopted a resolution on *sub judice* on 11 May 2000. The resolution, as amended, is as follows:

"That, subject to the discretion of the Lord Speaker,[1] and to the right of the House to legislate on any matter or to discuss any delegated legislation, the House in all its proceedings (including proceedings of committees of the House) shall apply the following rules on matters *sub judice*:

(1) Cases in which proceedings are active in United Kingdom courts shall not be referred to in any motion, debate or question.

(a) (i) Criminal proceedings are active when a charge has been made or a summons to appear has been issued, or, in Scotland, a warrant to cite has been granted.

(ii) Criminal proceedings cease to be active when they are concluded by a verdict and sentence or discontinuance, or, in cases dealt with by courts martial, after the conclusion of the mandatory post-trial review.

(b) (i) Civil proceedings are active when arrangements for the hearing, such as setting down a case for trial, have

---

[1] Procedure 2nd Rpt 2006–07.

been made, until the proceedings are ended by judgment or discontinuance.

(ii)   Any application made in or for the purposes of any civil proceedings shall be treated as a distinct proceeding.

(c)   Appellate proceedings, whether criminal or civil, are active from the time when they are commenced by application for leave to appeal or by notice of appeal until ended by judgment or discontinuance.

But where a ministerial decision is in question, or in the opinion of the Lord Speaker a case concerns issues of national importance such as the economy, public order or the essential services, reference to the issues or the case may be made in motions, debates or questions.

(2)   Specific matters which the House has expressly referred to any judicial body for decision and report shall not be referred to in any motion, debate or question, from the time when the Resolution of the House is passed, until the report is laid before the House.

(3)   For the purposes of this Resolution—

(a)   Matters before Coroners Courts or Fatal Accident Inquiries shall be treated as matters within paragraph (1)(a); and

(b)   "Question" includes a supplementary question."[1]

4.65   The House has agreed that the practice governing motions and questions relating to matters *sub judice* should be similar in both Houses of Parliament.[2] It is desirable that each House should be in the same position to debate a *sub judice* matter when the circumstances warrant it.

4.66   The rules governing *sub judice* do not apply to bills, Measures or delegated legislation or to proceedings on them. Nor do they apply to matters being considered by departmental inquiries and the like; but it is recognised that Parliament should not generally intervene in matters where the decision has been delegated to others by Parliament itself.

---

[1] LJ (1999–2000) 389.

[2] Procedure 1st Rpt 1963–64.

4.67    The Lord Speaker must be given at least 24 hours' notice of any proposal to refer to a matter which is *sub judice.* The exercise of the Speaker's discretion may not be challenged in the House.[1]

## MINISTERIAL ACCOUNTABILITY

4.68    The House has resolved that, in the opinion of this House, the following principles should govern the conduct of ministers of the Crown in relation to Parliament:

(1)    Ministers have a duty to Parliament to account, and be held to account, for the policies, decisions and actions of their departments and executive agencies;

(2)    It is of paramount importance that ministers should give accurate and truthful information to Parliament, correcting any inadvertent error at the earliest opportunity. Ministers who knowingly mislead Parliament will be expected to offer their resignation to the Prime Minister;

(3)    Ministers should be as open as possible with Parliament, refusing to provide information only when disclosure would not be in the public interest;

(4)    Ministers should require civil servants who give evidence before parliamentary committees on their behalf and under their directions to be as helpful as possible in providing accurate, truthful and full information;

(5)    The interpretation of "public interest" in paragraph (3) shall be decided in accordance with statute and the government's *Code of Practice on Access to Government Information,*[2] and compliance with the duty in paragraph (4) shall be in accordance with the duties and responsibilities of civil servants set out in the *Civil Service Code.*[3]

---

[1]    Procedure 1st Rpt 1994–95, Report of the Select Committee on the Speakership of the House of Lords, HL Paper 92 2005–06.

[2]    This Code was completely superseded by the Freedom of Information Act 2000, and had no effect after 1 January 2005.

[3]    HL Deb. 20 March 1997 cols 1055–62; LJ (1996–97) 404.

## Members and employees of public boards

4.69  Members of the House of Lords who are members of or employed by public boards, executive agencies or other public bodies, whether commercial or non-commercial in character, are not by reason of such membership debarred from exercising their right to speak in the House of Lords, even on matters affecting the boards of which they are members; and it is recognised that, in the last resort, only the members concerned can decide whether they can properly speak on a particular occasion.[1] Such members are subject to the normal rules on registration and declaration of interests.

4.70  The following guidance (known as the "Addison Rules"), based upon that given in 1951 by the then Leader of the House, Viscount Addison, after consultation and agreement between the parties, may be helpful to members of the House who are considering whether or not to take part in a particular debate:[2]

(a) when questions affecting public boards arise in Parliament, the government alone are responsible to Parliament. The duty of reply cannot devolve upon members of public boards who happen to be members of the House of Lords;

(b) it is important that, except where otherwise provided, public boards should be free to conduct their day-to-day administration without the intervention of Parliament or ministers. If board members who happen also to be members of the House of Lords were to give the House information about the day-to-day operations of the board or to answer criticism respecting it, the House would in fact be exercising a measure of parliamentary supervision over matters of management. It would also be difficult for the responsible minister not to give similar information to the House of Commons;

(c) there is no duty upon board members to speak in any debate or to answer questions put to them in debate. Nor should the fact that a member spoke in a particular debate be regarded as

---

[1]  Procedure 2nd Rpt 1970–71.

[2]  HL Deb. 21 March 1951, col. 1241.

a precedent for that member or any other member to speak in any other debate;

(d) the foregoing applies only to debates relating to public boards. Experience acquired as a member of a public board will often be relevant to general debates in which the same considerations do not arise, and the contributions of board members who are members of the House may be all the more valuable because of that experience.

# CHAPTER 5

# MEMBERS' CONDUCT

5.01 Members' conduct in the course of their parliamentary duties is governed by a Code of Conduct, agreed on 30 November 2009, and an accompanying Guide to the Code of Conduct, agreed on 16 March 2010, and amended on 9 November 2011. The full text of the Code, which came into effect at the start of the 2010 Parliament, is as follows:

## Code of Conduct for Members of the House of Lords

*Introduction*

1. The House of Lords is the second Chamber of the United Kingdom Parliament. As a constituent part of Parliament, the House of Lords makes laws, holds government to account, and debates issues of public interest.

2. Membership of the House is not an office, and does not constitute employment; most Members' primary employment is or has been outside Parliament. In discharging their parliamentary duties Members of the House of Lords draw substantially on experience and expertise gained outside Parliament.

3. The purpose of this Code of Conduct is

    (a) to provide guidance for Members of the House of Lords on the standards of conduct expected of them in the discharge of their parliamentary duties; the Code does not extend to Members' performance of duties unrelated to parliamentary proceedings, or to their private lives;

    (b) to provide the openness and accountability necessary to reinforce public confidence in the way in which Members of the House of Lords perform their parliamentary duties.

4. This Code applies to all Members of the House of Lords who are not either

    (a) on leave of absence;

    (b) suspended from the service of the House; or

    (c) statutorily disqualified from active membership.

5. Members are to sign an undertaking to abide by the Code as part of the ceremony of taking the oath upon introduction and at the start of each Parliament.

*General principles*

6. By virtue of their oath, or affirmation, of allegiance, Members of the House have a duty to be faithful and bear true allegiance to Her Majesty The Queen, Her heirs and successors, according to law.

7. In the conduct of their parliamentary duties, Members of the House shall base their actions on consideration of the public interest, and shall resolve any conflict between their personal interest and the public interest at once, and in favour of the public interest.

8. Members of the House:

    (a) must comply with the Code of Conduct;

    (b) should act always on their personal honour;

    (c) must never accept or agree to accept any financial inducement as an incentive or reward for exercising parliamentary influence;

    (d) must not seek to profit from membership of the House by accepting or agreeing to accept payment or other incentive or reward in return for providing parliamentary advice or services.

9. Members of the House should observe the seven general principles of conduct identified by the Committee on Standards in Public Life. These principles will be taken into consideration when any allegation of breaches of the provisions in other sections of the Code is under investigation:

    (a) Selflessness: Holders of public office should take decisions solely in terms of the public interest. They should not do so in order to gain financial or other material benefits for themselves, their family, or their friends.

    (b) Integrity: Holders of public office should not place themselves under any financial or other obligation to outside individuals or organisations that might influence them in the performance of their official duties.

    (c) Objectivity: In carrying out public business, including making public appointments, awarding contracts, or recommending individuals for rewards and benefits, holders of public office should make choices on merit.

    (d) Accountability: Holders of public office are accountable for their decisions and actions to the public and must submit themselves to whatever scrutiny is appropriate to their office.

(e) Openness: Holders of public office should be as open as possible about all the decisions and actions that they take. They should give reasons for their decisions and restrict information only when the wider public interest clearly demands.

(f) Honesty: Holders of public office have a duty to declare any private interests relating to their public duties and to take steps to resolve any conflicts arising in a way that protects the public interest.

(g) Leadership: Holders of public office should promote and support these principles by leadership and example.

*Rules of Conduct*

10. In order to assist in openness and accountability Members shall:

(a) register in the Register of Lords' Interests all relevant interests, in order to make clear what are the interests that might reasonably be thought to influence their parliamentary actions;

(b) declare when speaking in the House, or communicating with ministers or public servants, any interest which is a relevant interest in the context of the debate or the matter under discussion;

(c) act in accordance with any rules agreed by the House in respect of financial support for Members or the facilities of the House.

11. The test of relevant interest is whether the interest might be thought by a reasonable member of the public to influence the way in which a Member of the House of Lords discharges his or her parliamentary duties: in the case of registration, the Member's parliamentary duties in general; in the case of declaration, his or her duties in respect of the particular matter under discussion.

12. The test of relevant interest is therefore not whether a Member's actions in Parliament will be influenced by the interest, but whether a reasonable member of the public might think that this might be the case. Relevant interests include both financial and non-financial interests.

13. Members are responsible for ensuring that their registered interests are accurate and up-to-date. They should register any change in their relevant interests within one month of the change.

14. A Member must not act as a paid advocate in any proceeding of the House; that is to say, he or she must not seek by parliamentary means to confer exclusive benefit on an outside body or person from which he or she receives payment or reward.

15. Members are not otherwise debarred from participating in proceedings in regard to which they possess relevant interests, financial or non-financial; but such interests should be declared fully. Members of the House should be especially cautious in deciding whether to speak or vote in relation to interests that are direct, pecuniary and shared by few others.

*Enforcement of the Code of Conduct*

16. A House of Lords Commissioner for Standards is appointed to investigate alleged breaches of this Code, or of the rules governing Members' financial support or use of parliamentary facilities. Any such investigation is conducted in accordance with procedures set out in the Guide to the Code of Conduct.

17. After investigation the Commissioner reports his findings to the Sub-Committee on Lords' Conduct; the Sub-Committee reviews the Commissioner's findings and, where appropriate, recommends a disciplinary sanction to the Committee for Privileges and Conduct. The Member concerned has a right of appeal to the Committee for Privileges and Conduct against both the Commissioner's findings and any recommended sanction.

18. The Committee for Privileges and Conduct, having heard any appeal, reports its conclusions and recommendations to the House. The final decision rests with the House.

19. In investigating and adjudicating allegations of non-compliance with this Code, the Commissioner, the Sub-Committee on Lords' Conduct and the Committee for Privileges and Conduct shall act in accordance with the principles of natural justice and fairness.

20. Members shall co-operate, at all stages, with any investigation into their conduct by or under the authority of the House.

21. No Member shall lobby a member of the Committee for Privileges and Conduct or the Sub-Committee on Lords' Conduct in a manner calculated or intended to influence their consideration of a complaint of a breach of this Code.

*Advice and review*

22. The operation of the Register is overseen by the Sub-Committee on Lords' Conduct, assisted by the Registrar of Lords' Interests. The Registrar is available to advise Members of the House, and may consult the Sub-Committee when necessary.

23. A Member who acts on the advice of the Registrar in determining what is a relevant interest satisfies fully the requirements of the Code of Conduct in that regard. However, the final responsibility for deciding whether or not to participate in proceedings to which that interest is relevant rests with the Member concerned.

24. The Sub-Committee on Lords' Conduct reviews the Code of Conduct once each Parliament. Its findings, along with any recommended changes to the Code, are reported to the House.

25. The Sub-Committee also keeps the Guide to the Code of Conduct under regular review; recommended changes are reported to the House and will not take effect until agreed by the House.[1]

5.02 In accordance with paragraph 5 of the Code of Conduct, members are to sign an undertaking to abide by the Code as part of the ceremony of taking the oath upon introduction and at the start of each Parliament. Any member who has taken the oath but attends the House without having signed the undertaking is deemed to have breached the Code; it is for the Sub-Committee on Lords' Conduct to consider an appropriate sanction.

## The Guide to the Code of Conduct

5.03 The operation of the Code of Conduct is kept under review by the Sub-Committee on Lords' Conduct, a sub-committee of the Committee for Privileges and Conduct. As well as reviewing the Code itself once each Parliament, the Sub-Committee keeps the "Guide to the Code of Conduct" under regular review.[2] This Guide has been agreed by resolution of the House, and is binding upon members. Any change to the Guide must be reported to the House and no change can take effect until agreed by the House. Copies of the up-to-date text of the Guide are available online, from the Printed Paper Office or from the Registrar

---

[1] Minutes of Proceeding, 30 November 2009; amended 16 March 2010.

[2] Privileges 2nd Rpt 2009–10. A second edition of the Guide was published in November 2011.

of Lords' Interests. The Registrar is also available to advise members on the rules governing members' conduct.

5.04   What follows is a summary of key points within the Guide to the Code of Conduct which relate to members' conduct in the House and its committees. However, the Guide itself is the authoritative source of guidance on members' conduct.

## General principles and rules of conduct

5.05   Members are required both "to comply with the Code of Conduct" (paragraph 8(a)), and to act always "on their personal honour" (paragraph 8(b)). These paragraphs of the Code, taken together, mean that members are required not only to obey the letter of the rules, but to act in accordance with the spirit of those rules and the sense of the House. Members are under a general obligation to bear in mind the underlying purpose of the Code, which is to provide "openness and accountability".[1]

5.06   Members are required under paragraph 7 of the Code to base their actions on consideration of the public interest. Acceptance of financial inducement as an incentive or reward for exercising parliamentary influence would necessarily contravene this principle. Paragraph 8(c) of the Code therefore states that members "must never accept or agree to accept any financial inducement as an incentive or reward for exercising parliamentary influence".

5.07   Paragraph 8(d) of the Code describes the specific application of the principles described in paragraphs 7 and 8(c): members "must not seek to profit from membership of the House by accepting or agreeing to accept payment or other incentive or reward in return for providing parliamentary advice or services".

5.08   The prohibition on accepting payment in return for parliamentary *advice* means that members may not act as paid parliamentary consultants, advising outside organisations or persons on process, for example how they may lobby or otherwise influence the work of Parliament.

5.09   The prohibition on accepting payment in return for parliamentary *services* means that members may not, in return for payment or other incentive or reward, assist outside organisations or persons in influencing

---

[1] Privileges and Conduct 10th Rpt 2010–12.

Parliament. This includes acting as a "paid advocate" (see below), or making use of their position to arrange meetings with a view to any person lobbying members of either House, ministers or officials.

5.10   Paragraph 14 of the Code states that a member "must not act as a paid advocate in any proceeding of the House; that is to say, he or she must not seek by parliamentary means to confer exclusive benefit on an outside body or person from which he or she receives payment or reward."

5.11   This "exclusive benefit" principle would mean, for instance, that a member who was paid by a pharmaceutical company would be barred from seeking to confer benefit exclusively upon that company by parliamentary means. The way in which the benefit is conferred should be interpreted broadly: all proceedings of the House are included. The nature of the "exclusive benefit", on the other hand, should be interpreted narrowly. The same member would not be debarred from tabling an amendment, speaking or voting on matters relevant to, for instance, the pharmaceutical sector as a whole; National Health Service spending on drugs; or government policy on drug licensing and patents.

5.12   A member who seeks to confer benefit on an organisation in which he or she has a financial interest, but who considers that this does not constitute an "exclusive benefit", should make it clear in debate how he or she is acting not only in the interest of the organisation, but also the wider sector or community of which that organisation forms a part.

5.13   Paragraphs 8(c) and 8(d) of the Code (which prohibit payment for exercising parliamentary influence and payment for providing parliamentary advice and services) and paragraph 14 of the Code (which prohibits paid advocacy for exclusive benefit) do not apply to the Lords Spiritual, to ministers of the Crown, or to members or employees of non-departmental public bodies (whether commercial or non-commercial in character) in relation to those specific roles. Members and employees of public boards may take part in proceedings affecting the boards of which they are members or employees, subject to the usual rules on declaration of interests (see paragraph 4.69).

## Participation in proceedings

5.14   In accordance with paragraph 15 of the Code a member with a relevant interest is free to take part in the public business of the House subject to:

- the rules on financial inducements and parliamentary influence (paragraph 8 of the Code);

- the rules on paid advocacy (paragraph 14 of the Code);

- the rules on the registration and declaration of interests (paragraphs 10–12 of the Code); and

- the resolution of any conflict between personal and public interest in favour of the public interest (paragraph 7 of the Code).

5.15   However, paragraph 15 goes on to state that "Members of the House should be especially cautious in deciding whether to speak or vote in relation to interests that are direct, pecuniary and shared by few others." In other words, caution is especially required where a financial interest is direct (the member could personally benefit as a direct result of the proceeding) and shared by few others (the member is one of a small group of people in society who would so benefit).

5.16   More generally, a member who is unsure whether or not to participate in parliamentary proceedings in relation to which he or she has relevant interests should consider the following factors:

- the nature of the proceeding itself. There would, for instance, be more latitude in the case of a general debate than in proposing or voting on an amendment to legislation. Members with financial interests that are relevant to private legislation should exercise particular caution, and seek advice before deciding to participate in proceedings on that legislation.

- the nature of the member's intended contribution. A speech urging government investment in a sector in which the member had a financial interest might be open to misconstruction, whereas a speech canvassing issues of more general interest would not.

5.17   Members may consult the Registrar on these matters, but as paragraph 23 of the Code makes clear, "the final responsibility for deciding whether or not to participate in proceedings to which that interest is relevant rests with the member concerned".

### Registration and declaration of interests

5.18   Under paragraph 10 of the Code members are required to register and declare certain relevant interests. A relevant interest is one which might be thought by a reasonable member of the public to influence the way in which a member of the House of Lords discharges his or her parliamentary duties: in the case of registration, the member's parliamentary duties in general; in the case of declaration, his or her duties in respect of the particular matter under discussion.

5.19   Thus the House has two distinct but related methods for the disclosure of the relevant interests of its members. Registered interests are published in the Register of Lords' Interests, which is published online and updated daily. The main purpose of the Register is to give public notification on a continuing basis of those interests held by members that might reasonably be thought to have a general influence upon their parliamentary conduct or actions. The main purpose of declaration of interest is to ensure that fellow members of the House, ministers, officials and the public are made aware, at the point at which the member participates in proceedings of the House or otherwise acts in a parliamentary capacity, of any present or expected future interest that might reasonably be thought relevant to that particular action by the member. There is also a Register of Interests of Lords Members' Staff.

5.20   In cases of doubt members should seek the advice of the Registrar of Lords' Interests. A member who acts on the advice of the Registrar in determining what he or she is required to register or declare as a relevant interest fully satisfies the requirements of the Code of Conduct as regards registration or declaration.

## Registration

5.21   The Guide lists 10 categories within which members are required to register all financial or non-financial interests held by them, and in certain cases by their spouse or partner, which are relevant for the purposes of registration. Full details are given in the Guide, pages 12–18.

## Declaration

5.22   Under paragraph 10(b) of the Code of Conduct, members must "declare when speaking in the House, or communicating with ministers or public servants, any interest which is a relevant interest in the context of the debate or the matter under discussion". This provision should be interpreted broadly. Thus "speaking in the House" covers members' participation in the work of select committees of the House. "Public servants" includes servants of the Crown, civil servants, employees of government agencies or non-departmental public bodies, and members, officers and employees of local authorities or other governmental bodies.

5.23 The "matter under discussion" is normally the item of business as it appears on the Order Paper. Thus in the case of a bill, the subject-matter is the bill as a whole. A full declaration of any interests relevant to a bill should be made at least on the occasion of the member's first intervention at each stage of the bill's progress.

5.24 Members should declare interests briefly, but in such a way that their declaration is comprehensible, specific, and unambiguous, without either demanding prior knowledge of their audience or requiring reference to other documents, including the Register. An exception may be made at Oral Questions or other time-limited proceedings, where it may be for the convenience of the House that members should not take up time by making lengthy or repeated declarations of interest. On such occasions a brief reference to the published Register may be appropriate, though this only suffices for registered interests.

5.25 Members should not take up the time of the House, particularly during time-limited proceedings, by declaring trivial, frivolous or irrelevant interests.

5.26 Members are also required to draw attention to any relevant registrable interests when tabling written notices in *House of Lords Business*. The symbol [I] appears after the member's name in *House of Lords Business*. The Table Office also arranges for online publication of the specific interest.

### Members' financial support

5.27 Membership of the House of Lords is not salaried. Members of the House are, however, entitled to claim financial support in respect of their parliamentary work. The House Committee is responsible for proposing rules on the financial support available to members, which are reported to and agreed by the House. The available support and the rules relating to the scheme are set out in the *Guide to financial support for Members*.

5.28 Paragraph 10(c) of the Code of Conduct states that members shall "act in accordance with any rules agreed by the House in respect of financial support for Members". A breach of such rules therefore constitutes a breach of the Code of Conduct and could lead to an investigation by the House of Lords Commissioner for Standards.

5.29 The Finance Director is responsible for the administration of the scheme, and any member may seek the written advice of the Finance Director before determining what use to make of the scheme. The responsibility for deciding what use to make of the scheme rests with the member concerned.

## Use of facilities and services

5.30 The House provides various facilities and services for members, the cost of which is either met in full or subsidised by the public purse. These facilities and services are provided primarily to support members in their parliamentary work. The domestic committees are responsible for proposing rules on the use of facilities by members, which are reported to and agreed by the House. The available facilities and services and the rules relating to their use are set out in the *Handbook on facilities and services for Members of the House of Lords.*

5.31 Paragraph 10(c) of the Code of Conduct states that members shall "act in accordance with any rules agreed by the House in respect of … the facilities of the House". A breach of the rules therefore constitutes a breach of the Code of Conduct and could lead to an investigation by the House of Lords Commissioner for Standards. The *Handbook* identifies which official is responsible for the provision of each facility or service and a member who acts on the advice of that official in determining what use to make of a facility fully satisfies the requirements of the Code of Conduct in that regard.

## Enforcement

5.32 The procedure for investigating complaints is set out in full in the Guide to the Code of Conduct. In summary, responsibility for investigating alleged breaches of the Code rests with the House of Lords Commissioner for Standards, who is an independent officer appointed by the House as a whole. Following his investigation, the Commissioner reports findings of fact to the Sub-Committee on Lords' Conduct and offers his own conclusion on whether the Code has been breached. The Sub-Committee reviews the Commissioner's findings, may comment on them and, where appropriate, recommends a sanction. The reports of the Commissioner and Sub-Committee are presented to the Committee for Privileges and Conduct, and the member concerned has a right of appeal against both the Commissioner's findings and any recommended sanction. Having heard any appeal, the Committee for Privileges and Conduct reports to the House and the final decision rests with the House.

## Disciplinary powers

5.33 The Houses possesses an inherent power to discipline its members; the means by which it chooses to exercise this power falls within the regulation by the House of its own procedures. The duty imposed upon members, by virtue of the writs of summons, to attend Parliament, is subject to various implied conditions, which are reflected in the many rules governing the conduct of members which have been adopted over time by the House. The House has no power, by resolution, to require that the writ of summons be withheld from a member otherwise entitled to receive it; as a result, it is not within the power of the House by resolution to expel a member permanently.[1] The House does possess the power to suspend its members for a defined period not longer than the remainder of the current Parliament.[2]

5.34 In the event of a member being suspended, the member concerned is expected to leave the Chamber without delay.[3] Suspended members have no access to the precincts of the House of Lords estate (including as guests) or to services provided to members. Suspended members' security passes are cancelled, as are those of their staff, spouses and partners. Suspended members are ineligible to claim financial support from the House during the period for which they are suspended, are not entitled to receive parliamentary papers from the Printed Paper Office, and cannot use any parliamentary ICT applications.[4]

---

[1] See Report of the Joint Committee on Parliamentary Privilege, HL Paper 43-I, 1998–99, paragraphs 272, 279.

[2] Privileges 1st Rpt 2008–09. See HL Deb. 20 May 2009, cols 1394–1418.

[3] Procedure Committee minutes 18 May 2009.

[4] House Committee minutes 19 May 2009.

# CHAPTER 6
# STATEMENTS, QUESTIONS AND MOTIONS

## STATEMENTS

### Personal statements

6.01    Members may by leave of the House make a short factual statement of a personal character, such as a personal apology, a correction of information given in a speech made by them in the House or a reply to allegations made against them in the House. Personal statements are usually made at the beginning of business and are not debatable.

### Ministerial statements (oral)[1]

6.02    Statements by ministers on matters of public importance may be made by leave of the House without notice.[2] Such statements are commonly synchronised in the two Houses. Annunciators in the House also show this information.

### *Timing*

6.03    If the responsible minister is a member of the House of Commons, the statement is made first in that House and may be repeated in the House of Lords. The timing is agreed through the usual channels.[3] Where a statement of exceptional length has been made in full to the House of Commons and made available in the Printed Paper Office before it is due to be repeated in the House of Lords, the minister in the Lords may (with the agreement of the usual channels) draw the attention of the House to the statement made earlier without repeating it, and the House then proceeds immediately to the period for exchanges

---

[1]    Procedure 2nd Rpt 1984–85.

[2]    SO 35.

[3]    When considering whether to require repetition of a Statement made in the Commons on a Wednesday, the usual channels bear in mind the extra pressure on business created by the late start, and consider the additional options of (i) a Private Notice Question on the subject of the Statement and (ii) taking the Statement the next day (Procedure 2nd Rpt 2005–06).

with the Opposition front bench or benches. In such circumstances the text of the statement is reproduced in full in the Official Report.[1]

6.04    If the responsible minister is a member of the House of Lords, the statement is usually made after questions (on Fridays, at the beginning of business).

6.05    If the House is in committee, it is resumed on the motion of a member of the government for the purpose of hearing the statement. When the statement and exchanges following it are finished, the House again resolves itself into a committee, on the motion of the Lord in charge of the bill. On days when there are two balloted debates or time-limited debates, any Commons statement repeated in the House is normally taken between the two debates. Only in exceptional circumstances are such debates interrupted for a statement.

6.06    There is no limit on the number of ministerial statements that can be made in one day, but lengthy interruption of the business of the House is not desirable. If the Lords are not sitting on a day on which a statement is made in the Commons, it is not the practice to repeat it when the Lords next sit, save in the case of an exceptionally important statement.

*Discussion on a statement*

6.07    Ministerial statements are made for the information of the House, and although brief questions[2] from all quarters of the House are allowed, statements should not be made the occasion for an immediate debate.[3] The time for the Opposition front bench or benches and the minister's reply to them should be limited to 20 minutes;[4] ministers should not, however, cut short their replies, even if this means going beyond the 20-minute limit.[5] The period of questions and answers which then follows for backbench members should not exceed 20 minutes from the end of

---

[1]  Procedure 8th Rpt 2010–12. See Official Report for 29 November 2011.

[2]  Procedure 8th Rpt 2010–12.

[3]  SO 35; often restated by the Procedure Committee, most recently in 1st Rpt 2002–03.

[4]  Procedure 1st Rpt 1998–99.

[5]  Procedure 1st Rpt 2000–01.

the minister's initial reply to the Opposition.[1] If a debate upon a statement is desired, a notice should be tabled for a later date.

6.08   As a matter of courtesy, members who wish to ask questions on an oral statement should be present to hear the whole of the statement read out.[2]

*Publication in Hansard*

6.09   Where a statement contains material which is too lengthy or too complicated to be given orally in the House the additional material may be published in Hansard without being given orally.[3]

6.10   Where a Commons statement is not repeated an italic reference to the appropriate place in the Commons Hansard is made on the cover of the Lords daily Hansard.[4]

## Written statements

6.11   Written statements may be made when the House is sitting, by ministers or the Chairman of Committees. Notice is not required. Written statements made by a Lords minister repeating Commons statements may also be published in editions of Hansard produced when the House is not sitting. Written statements are placed in the Library as soon as they are made, and are printed in Hansard.[5]

# QUESTIONS AND MOTIONS

## Questions and Motions: general principles

6.12   Questions and motions are expected to be worded in accordance with the practice of the House. The Clerks are available to assist members in drafting questions and motions, and the advice tendered by

---

[1]  Procedure 1st Rpt 1989-90; 1st Rpt 1994–95. On 26 January 2004, additional time was allowed for an intervention by the Lord Chief Justice (HL Deb. col. 12). On 10 June 2009, the Convenor of the Crossbench Peers was permitted to intervene during the time for the front benches, and the time allowed for backbenchers was extended to 40 minutes (HL Deb. col. 638).

[2]  Procedure 3rd Rpt 2010–12.

[3]  Procedure 4th Rpt 1963–64; 3rd Rpt 1984–85; 1st Rpt 1987–88.

[4]  Procedure 1st Rpt 1987–88; 1st Rpt 1998–99.

[5]  Procedure 1st Rpt 2003–04.

the Clerks should be accepted.[1] However, there is no official who has authority to refuse a question or motion on the ground of irregularity. Members are responsible for the form in which their questions and motions appear in House of Lords Business, subject to the sense of the House which is the final arbiter.

6.13   It is open to any member of the House to call attention to a question or motion which has appeared on the day's order paper or in the future business section of *House of Lords Business*, and to move that leave be not given to ask the question or move the motion, or to move that it be removed from *House of Lords Business*. Such a motion should only be used in the last resort; it is debatable and is decided by the House.[2]

## Questions

### The nature of parliamentary questions

6.14   The purpose of parliamentary questions is to elicit information from the government of the day, and thus to assist members of both Houses in holding the government to account. The House has resolved that it is of "paramount importance" that ministers should give "accurate and truthful" information to Parliament, and that they be as "open as possible" in answering questions.[3] Such requirements are inherent in ministerial accountability to Parliament. A parliamentary question is not a "request for information" under the Freedom of Information Act 2000.

### Form and scope of questions

6.15   Parliamentary questions should relate to matters of government responsibility. Questions should be as short and clear as possible and are drafted so as to be precise in their requests for information. Statements of fact should be included in questions only to the extent necessary to elicit the information sought. Questions should be worded neutrally, and should not presuppose their own answer. They should not contain expressions of opinion or argument. It is not in order to italicise or

---

[1]   Procedure 1st Rpt 1985–86.

[2]   LJ (1982–83) 108.

[3]   LJ (1996–97) 404.

underline words in the text of motions or questions in order to give them emphasis.[1]

6.16 Questions are normally addressed to "Her Majesty's Government", rather than to a particular department or minister. It is for the government to decide which department or minister should answer a particular question. There are certain exceptions, including oral questions addressed to Secretaries of State sitting in the House of Lords, which may be taken in a designated question time. Such questions are addressed to "the Secretary of State for [department]" (see paragraph 6.25). For questions addressed to the Leader of the House or the Chairman of Committees see below, paragraph 6.21.

6.17 In drafting a question, thought should be given to the nature and scope of the response:

- Oral questions are not intended to give rise to debate, and should be drafted in such a way that the minister can make his or her initial reply in no more than 75 words. Proceedings on each question, including supplementary questions and answers, are normally limited to a total of seven or eight minutes.

- Questions for written answer should usually be answerable using no more than two columns of Hansard. The government apply a "disproportionate cost threshold", currently set at £800,[2] to written questions, and may decline to answer questions where the cost of answering would exceed this figure.

*What makes a question inadmissible?*

6.18 Although the House allows more latitude than the House of Commons, questions are generally regarded as inadmissible if they fall into one or more of the following categories:

- Questions that cast reflections on the Sovereign or the Royal Family.

- Questions that relate to matters *sub judice*.

---

[1] Procedure 1st Rpt 1985–86, 9th Rpt 1970–71.

[2] HL Deb., 20 January 2010, col. WS60.

- Questions that relate to matters for which the Church of England is responsible.[1]

- Questions that relate to matters devolved to the Scottish Parliament, the Welsh Assembly or the Northern Ireland Assembly.

- Questions that contain an expression or a statement of opinion, or whose purpose is to invite the government to agree to a proposition, or to express an opinion.

- Questions that are phrased offensively. The principles of Standing Order 32 (asperity of speech) also apply.

### Government responsibility

6.19 In addition, questions which are not matters for which the government are responsible are regarded as inadmissible. In judging government responsibility, members should take account of the following guidance:

- Questions should relate to ministers' official duties, rather than their private affairs or party matters.

- Where government functions are delegated to an executive agency, accountability to Parliament remains through ministers. When a minister answers a parliamentary question, orally or in writing, by reference to a letter from the chief executive of an agency, the minister remains accountable for the answer, which attracts parliamentary privilege, and criticism of the answer in the House should be directed at the minister, not the chief executive.

- Questions should not ask about opposition party policies.

- Questions should not ask the government for a legal opinion on the interpretation of statute or of international law, such matters being the competence of the courts.

- Questions should not ask about matters which are the particular responsibility of local authorities or the Greater London Assembly.

- Questions should not ask about the internal affairs of another country (save for questions about human rights or other matters

---

[1] Procedure 2nd Rpt 1988–89.

covered by international conventions to which the United Kingdom is party).[1]

- In general, questions should not contain accusations against individuals. The names of individuals or bodies are not introduced into questions invidiously or for the purpose of advertisement.

- Questions should not ask the government about the accuracy of statements in the press, where these have been made by private individuals or bodies.

- Questions should not ask about events more than 30 years ago without direct relevance to current issues.

- The tabling of questions on public utilities, nationalised industries and privatised industries is restricted to those matters for which the government are in practice responsible.

- Questions should not be hypothetical, and should address issues of substance. Questions which are "trivial, vague or meaningless"[2] are not tabled.

*Questions relating to the business of either House*

6.20 The government are not responsible for the business or decisions of either House of Parliament. Questions should not criticise the decisions of either House.

6.21 In respect of the House of Lords, questions may be addressed to certain members of the House as holders of official positions but not as members of the government. Thus the Leader of the House has been questioned on matters of procedure, and the Chairman of Committees on matters falling within the duties of his office or relating to the House Committee and other domestic committees.

6.22 Questions are not tabled about the internal affairs of the House of Commons. Questions should not ask about House of Commons select committee reports to which the government have yet to publish their response. Nor do questions usually refer to evidence given before a Commons select committee.

---

[1] See also *Erskine May*, p. 361.

[2] *Erskine May*, p. 365.

## Wording of questions

6.23    The Clerks can advise on how questions may be amended to conform to House style—for instance, the use of punctuation and abbreviations, the standard form for references to previous answers, and so on. Questions should use plain English and should generally be understandable without reference to other documents (with the exception of Hansard).

## Question time

6.24    Question time in the House of Lords takes place at the start of business on Mondays, Tuesdays, Wednesdays and Thursdays. Question time may not exceed 30 minutes.[1]

6.25    In December 2009 the House agreed, on a trial basis, that Secretaries of State sitting in the House of Lords should each, on one Thursday each month, answer three oral questions addressed to them in their ministerial capacity.[2] Although no Secretaries of State sat in the House of Lords in the first session of the 2010 Parliament, the procedure itself was made permanent in November 2011, with a view to its revival as appropriate.[3] Questions to Secretaries of State take place immediately after oral questions, and last for up to 20 minutes. Arrangements for selecting such questions, by ballot, are described below (paragraph 6.35). Except where indicated in the following paragraphs, the procedure for Secretary of State's questions is identical to that for normal oral questions.

## Tabling oral questions

6.26    Oral questions, marked * in *House of Lords Business*, are asked for information only, and not with a view to stating an opinion, making a speech or raising a debate.[4] The arrangements for tabling such questions are as follows:

- oral questions may be tabled up to four weeks, including recesses, in advance of the date on which they are to be asked (e.g. a question

---

[1]   Procedure 1st Rpt 1990–91.

[2]   Procedure 1st Rpt 2009–10.

[3]   Procedure 8th Rpt 2010–12.

[4]   SO 34.

to be asked on Monday 31 March may not be tabled before Monday 3 March);

- oral questions are accepted by the Table Office (or the Duty Clerk in recesses) from 2 p.m. on the day on which they become available;

- no oral question may be tabled less than 24 hours before the start of the sitting at which it is due to be asked (or after 2.30 p.m. on Friday for Monday);

- the number of oral questions is limited to four;

- no member of the House may have more than one oral question on the order paper at any one time,[1] but topical questions and Secretary of State's questions are excluded from this rule;

- when oral questions become available, priority in tabling them is afforded to members in person, followed by members telephoning the Table Office in person; questions are offered to members who have contacted the Table Office either via email or fax, or whose questions have been brought in by others, from 2.15 p.m.[2]

*Asking the question*

6.27   Oral questions are asked by leave of the House. The form of words to be used in asking a question is:

*"My Lords, I beg leave to ask the question standing in my name on the order paper."*[3]

6.28   If a member of the House is not present to ask a question, the question may be asked by another member with the permission of the member named on the order paper.[4] On such occasions, the member who is in fact to ask the question should inform the Table, who will inform the government. The unanimous leave of the House is required for one member's question to be asked by another when the authority of the member named on the order paper has not been given.[5] If the Clerk

---

[1]   Procedure 1st Rpt 1998–99.

[2]   Procedure Committee minutes, 14 February 2011.

[3]   Procedure 1st Rpt 1967–68.

[4]   Procedure 2nd Rpt 1984–85.

[5]   SO 42(2).

of the Parliaments knows that an oral question is not going to be asked, he informs the House before he calls the first question;[1] the full 30 minutes is available for the remaining questions.

### Ministers' replies and supplementary questions

6.29   Ministers' initial answers should not generally exceed 75 words. Supplementary questions may be asked but they should be short and confined to not more than two points.[2] If a supplementary question exceeds these guidelines, the minister need only answer the two main points. Supplementary questions should be confined to the subject of the original question, and ministers should not answer irrelevant questions.[3] The essential purpose of supplementaries is to elicit information, and they should not incorporate statements of opinion. They should not be read. The member who tabled the question has no automatic right to ask a final supplementary question.

6.30   Members should not take up the time of the House during question time by making trivial declarations of non-financial and non-registrable interests. Questioners should not thank the government for their answers, nor ministers thank questioners for their questions.[4]

6.31   Where a minister's answer contains material that is too lengthy or too complicated to be given orally in the House, it may be published in Hansard.[5]

### Topical (balloted) oral questions

6.32   The fourth space for an oral question each Tuesday, Wednesday and Thursday is reserved for a question which is topical. The questions are chosen by ballot.[6]

6.33   Members may enter the ballot even if they already have one oral question on the order paper; but they may not enter the ballot if they already have an oral question on the order paper for the day concerned. No

---

[1]  Procedure 1st Rpt 1999–2000.

[2]  Procedure 1st Rpt 1984–85; 1st Rpt 1987–88.

[3]  Restated in Procedure 1st Rpt 2002–03.

[4]  Procedure 6th Rpt 2010–12.

[5]  Procedure 4th Rpt 1963–64.

[6]  Procedure 5th Rpt 2001–02; 3rd Rpt 2003–04.

member may ask more than four[1] topical oral questions in one session. The Clerks discourage members from tabling questions which are clearly not topical and indicate to members which questions have already been tabled for ballot. No more than one question on a subject may be accepted for inclusion in the ballot and priority is given to the first which is tabled.

*The ballot*

6.34   The timetable for the ballot for topical questions during any sitting week is:

| Day question is to be asked | Ballot opens | Ballot drawn | Questions appear in *HL Business* |
|---|---|---|---|
| Tuesday | Previous Wednesday, after oral questions | Friday 1 p.m. | Monday or Tuesday morning |
| Wednesday | Previous Thursday, 3 p.m. | Monday 1 p.m. | Tuesday morning |
| Thursday | Previous Friday, 3 p.m. | Tuesday 1 p.m. | Wednesday morning |

All questions for the ballot should be submitted to the Table Office.

*The ballot for Secretary of State's questions*

6.35   The three questions addressed to Secretaries of State, which are asked on a Thursday, are selected by means of a ballot which takes place at 1 p.m. the preceding Monday. The ballot opens one week earlier. The timetable is thus as follows:

---

[1]  Procedure 5th Rpt 2001–02; 3rd Rpt 2003–04. The limit was increased to five for the long 2010–12 session (Procedure 3rd Rpt 2010–12).

| Day questions are to be asked | Ballot opens | Ballot drawn | Questions appear in *HL Business* |
|---|---|---|---|
| Thursday | Monday of the preceding week, 10 a.m. | Monday of the same week, 1 p.m. | Tuesday morning |

*Private notice questions*[1]

6.36   A private notice question (PNQ) gives members of the House the opportunity to raise urgent matters on any sitting day. A PNQ should be submitted in writing to the Lord Speaker by 12 noon on the day on which it is proposed to ask it, or by 10 a.m. on days when the House sits before 1 p.m. The decision whether the question is of sufficient urgency and importance to justify an immediate reply rests with the Lord Speaker, after consultation.[2]

6.37   PNQs are taken immediately after oral questions, or on Friday at a time agreed by the Lord Speaker, the Lord asking the question and the usual channels. They should not be made the occasion for immediate debate.[3] Proceedings on PNQs follow the rules for oral questions. In particular, supplementary questions should be short and confined to not more than two points. Proceedings on a PNQ are limited to 10 minutes. For these reasons it may at times be more convenient for the House if the PNQ procedure is not used but instead the government makes a statement on the matter which the PNQ is intended to raise. Circumstances in which statements may be more appropriate than PNQs include: when a long answer is required; when the responsible minister is a member of the House of Lords; when the House of Commons is not sitting.[4]

6.38   When the answer to an Urgent Question tabled in the Commons is, by agreement between the usual channels, to be repeated in the

---

[1]  SO 35; Procedure 1st Rpt 1959–60; 5th Rpt 1971–72.

[2]  Procedure 3rd Rpt 2005–06; 2nd Rpt 2009–10.

[3]  SO 35.

[4]  Procedure 2nd Rpt 1990–91.

Lords, it is repeated in the form of a statement, synchronised with the answer in the Commons. In November 2012 the House agreed, on a trial basis, that in such cases the repetition of the answer should be followed by ten minutes of question and answer, to which the rules governing PNQs apply.[1]

6.39   When an oral question in the House of Commons is deferred by a minister in that House to be answered at the end of normal question time,[2] the PNQ procedure may be used in order to repeat the question and answer in the Lords.

### Questions for written answer

6.40   Members may also table "Questions for Written Answer".[3] Questions may be tabled only on sitting days, and on two days during the summer recess, normally the first Monday in September and the first Monday in October.[4] Guidance on the wording of written questions is given at paragraphs 6.12–6.23. Answers to written questions are sent directly to the member by a Lords minister in the relevant department and are published in Hansard. Answers are issued to the Press Gallery from 4.30 p.m., with no embargo on use and publication.

6.41   When a minister undertakes in the House to write to a member on a matter of general interest to the House, it is open to that member or any other member to ensure that the minister's reply is available to the House by putting down a question for written answer.[5]

### Answers

6.42   Written questions, including those tabled in the summer recess, are expected to be answered within 10 working days.[6] Answers are sent to members by post. When the House is in recess, answers should be sent to the member concerned within 10 working days. They are printed

---

[1]  Procedure 2nd Rpt 2012–13.

[2]  See *Erskine May*, p 353.

[3]  SO 44; Procedure 1st Rpt 1990–91.

[4]  Procedure 3rd Rpt 2006–07. The Leader of the House has discretion to vary the standard pattern of dates, by agreement with the usual channels, in case of exceptional recess dates.

[5]  Procedure 7th Rpt 1971–72.

[6]  Procedure 3rd Rpt 2009–10.

in Hansard either on the next sitting day, or, in the case of the summer recess, on the day following the second tabling day, with a reference to the date of the answer. Where appropriate, written questions may be answered on the day on which they are tabled. The length of ministerial answers to written questions should not exceed two columns of Hansard, and the normal practice is for longer answers to be placed in the Library of the House; a covering reply stating that the information has been placed in the Library is published in Hansard.[1] The Leader of the House advises on individual cases of difficulty.[2]

### Limits on number of written questions

6.43 Members of the House of Lords are not entitled to table more than six written questions on any one day, or more than 12 written questions per sitting week.[3] The tabling of a series of different requests for information in the form of a single question is deprecated.[4]

### Questions for short debate

6.44 A question for short debate is distinguishable from a motion in that there is no right of reply.[5] Such a question may be tabled for any day on which the House is sitting. Members should table such questions in the list contained in *House of Lords Business*, and then consult the Government Whips' Office to agree upon a suitable date when the question can be asked.[6] The date of tabling is given in *House of Lords Business*; if the question has not been asked within six months of tabling, it is removed from the list. Members are limited to one question for short debate in *House of Lords Business* at any one time.[7] A ballot is conducted to determine the order in which questions for short debate

---

[1] Procedure 4th Rpt 1998–99.

[2] Procedure Committee minutes, 4 April 2000.

[3] Procedure 2nd Rpt 1988–89, 3rd Rpt 2006–07, 11th Rpt 2010–12.

[4] Procedure 1st Rpt 1977–78.

[5] SO 36.

[6] Procedure 6th Rpt 2005–06.

[7] Procedure 8th Rpt 2010–12.

tabled on the day of State Opening are entered in *House of Lords Business.*[1]

## Timing of questions for short debate

6.45    Questions for short debate are entered last on the order paper,[2] and more than one question for short debate should be put down only on a day when business appears to be light. They are taken either as last business (in which case they are subject to a time limit of 1½ hours[3]) or during the lunch or dinner break (in which case they last for a maximum of one hour[4]). Thus questions for short debate should be limited in scope.[5]

6.46    Questions for short debate may be taken in a Grand Committee with the concurrence of those concerned. No business of the House motion is required. Such questions are time-limited to 1 or 1½ hours.[6]

## Guidance on the conduct of questions for short debate

6.47    Whether a question for short debate is taken as last business or in a lunch or dinner break, the questioner is guaranteed 10 minutes and the minister 12 minutes. The remaining time is divided equally between all speakers on the list; there is no guaranteed time for opposition frontbenchers. If the list of speakers is small, the maximum allocation for all speeches is 10 minutes, except for the minister, who is still guaranteed 12 minutes.

6.48    No member may speak more than once except with the leave of the House. If a member does speak more than once it should be only for the purpose of explaining a material point in his or her speech and not to introduce new subjects for debate.[7]

- The member who asks the question has no right of reply since no motion has been moved.

---

[1]   Procedure 10th Rpt 2010-12.

[2]   SO 40(9).

[3]   Procedure 1st Rpt 1994–95.

[4]   Procedure 3rd Rpt 1993–94.

[5]   Procedure 8th Rpt 2010–12.

[6]   Resolution of the House 31 January 2005; Procedure 5th Rpt 2006–07.

[7]   SO 30(2).

- It is not in order for members to continue the debate after the government's reply has been given, except for questions to the minister before the minister sits down.

## Motions

*General*

6.49   In a normal full session every Thursday[1] from the beginning of the session until the end of January[2] is set aside for general debates. The House has agreed that it is desirable that there should be regular debates on general topics, and on select committee reports, in prime time.[3]

6.50   Motions are tabled on the order paper in the name of one member only. It is not the practice to add names of other members in support of a motion.

- The leave of the House is not sought when a motion is moved. The motion is moved as follows: *"I beg to move the motion standing in my name on the order paper"*.[4]

- Every motion, after it has been moved, must be proposed in the form of a Question from the Woolsack before debate takes place upon it.

- Motions, other than for the Humble Address in reply to the Queen's Speech, are not seconded.

- At the conclusion of the debate, after every member who wishes to speak has spoken, the mover has the right of reply. At the end of his or her speech in reply, the mover may either withdraw the motion or press it. If it is pressed, the Lord on the Woolsack or in the Chair then completes the Question on the motion, if necessary reading its terms.

---

[1]   Procedure 6th Rpt 2005–06.

[2]   Procedure 3rd Rpt 2010–12.

[3]   Procedure 5th Rpt 2001–02.

[4]   If a member of the House is absent when a motion standing in his or her name is called and has authorised another member to act on his or her behalf, that member may do so, explaining the situation. Otherwise, the motion cannot be proceeded with on that day unless unanimous leave is granted by the House. See paragraph 3.37.

- It is contrary to the practice of the House for a Question once decided to be put again in the same session.

6.51    General guidance on the wording of questions and motions, and on Government responsibility, may be found above at paragraphs 6.12–6.23.

6.52    The two types of motion are

- resolutions;
- "take-note" motions.

## Resolutions[1]

6.53    Resolutions may be put down in cases where a member wishes the House to make a definite decision on a subject, if necessary on a vote. A resolution, if passed, constitutes the formal opinion or decision of the House on the matter.

6.54    Resolutions begin with the words "To move to resolve ..." or "To move that this House ...", and it is in order to incorporate statements of opinion or the demonstration of a point of view.

## Motions to take note

6.55    Most debates take place on a motion "That this House takes note of ...". This formula enables the House to debate a situation or a document without coming to any positive decision. Such motions are usually agreed to, since they are neutral in wording, and there is neither advantage nor significance in opposing them. The opinion of the House is expressed in the speeches made in the debate rather than on a division. The formula is regularly used for debates on the general debate day and for select committee reports. It is also appropriate when a minister wishes to put down a neutral motion.

6.56    "Take note" motions should be short and neutrally phrased to avoid provocative or tendentious language, although members are not prevented from advancing controversial points of view in the course of debate. A "take note" motion should not include a statement of opinion

---

[1] Procedure 1st Rpt 1985–86.

or demonstrate a point of view. "Take note" motions are not amendable.[1]

6.57 General debates may be held in Grand Committee;[2] the proceedings are the same as those that take place in the Chamber.

### Balloted debates

6.58 One Thursday in each month from the start of the session to the end of December[3] is set aside for two balloted debates.[4] These balloted debates are limited to 2½ hours each, and their subjects should be narrow enough to be debated within the time limit. These debates may be initiated only by backbench and Crossbench members and a member may initiate only one balloted debate per session.

6.59 The choice of the two subjects is made by ballot, which is carried out by the Clerk of the Parliaments, two or three weeks before the debates are due to take place. A member wishing to initiate a balloted debate must give notice by tabling the motion in *House of Lords Business* under Motions for Balloted Debate. It is not in order to put down a motion for a balloted debate which is the same, or substantially the same, as a motion that is already entered for the ballot.[5] It is assumed, unless notice to the contrary is given to the Table Office, that any member who has a motion down for the ballot is willing and able to move his motion on the day appointed.

6.60 The purpose of these debates is to provide a forum for discussion rather than questions which the House may decide on a division. They always take place on "take note" motions, which should worded neutrally.

6.61 When a motion has been set down for a particular day, it may be amended in form but not in substance: that is to say, a member who has been successful in the ballot may not substitute another subject for that originally proposed.

---

[1] Minutes of Proceedings, 8 November 2011.

[2] Procedure 9th Rpt 2010–12.

[3] Procedure 6th Rpt 2010–12.

[4] Procedure 1st Rpt 1974. They were formerly called "short debates".

[5] Procedure 5th Rpt 1974–75.

*Time-limited debates*[1]

6.62   The House may limit debates, either in the House itself or in Grand Committee, to a specific number of hours. A business of the House motion in the name of the Leader of the House (of which notice is required) must be moved before the start of the debate if a time limit is to be applied. Within the overall limit, the amount of time allotted to particular speakers is calculated in advance and stated on the speakers' list.

6.63   Speaking time is allocated equally between all the speakers on the speakers' list, subject to a guaranteed minimum number of minutes being given to the mover of the debate, the official opposition frontbencher or frontbenchers and the minister replying. The table below shows these guaranteed minimum allocations of time for debates of various lengths, in minutes.

|  | LENGTH OF DEBATE | | |
| --- | --- | --- | --- |
|  | 4 hrs or over | 2 hrs or over | Less than 2 hrs |
| Mover | 20 | 15 | 12 |
| Opposition frontbencher(s) | 12 | 10 | 8 |
| Minister replying | 25 | 20 | 15 |

6.64   For speaking time in Questions for Short Debate, see paragraph 6.47.

6.65   If the number of speakers on the speakers' list is small, every speaker enjoys an equal speaking time (up to the recommended maximum of 15 minutes for any speech), except for the minister in reply who has at least the guaranteed minimum time set out in the table.

6.66   At the appropriate time, whoever is speaking is expected to give way to the front benches.

6.67   The digital clocks in the Chamber show the number of minutes that have already elapsed since the start of each speech.

---

[1] Procedure 2nd Rpt 1983–84; 2nd Rpt 1990–91; 3rd Rpt 1992–93.

6.68 Speakers in time-limited debates should respect the time guidelines and keep their speeches short, so that all those who wish to speak may do so. Members may also speak briefly in the gap (for a maximum of 4 minutes) if time allows, subject to the guidance set out in paragraph 4.28). During time-limited debates, speeches should be interrupted only if time allows.

6.69 If time-limited debates are interrupted by other business, for example by a statement, the time limit is extended correspondingly and an appropriate announcement made to the House.

6.70 If the debate on a motion is still continuing at the end of the time allotted to it, the Clerk at the Table rises, and the Lord on the Woolsack brings the debate to an end by either putting the Question forthwith or asking whether the mover of the motion wishes to withdraw it.[1]

*Amendments to motions*

6.71 A motion for debate, other than a "take note" motion, may be amended with or without notice.

6.72 In principle the discussion of an amendment to a motion is a separate debate, which must be concluded before the House returns to the original motion (or the original motion as amended). However, in practice, once a motion and an amendment to it have been moved, the rest of the debate takes place on that amendment, and the members in whose names the motion and any subsequent amendments stand speak in this debate to indicate the reasons why they prefer their own form of words. When the first amendment has been disposed of, any remaining amendments and the original motion (as amended) are usually put and decided without further debate.

6.73 The following principles apply to a debate during which amendments, and possibly amendments to amendments, are proposed to a motion:

- a motion, an amendment to the motion, and any amendment to the amendment, must each be moved and proposed in the form of a Question from the Woolsack before they can be further debated;

---

[1] SO 37(1).

- a member of the House who moves a motion, an amendment to it or any amendment to the amendment, may speak for that purpose and has a right of reply on his or her motion or amendment;

- a member whose motion is sought to be amended by one or more proposed amendments may make separate speeches dealing with each amendment, but may not move any amendment; if, having seen the terms of any proposed amendment, the mover seeks to modify the motion he or she should indicate in moving the motion the terms of the motion which he or she is actually moving so that the original Question can be put in that amended form;

- a member who has neither moved the original motion nor any amendment to it may speak once on the motion and once on any amendment or on any amendment to that amendment;

- a member who moves an amendment should not speak separately on the original motion, but has a right of reply on his or her amendment.

6.74   At the end of the debate on an amendment to a motion, the Lord on the Woolsack states the terms of the original motion and of the amendment and then puts the Question *"that this amendment be agreed to".*

6.75   If there is an equality of votes in a division on such an amendment, the amendment is disagreed to.

6.76   If there is more than one amendment to a motion, the amendments are dealt with in the order in which they relate to the motion, or, if they relate to the same place in the motion, in the order in which they were tabled.

6.77   If amendments are moved to an amendment, such amendments are dealt with in the order in which they stand on the order paper, in the same manner as if they were amendments to a motion, until all are disposed of. Then the original amendment is dealt with.

6.78   If any amendment is agreed to, at the end of the debate the Lord on the Woolsack puts the Question:

*"That the original motion, as amended, be agreed to".*

*Committees on motions*

6.79   On rare occasions when the House considers that the structure of debate set out above is too restrictive, it can go into committee on a motion, so that the limit on the number of times a member may speak is removed. The motion to do so may be moved without notice.

### Adjournment of debates lasting more than one day

6.80   A motion for the adjournment of a debate may be moved at any time during the debate without notice and may be debated. But when it has been arranged in advance for a debate to be adjourned (for example, the debate on the Queen's Speech), it is usual for its adjournment to be moved formally by the member who will speak first when the debate is resumed. The House may make an order, without notice, for adjourned business to be taken later the same day, or taken as first business on another day.[1]

### Withdrawal of motions

6.81   If, at the conclusion of the debate, the mover decides not to seek the opinion of the House, he or she asks leave to withdraw the motion or amendment. A motion or amendment may be withdrawn only by unanimous leave of the House, though it is rare for any objection to be made.

6.82   The member in whose name the motion stands should conclude the debate by saying:

*"I beg leave to withdraw the motion"*

6.83   No formal motion for withdrawal is made and no formal Question is put. The Lord on the Woolsack asks the House:

*"Is it your Lordships' pleasure that the motion be withdrawn?"*

6.84   A single dissenting voice is sufficient to prevent withdrawal.[2] If there is none, the Lord on the Woolsack adds:

*"The motion is, by leave, withdrawn."*

6.85   If any member dissents, the Lord on the Woolsack must put the Question on the motion.

6.86   When a member begs leave to withdraw a motion, other members are not precluded from rising to speak; and if they continue the debate the mover may again beg leave to withdraw the motion at a later

---

[1]  SO 45.
[2]  SO 31.

stage. If, however, the Lord on the Woolsack has asked the House whether leave to withdraw be granted, and any member has objected, the mover cannot again seek leave to withdraw his motion, which must be decided on Question.

# CHAPTER 7
# DIVISIONS

## General principles

7.01    At the end of a debate on a motion or amendment which has not been withdrawn, the Lord on the Woolsack or in the Chair puts the Question to the House ("*The Question is …*") and then says:

> *"As many as are of that opinion will say "Content". The contrary "Not-content"."*

If there is a response from only one side, the Lord on the Woolsack or in the Chair then says:

> *"The Contents [Not-contents] have it."*

The Question is agreed to or disagreed to accordingly.

7.02    If there is a response from both sides, but one side appears more numerous than the other, the Lord on the Woolsack or in the Chair says:

> *"I think the Contents [Not-contents] have it."*

If this expression of opinion is not challenged, the Lord on the Woolsack or in the Chair says:

> *"The Contents [Not-contents] have it."*

The Question is then decided accordingly. A motion or amendment that is decided in the negative without a division taking place is described as having been "negatived".

7.03    If this expression of opinion is challenged, the Lord on the Woolsack or in the Chair may repeat it until the challenge is abandoned or until satisfied that a division is inevitable.[1] This process is known as "collecting the voices". If the challenge is maintained, even by only one member, a division must be called.[2] The Lord on the Woolsack or in the Chair says:

> *"Clear the Bar."*

7.04    The area immediately behind the Bar of the House and the division lobbies are then cleared of visitors. The galleries, the space within the rails around the Throne, the Clerks' box, the officials' box, and the

---

[1] Procedure 2nd Rpt 1981–82.
[2] SO 53.

seats below Bar are not cleared, unless the House so orders. The doors at the ends of the division lobbies are locked.

7.05   During the three minutes after the order has been given for the Bar to be cleared, two Tellers are appointed by the members wishing to vote "Content" and two by those wishing to vote "Not-content". The Tellers give their names in at the Table where they receive their Tellers' wands and they state to the Clerk whether they are appointed by the Contents or the Not-contents.[1]

7.06   Once two tellers and two clerks are in place in a lobby, the tellers have discretion to start counting members through that lobby, and the doors at the exit from the lobby are unlocked. At the end of three minutes, the Lord on the Woolsack or in the Chair again puts the Question, and if the doors at the exit from one or both lobbies have yet to be unlocked, they are unlocked at this point.

7.07   If only one side replies when the Question is repeated after three minutes, the Lord on the Woolsack or in the Chair says:

*"The Contents [Not-contents] have it."*

and no division takes place.

7.08   If one or more voices from each side shouts "Content" and "Not-content", the Lord on the Woolsack or in the Chair proceeds with the division by saying:

*"The Contents will go to the right by the Throne. The Not-contents to the left by the Bar."*

7.09   The members wishing to vote "Content" then go through the door to the right of the Throne through the lobby on the spiritual side, and re-enter the House through the door beyond the Bar of the House. The members wishing to vote "Not-content" go through the door beyond the Bar on the temporal side and re-enter the House through the door to the left of the Throne.

7.10   A member may, usually on the ground of disability, vote in the Chamber.[2] Such votes, and those of the Lord on the Woolsack or in the Chair, are taken in the Chamber by the Clerk.

---

[1]   The procedure to be followed if the correct number of Tellers is not appointed is set out at paragraphs 7.21–7.22.

[2]   SO 54.

7.11   A member may vote in a division even if not in the House to hear the Question put.[1]

7.12   One Teller from each side and two Clerks go to each lobby to record the numbers and names of those voting. Members voting divide into two streams in each lobby.[2] They must give their names to the Clerks. Members do not bow to the Tellers.[3]

7.13   At the end of eight minutes from the time when the Bar is ordered to be cleared, or longer at the discretion of the Lord on the Woolsack or in the Chair,[4] the House or committee is again informed of the Question which is the subject of the division. The doors of the Chamber are locked; and from that moment only members who are already in the Chamber or the lobbies may vote.[5] When the Tellers are satisfied that all members who wish to vote in their respective lobbies have done so, they return to the Table. They tell the Clerk how many votes they have recorded. The Clerk adds the vote of the Lord on the Woolsack or in the Chair, and any member voting in the Chamber, and hands the result to one of the Tellers for the winning side. That Teller gives it to the Lord on the Woolsack or in the Chair who reads it to the House or committee in this form:

"There have voted:

Content: —

Not-content:—

And so the Contents [Not-contents] have it."

7.14   The three other Tellers remain at the Table until the numbers have been announced, at which point all four hand back their wands.

---

[1]   In 2011 the House resolved, in respect of proceedings in the Grand Committee on the Welfare Reform Bill taking place in Committee Room 4A, that members with restricted mobility who (a) had given advance notification to the Clerk of the Parliaments, and (b) were present in the Grand Committee by the time the question was repeated three minutes after a division in the House being called, should be entitled to vote in their places in the Grand Committee. See Minutes of Proceedings, 6 October 2011.

[2]   Procedure 3rd Rpt 1992–93.

[3]   Procedure 1st Rpt 1969–70.

[4]   Procedure 2nd Rpt 1992–93.

[5]   Members who are already queuing to enter the Chamber when the Question is repeated after eight minutes are allowed to enter the Chamber before the doors are locked.

7.15 For details of the procedures to be followed by Tellers, see appendix A page 246.

7.16 Division lists showing how members voted are published on the parliamentary intranet and on the Internet. They are printed in Hansard and in the Journals.[1]

## Voting in wrong lobby

7.17 Any member who by mistake votes in the wrong lobby must wait until the others in that lobby have voted, and then ask the Tellers not to count his or her vote. The Tellers then accompany the member concerned to the Table, and tell the Clerk what has happened. They then ask the member which way he or she wishes to vote. That vote is taken by the Clerk in the House, and recorded accordingly.[2]

## Voting in both lobbies

7.18 If any member votes in both lobbies in one division, his or her name is struck off the list of those voting in that division, and the vote is disregarded.

## Votes of the Lord Speaker and Chairman

7.19 The Lord Speaker is expected not to vote.[3] The Deputy Speaker, or Deputy Chairman in Committee of the whole House, may vote, but does not have a casting vote.

## Discrepancies

7.20 If the Tellers' figures, as announced in the House, do not tally with the division lists taken by the Clerks, the following action is taken:[4]

    (a) the responsibility for counting the votes rests with the Tellers, and once their figures have been announced to the House, these figures are authoritative, unless and until corrected by a further announcement in the House;

---

[1] SO 58.

[2] SO 55.

[3] Procedure 4th Rpt 2005–06.

[4] Procedure 1st Rpt 1966–67.

(b) if a discrepancy is discovered between the Tellers' figures and the lists of the division Clerks, this should be reported as soon as possible to the Tellers with a view to reconciling the discrepancy;

(c) if the Tellers agree that a correction is needed, this correction should be announced to the House at the earliest convenient moment from the Woolsack or the Chair;

(d) if the correction involves the reversal of a decision of the House and the House has taken further action on the basis of the mistaken announcement, any proceedings taken on the basis of that announcement should, unless irreversible, be voided;

(e) if after consultation with the Tellers no reconciliation is possible and the discrepancy remains unexplained, a note is added to the division list in the Official Report and in the Journals, drawing attention to the discrepancy between the numbers announced and the names recorded.

## Insufficiency of Tellers

7.21   If after three minutes from the time when the Bar is ordered to be cleared, one side has appointed Tellers, but no Teller, or only one Teller, has been appointed by the other side, a division cannot take place;[1] and the Lord on the Woolsack or in the Chair declares the Question decided in favour of the side which has appointed two Tellers, using the following words:

> "My Lords, Tellers for the Contents [Not-contents] have not been appointed pursuant to Standing Order No. 53. A division, therefore, cannot take place, and I declare that the Not-contents [Contents] have it."[2]

7.22   If both sides fail to appoint Tellers, a division cannot take place and the Question is decided in accordance with SO 56 (see below). The Lord on the Woolsack or in the Chair informs the House:

> "My Lords, Tellers have not been appointed either for the Contents or for the Not-contents pursuant to Standing Order No. 53. A

---

[1]  SO 53(2).

[2]  Procedure 2nd Rpt 1968–69.

*division, therefore, cannot take place, and in accordance with Standing Order No. 56 [... adding the appropriate formula which will be supplied by the Clerk at the Table]."*

## Equality of votes

7.23   If the Contents and Not-contents are equal in number[1] or if both sides fail to appoint tellers, the Question is decided on the principle contained in SO 56 that legislation is allowed to proceed in the form which is before the House unless there is a majority in favour of rejecting or amending it; and that other motions are rejected unless there is a majority in their favour.[2] If there is an equality of votes on a division, the Clerk delivers the result to the Lord on the Woolsack or in the Chair, who reads out the numbers of those voting in the normal way and announces the result as follows:

(a) on a motion for a stage of a bill, or on an amendment to such a motion:

*"There being an equality of votes, in accordance with Standing Order No. 56, which provides that no proposal to reject a bill shall be agreed to unless there is a majority in favour of such rejection, I declare the motion agreed to [the amendment disagreed to]."*

(b) on an amendment to a bill:

*"There being an equality of votes, in accordance with Standing Order No. 56, which provides that no proposal to amend a bill in the form in which it is before the House shall be agreed to unless there is a majority in favour of such an amendment, I declare the amendment disagreed to."*

(c) on an amendment to an amendment:

*"There being an equality of votes, in accordance with Standing Order No. 56, which provides that the Question before the House shall be resolved in the negative unless there is a majority in its favour, I declare the amendment to the amendment disagreed to."*

---

[1]   Procedure 1st Rpt 1962–63.

[2]   SO 56 superseded the ancient rule, *"Semper praesumitur pro negante".*

(d) on the Question in committee of the whole House that "a clause stand part" of a bill or that "this be a Schedule" to a bill, since the effect of resolving this Question in the negative would be to amend the bill:

*"There being an equality of votes, in accordance with Standing Order No. 56, which provides that no proposal to amend a bill in the form in which it is before the House shall be agreed to unless there is a majority in favour of such amendment, I declare the Question resolved in the affirmative."*

(e) on consideration of a Commons amendment, since the form of the bill before the House is taken to be the bill as amended by the Commons:

*"There being an equality of votes, in accordance with Standing Order No. 56, which provides that no proposal to amend a bill in the form in which it is before the House shall be agreed to unless there is a majority in favour of such amendment, I declare the Commons amendment agreed to."*

(f) on a motion to insist, or not to insist, on an amendment to which the Commons have disagreed, since the form of the bill before the House is taken to be the bill as amended by the Commons:

*"There being an equality of votes, in accordance with Standing Order No. 56, which provides that no proposal to amend a bill in the form in which it is before the House shall be agreed to unless there is a majority in favour of such amendment, I declare the amendment not insisted on."*

(g) on a motion to approve an affirmative instrument:

*"There being an equality of votes, in accordance with Standing Order No. 56, which provides that no proposal to reject subordinate legislation shall be agreed to unless there is a majority in favour of such rejection, I declare the motion agreed to."*

(h) on a prayer to annul a statutory instrument, a resolution to annul a special procedure order, or an amendment to a motion to approve an affirmative instrument, the effect of which would be to reject the instrument:

*"There being an equality of votes, in accordance with Standing Order No. 56, which provides that no proposal to reject*

subordinate legislation shall be agreed to unless there is a majority in favour of such rejection, I declare the motion/amendment disagreed to."

(i) on any other motion or amendment:

"There being an equality of votes, in accordance with Standing Order No. 56, which provides that the Question before the House shall be resolved in the negative unless there is a majority in its favour, I declare the motion/amendment disagreed to."

## Quorum on divisions

*General and procedural questions*

7.24 There is no quorum for divisions on general or procedural questions.[1]

*Bills and subordinate legislation*

7.25 The quorum is 30 for divisions on bills and subordinate legislation.

7.26 If fewer than 30 members vote in a division on a bill or amendment or on any Question for the approval or disapproval of subordinate legislation, the Lord on the Woolsack or in the Chair declares the Question not decided, as follows:[2]

(a) on a stage of a bill, on an amendment to a motion relating to such a stage, or on a motion to approve or annul subordinate legislation:

"As it appears that fewer than thirty members have voted, in accordance with Standing Order No. 57, I declare the Question not decided and the debate thereon stands adjourned."

The debate on the undecided Question is adjourned to a subsequent sitting. The House proceeds to the next business

[1] Procedure 1st Rpt 1958–59.
[2] SO 57.

on the order paper. Members who have spoken are permitted to speak again on any subsequent proceedings.[1]

(b) in Committee of the whole House:

*"As it appears that fewer than thirty members have voted, in accordance with Standing Order No. 57, I declare the Question not decided; and, pursuant to the Standing Order, the House will now resume."*

The debate on the undecided Question is adjourned to a subsequent sitting and the House is resumed. The next business on the order paper is taken. On any subsequent proceedings in committee on the bill, the committee proceeds with the consideration of the Question on which no decision was taken because of the absence of a quorum.

(c) on the consideration of an amendment to a bill at any stage other than Committee of the whole House:

*"As it appears that fewer than thirty members have voted, in accordance with Standing Order No. 57, I declare the Question not decided and the further proceedings on the bill stand adjourned."*

The debate on the amendment and the remaining proceedings on the stage of the bill in question are adjourned to a subsequent sitting. The House proceeds to the next business on the order paper. Members who have spoken are permitted to speak again on any subsequent proceedings.

## Proxies

7.27   The use of proxies in a division was discontinued in 1868. Two days' notice is required for any proposal to revive proxies.[2]

## Protests

7.28   Any member has the right to record a protest against any decision of the House, and may give reasons for the protest. The protest must be entered in the Protest Book, and signed before the rising of the House

---

[1]   Procedure 1st Rpt 1963–64.

[2]   SO 60.

on the next sitting day.[1] Members of the House may add their names to a protest, either without remark or with reasons why they have appended their names. Every protest is entered in the Journals. Members may not enter a protest unless they were present for, and in the case of a division, voted on, the matter at issue.[2]

7.29  Any member who is considering recording a protest should contact the Table Office.

---

[1]  Leave has been given to enter a protest after the period limited by SO 59.

[2]  This restriction may be dispensed with on motion.

# CHAPTER 8
# PUBLIC BILLS

## Stages of a public bill

8.01  Public bills in the House of Lords have five main stages:

- introduction and first reading;
- second reading;
- committee;
- report;
- third reading and passing.

Further stages may also be necessary as a result of communications between the two Houses (see paragraphs 8.158–8.178).

## Successive stages of a bill to be taken on different days

8.02  Under SO 46, no two stages of a bill may be taken on one day, except if a bill is not amended in Committee of the whole House, in which case the report stage may be taken immediately thereafter. So, if it is intended to take more than one stage of a bill on one day, other than the report stage of a bill which has not been amended in Committee of the whole House, SO 46 must be suspended or dispensed with; SO 86 requires that notice of this must be given.[1]

8.03  SO 86 also provides that on occasions of grave national emergency a bill may be passed through all its stages on one day without notice. In such cases SOs 46 and 86 are read at the Table by the Clerk and a resolution is moved that it is essential for reasons of national security that a bill or bills should immediately be proceeded with and that the provisions of SO 46 should be dispensed with to enable the House to proceed that day with every stage of the bill or bills which it thinks necessary.[2]

---

[1] SO 86.
[2] LJ (1971–72) 159.

## Recommended minimum intervals between the stages of a bill

8.04 The following minimum intervals between stages of public bills should be observed:[1]

(a) two weekends between the first reading (whether of a new bill or one brought from the Commons) and the debate on second reading;

(b) fourteen days between second reading and the start of the committee stage;

(c) on all bills of considerable length and complexity, fourteen days between the end of the committee stage and the start of the report stage;

(d) three sitting days between the end of the report stage and third reading.[2]

8.05 When these minimum intervals are departed from, notice is given by means of a § against the bill in *House of Lords Business*. However, such notice is not required when SO 46 has been suspended or dispensed with.

8.06 For any legislation subject to expedited procedures ("fast-tracked") the Explanatory Notes accompanying the legislation will contain a full explanation of the reasons for using a fast-track procedure.[3]

8.07 Reasonable notice should whenever possible be given for consideration of Commons amendments, taking into account the number and scale of amendments and the availability of papers relating to them.[4]

## Carry-over

8.08 Subject to the procedure described in the following paragraph, any public bill which does not receive Royal Assent in the session in which it is introduced falls at the end of that session.

---

[1] Procedure 2nd Rpt 1976–77.

[2] The fourteen-day periods are inclusive of the day on which the previous stage is concluded. The three-day period is exclusive.

[3] Written Statement by the Leader of the House, 15 December 2009.

[4] Procedure 1st Rpt 1987–88; Procedure 1st Rpt 1991–92.

8.09 The two Houses have agreed that government public bills can be "carried over" from one session to the next in the same way as private and hybrid bills, in the House in which they originated.[1] In the Lords:

- eligibility of bills for carry-over is settled by informal discussion through the usual channels;

- bills are carried over by *ad hoc* motions;

- a Commons bill carried over in the Commons is treated in the same way as any other bill brought from the Commons;

- a bill that has been carried over falls if it does not reach the statute book by the end of the session following that in which it was introduced.

8.10 The carry-over procedure does not apply over a dissolution.

## Introduction and first reading

8.11 Any member may introduce a bill without notice and without leave.

8.12 A member wishing to introduce a bill should inform the Legislation Office not later than the working day before the day of introduction, and should discuss the bill with the Office in draft. The final text must be handed in to the Office before introduction.

## Devolution

8.13 The powers of the House to legislate on devolved matters are unaffected by the devolution legislation.[2]

8.14 The government have stated that "there would be instances where it would be more convenient for legislation on devolved matters to be passed by the United Kingdom Parliament, [though] Westminster would not normally legislate with regard to matters within the

---

[1] Procedure 3rd Rpt 1997–98. In the Lords, the Constitutional Reform Bill [HL] was carried over from session 2003–04 to 2004–05, and the Trusts (Capital and Income) Bill [HL] from 2010–12 to 2012–13. In the Commons, the power to carry over has been used more frequently. The House of Lords has agreed that it should be possible for government bills in their second House to be carried over if they have been the subject of pre-legislative scrutiny (Procedure, 5th Rpt 2001–02), but this principle has not been endorsed by the Commons.

[2] Scotland Act 1998, s. 28(7); Northern Ireland Act 1998 s. 5(6); Government of Wales Act 2006, ss. 93(5), 107(5).

competence of the [devolved] parliament without the consent of that parliament".[1] When the Scottish Parliament, the National Assembly for Wales or the Northern Ireland Assembly has passed a Legislative Consent Motion, this is indicated in the list of bills in progress in *House of Lords Business*.

## Procedure on introduction: Lords bills

8.15 A member who wishes to present a bill rises at the beginning of public business after oral questions or (exceptionally) at the end of public business immediately before the adjournment of the House,[2] and introduces the bill by saying:

*"My Lords, I beg to introduce a bill to [long title of bill]. I beg to move that this bill be now read a first time."*

8.16 The Question is put from the Woolsack. The first reading of a bill is agreed to without dissent or debate, both as a matter of courtesy and because the House usually has no knowledge of the bill until it is published.

8.17 A bill may be introduced by a member on behalf of another member.

## Procedure on introduction: Commons bills

8.18 A bill which has been introduced in the Commons and which has passed through all its stages in that House is brought to the Lords by a Commons Clerk with a message stating that the Commons have passed the bill. The message is read by the Clerk at the Table as soon as the item of business in progress has ended, and the first reading of the bill (whether a government bill or a private member's bill) is moved immediately by a government Whip.

8.19 As with Lords bills, the first reading of a bill brought from the Commons is agreed to without discussion, both as a matter of courtesy

---

[1] HL Deb. 28 October 1998, cols 1947–52. The "Sewel convention". This was stated in proceedings on the Scotland Bill, and it is reflected in the Concordat between the Government and the Scottish Government about bills. The Concordat states that in practice consultation with the Scottish Government is sufficient, on the ground that the Executive will then consult the Scottish Parliament. This principle applies to the other devolved assemblies.

[2] SO 41(3).

to the Commons and because at this stage no member has formally taken charge of it.

8.20 The member taking charge of a Commons bill should inform the Public Bill Office.

## Bills brought up and printed when Lords not sitting

8.21 A bill passed by the Commons may be carried up to the Lords when the Lords are not sitting. Under SO 50 it is deemed to have been brought from the Commons on that day and the bill and any explanatory notes may be published before first reading if this is for the convenience of the House.

## Publishing of bills and explanatory notes

8.22 After the first reading of a bill an order is made for the bill and any explanatory notes to be published. By convention, Consolidated Fund Bills and Appropriation Bills are not printed for the Lords, nor are provisional order confirmation bills unless subsequently amended on consideration on report. On occasion other bills may not be printed, including bills which are to be taken through the House urgently.

8.23 A bill introduced in the Lords is endorsed with the name of the member of the House who has introduced it. It is not the practice to add other names. A bill brought from the Commons is not endorsed with the name of the member taking charge of the bill.

### Explanatory notes

8.24 For most government bills explanatory notes are produced by the responsible department at the time the bill is introduced. Such notes cover the financial and manpower implications of the bill and any regulatory aspects (though any regulatory appraisal is usually produced separately). Notes must be neutral in tone and must not seek to promote the bill or the policy underlying it.[1] Explanatory notes are also produced for Commons amendments to Lords bills. In some cases departments may prepare notes for private members' bills, with the consent of the member in charge of the bill, whose authority must be communicated to the Legislation Office before the notes can be

---

[1] Procedure 2nd Rpt 1997–98.

published. Explanatory notes may also be produced by private members themselves: members should submit a draft to the Legislation Office before introduction in order to ensure that these are in proper form.

## European Convention on Human Rights

8.25 Under s.19 of the Human Rights Act 1998 the minister in charge of a government bill must make a statement before second reading as to whether in his view the provisions of the bill are compatible with the European Convention on Human Rights, and publish the statement in such manner as he or she considers appropriate.[1] This requirement extends to provisional order confirmation bills. The statement is usually set out on the cover page of a bill as first printed for each House; where bills are not printed for the Lords the statement is publicised by means of a written statement.

8.26 The minister who makes the statement should under normal circumstances move the second reading of the bill. If that minister is unable to do so, another minister should do so on the basis that he or she is acting on behalf of the minister who has made the statement.[2]

## Notice of subsequent stages

8.27 The member who is in charge of a bill gives notice of a date for second reading, and for the stages thereafter, in *House of Lords Business*.

8.28 Any member may move any stage of a bill on behalf of the member in charge of the bill. Bills once introduced are in the possession of the House and not in the sole ownership of the member in charge.[3]

## Government and private members' bills

8.29 There is no procedural distinction between bills sponsored by a minister and those introduced by other members of the House, save in respect of carry-over and human rights statements. In practice the House normally accords priority to proceedings on government bills except where private members' bills are not expected to give rise to debate. But there is no concept of government or private members' "time" in the

---

[1] This requirement does not apply to private members' bills.

[2] Procedure 1st Rpt 2001–02.

[3] HL Deb. 19 July 1989, cols 788–91; Procedure 3rd Rpt 1992–93.

Lords, nor any specific time when government or private members' bills are taken.

## Commons bills not taken up within twelve sitting days

8.30   Under SO 49, if a bill brought up from the Commons remains for twelve sitting days without any member having given notice of a date for second reading, it cannot be proceeded with except after eight days' notice. Motions to dispense with SO 49 have been agreed to.[1]

## Withdrawal of bills

8.31   A Commons bill may not be withdrawn at any stage in the House of Lords.

8.32   At any time after first reading, a bill originating in the House of Lords may, with the agreement of the House, be withdrawn by the Lord who presented it. This may be achieved by the member in charge of the bill, having moved the motion for a stage of the bill begging leave to withdraw that motion. Unanimous leave of the House is required for any motion to be withdrawn, so that a single dissenting voice prevents leave being given and the Question must in that case be put and decided. The granting of leave to withdraw a stage of a bill is treated as withdrawal of the bill, unless the member in charge of the bill indicates that he intends to proceed with the bill on another day.

8.33   If a bill is between stages, a separate motion, of which notice is given, should be tabled, "*That the bill be withdrawn*". Such a motion does not require unanimous agreement.

## Delegated Powers and Regulatory Reform Committee[2]

8.34   All bills other than consolidation, money and supply bills are considered by the Delegated Powers and Regulatory Reform Committee, which reports to the House in relation to any delegated powers they contain. These reports are highlighted by means of an italic note against a bill in *House of Lords Business*. The committee aims to report before the committee stage begins, though the House is under no obligation to delay proceedings if the committee has not reported by that time. If time

---

[1]   LJ (1979–80) 1358, LJ (1999–2000) 627.

[2]   The work of the Committee is described at paragraphs 11.49–11.51.

allows, the committee may also report on government amendments, if these involve significant delegated powers.[1]

### Constitution Committee

8.35 The Constitution Committee examines the constitutional implications of all public bills coming before the House. Constitution Committee reports on public bills may be highlighted by means of an italic note against a bill in *House of Lords Business*.

### Pre-legislative scrutiny

8.36 Government bills which are published in draft may be considered and reported on, before they are introduced, by a select or joint committee appointed for that purpose. At least 3–4 months (excluding long recesses) is normally required to hear evidence and report. Such "pre-legislative scrutiny" does not have the effect of eliminating any stages when the bill itself is considered by the House.

## SECOND READING

8.37 The second reading is the stage at which the general principles of the bill are considered. The member in charge of the bill says, *"My Lords, I beg to move that this bill be now read a second time",* and makes the case for the bill. In debate, other members of the House may indicate, in general terms, how the bill might be amended, but discussion of points of detail should normally be left to the committee stage.

### Opposition to second reading

8.38 A bill may be opposed on second reading by an amendment to the effect that "this House declines to give the bill a second reading". The amendment may add a reason (a "reasoned amendment"). The agreement of the House to such an amendment, with or without a reason, means automatic rejection of the bill. The question as amended is not put, and the bill is removed from the list of bills in progress.

8.39 It is possible to oppose the motion "That this bill be now read a second time", without tabling an amendment, but this is uncommon,

---

[1] Procedure 1st Rpt 1999–2000.

because notice of such opposition, which is desirable in the interests of good order, cannot be given on the order paper.

## Second reading agreed to with amendment

8.40 Amendments may be moved which do not seek to negative the second reading but invite the House to put on record a particular point of view in agreeing to the second reading.

8.41 Notice is required on the order paper of any amendment to the motion for second reading. If notice has been given of more than one amendment, they are dealt with in the order in which they relate to the motion, or, if they relate to the same place in the motion, in the order in which they were tabled. In such cases it is usual for the whole debate to take place on the first amendment, and for the members who tabled the other amendments to speak in this debate. When the debate is concluded, the Question is put on each amendment successively, or on so many of them as need to be disposed of before a positive decision is reached. The Question on the original motion or on the original motion as amended is then finally put and decided.

## Motion for adjournment of second reading debate

8.42 It is also possible to move that the second reading debate be adjourned, with or without notice or reasons. Such a motion, if agreed to, does not prevent the motion for the second reading being put down for a subsequent day.

## Consideration in a Second Reading Committee

8.43 Second reading debates on certain Law Commission bills are held in the Moses Room.[1] Following first reading, a motion is tabled, with at least three sitting days' notice, to refer the bill to a "Second Reading Committee". The committee debates the bill, and reports to the House that it has considered the bill. The second reading motion is then normally taken without debate in the House, though it remains possible, in the event of opposition, for amendments to be tabled or a vote to take place on the motion. Law Commission bills are normally committed to a special public bill committee (see below).

---

[1] Procedure 1st Rpt 2007–08, 2nd Rpt 2010–12.

# COMMITMENT

8.44  After second reading, either immediately or at a later date, bills are committed to a committee on a motion in the name of the member in charge of the bill. Bills are usually committed to a Committee of the whole House or a Grand Committee.[1] The forms of words are *"That this bill be committed to a Committee of the whole House"* or *"to a Grand Committee".*

8.45  In certain cases bills may be committed to other types of committee. These include public bill committees, special public bill committees and select committees, which are described at paragraphs 8.104–8.122.

8.46  The House sometimes wishes, after committing a bill to one kind of committee, to commit it to another instead. The motion is "That the order of commitment of [date] committing the bill to an [original committee] be discharged and that the bill be committed to a [new committee]."

8.47  In order to save the time of the House, supply bills and money bills are not usually committed. This is the invariable practice in the case of supply bills and the normal practice for money bills.[2] Immediately after the second reading the member in charge of the bill moves *"That this bill be not committed"* and the Question is put. If it is agreed to, the next stage is third reading. A bill which has not been committed is described as having had its committee stage "negatived".

## Instructions

8.48  Instructions to any committee on a bill may be moved after the second reading.

8.49  Instructions may be either mandatory or permissive. The most common mandatory instruction directs the committee to consider the clauses and Schedules in an order other than that of the bill. Permissive

---

[1]  The Protection of Freedoms Bill 2010–12 was committed in part fo a Grand Committee and in part to a Committee of the whole House (Minutes of Proceedings, 8 November 2011). In such cases the proceedings take place sequentially and the bill is reported in respect of the clauses and Schedules separately from each committee.

[2]  SO 47(1), Procedure 1st Rpt 1970–71.

instructions enable a committee to do something that it could not otherwise do, such as divide a bill into two.

8.50 Instructions to extend the scope of a bill (that is, to make admissible amendments which would otherwise be excluded by the rules of relevance) are not in order.[1]

# AMENDMENTS

### Tabling of amendments

8.51 Amendments may be moved in committee, on report and on third reading. The following section describes general procedure for dealing with amendments. Issues specific to particular stages are described in the sections relating to those stages.

8.52 Amendments may be tabled in the Legislation Office at any time after second reading. When the second reading and committee stages are expected to take place on the same day, amendments are accepted before second reading. The late tabling of amendments is strongly deprecated since members have only a limited time to consider them and, if necessary, move amendments to them.[2]

8.53 Amendments which are intended to be published the next working day should be tabled between 10 a.m. and 5 p.m. on Mondays to Thursdays, and 10 a.m. and 4 p.m. on Fridays. Amendments may be tabled with the duty Clerk during recesses, between 10 a.m. and 4 p.m.

### Admissibility of amendments

8.54 The House observes the following general rules regarding the admissibility of amendments:

- amendments must be relevant to the subject matter of the bill[3] and amendments to a clause or Schedule must be relevant to the clause or Schedule to which they are proposed;

- amendments proposed at committee or any other stage must not be inconsistent with a previous decision taken at that stage,[1] except

---

[1] Procedure 2nd Rpt 1990–91.

[2] Procedure 2nd Rpt 1976–77.

[3] See HL Deb. 6 February 1968, cols 1075–1086.

where alternative amendments are proposed to the same place in the bill;

- amendments to a Schedule are not in order if they go beyond the scope of, or are contrary to, the relevant clause which has been agreed to;

- amendments to the long title are not in order unless they are to rectify a mistake in the original title, to restate the title more clearly, or to reflect amendments to the bill which are relevant to the bill but not covered by the former long title;

- clause headings, and headings placed above parts of the bill or above groups of clauses, are technically not part of the bill and so are not open to amendment. Punctuation is also technically not part of the bill.

8.55 The Legislation Office advises on whether an amendment is admissible and it is expected that this advice will be taken. If a member insists on tabling an amendment which the Legislation Office has advised is inadmissible, that office writes to the Leader of the House, copying the advice to the other Leaders, the Chief Whips and the Convenor. The Leader of the House draws the House's attention to the advice when the amendment is called, and asks the House to endorse the advice of the Legislation Office. The reason for this is that the admissibility of an amendment can ultimately be decided only by the House itself, there being no authority that can in advance rule an amendment out of order.

8.56 Tabling amendments to bills originating in the House of Commons is unprofitable if such amendments appear to be material and intolerable infringements of Commons financial privilege, in that they impose a charge not covered by the terms of the money or Ways and Means resolutions in the Commons, unless there is reason to believe that the Commons will pass a supplementary financial resolution (see paragraph 8.181).

## Printing of amendments

8.57 All amendments to a particular bill tabled on the same day are printed in one daily sheet, and are not numbered at this stage. The names

---

[1] SO 38.

of members supporting an amendment are printed above it, up to a maximum of four names, or five if the member in charge of the bill adds his or her name.[1]

## Rules of marshalling

8.58   Subject to the rules listed below, amendments are printed in the order of their page, line and word references in the bill, taking account of any instruction that has been tabled. The rules are as follows:

- amendments to the preamble and the long title, in that order, are taken last;
- amendments to leave out words take precedence over amendments to leave out the same words and insert others;
- amendments to leave out a shorter block of text (e.g. lines 1–5) take precedence over amendments to leave out a longer block of text (e.g. lines 1–20);
- amendments to leave out any block of text other than a complete clause or Schedule come before amendments to that text;
- amendments to a clause are considered before the Question that the clause stand part of the bill;
- amendments to leave out a clause and substitute another are considered after any amendments to the clause;
- because each clause and Schedule must be stood part of the bill in committee, an amendment to leave out a clause or Schedule in committee is not technically an amendment, but a statement of intention to oppose the Question that the clause or Schedule stand part of the bill. Notice is usually given of such intention and printed in italics, without being numbered, on the marshalled list. On report and third reading an intention to leave out a clause or Schedule is indicated by tabling an amendment;[2]
- amendments to divide a clause are taken after the clause has been stood part of the bill;[3]

---

[1]   Procedure 1st Rpt 1974–75.

[2]   HL Deb. 11 June 1964, cols 986–1001; Procedure 1st Rpt 1983–84.

[3]   e.g. HL Deb. 21 January 1997, col. 586.

- amendments to transpose a clause or clauses, or part of a clause, to another place in the bill are taken after the clause (or the last of the affected clauses) has been stood part of the bill;

- amendments to insert a new clause are considered at the place in the bill where it is proposed that the new clause is to be inserted;

- amendments to new clauses or amendments to other proposed amendments are considered immediately after the Question on the original amendment has been put for the first time, in the order in which they relate to the text of the original amendment, and are disposed of before the Question on the original amendment, or the original amendment as amended, is finally put;

- where alternative amendments are tabled to the same place in the bill, they are marshalled in the order in which they are tabled, except that priority is given to an amendment tabled by the member in charge of the bill. A decision may be taken on each in turn, even if the second amendment is in substitution for the first amendment to which the committee has already agreed.

8.59    Accordingly amendments are marshalled as follows:

## Clause 1

Amendment No.

1.    Page 1, line 5, leave out subsection (1)

2.    Page 1, line 5, leave out subsection (1) and insert– "(1) —"

3.    Page 1, line 6, leave out "word"

4.    Page 1, line 6, leave out "word" and insert "words"

5.    Page 1, line 6, after "word" insert "usually"

6.    Page 1, line 7, leave out "4" and insert "5"

7.    Page 1, line 7, leave out "4" and insert "6"

8.    Page 1, line 7, leave out "4" and insert "7"

(If amendment 6 is agreed to, the Question is put on amendment 7 thus:

"Page 1, line 7, leave out "5" and insert "6""

and on amendment 8 thus:

"Page 1, line 7, leave out "5" [or "6"] and insert "7"".)

9.    *Lord A gives notice of his intention to oppose the Question that Clause 1 stand part of the bill* [at committee] or

Leave out Clause 1 [at report or third reading]

10. Leave out Clause 1 and insert the following new Clause—"—"
11. Transpose Clause 1 to after Clause 46

## Marshalled lists

### At committee and report stages

8.60 Two working days before consideration of a bill is due to take place, the various amendments are numbered and published as a "marshalled list", arranged in the order they will be considered, taking account of any instruction. If further amendments are tabled on the day before that appointed for consideration they are printed on supplementary sheets or are incorporated in a revised marshalled list. Any amendments not previously published, and amendments which have been altered since they were last published, are marked with a ★ on the marshalled list, but are otherwise treated identically to other amendments.[1] When the stage is not completed in one day, further amendments may be tabled, which are printed on sheets supplementary to the marshalled list and on further marshalled lists.

### At third reading

8.61 Marshalled lists for third reading are produced in the same way as those for committee and report, except that amendments must be tabled by the working day before the stage. The list is usually published on the day of the stage.

## Manuscript amendments

8.62 Whenever possible, amendments should be tabled in time for inclusion in the marshalled list. However, except on third reading, it is in order to move, as manuscript amendments, amendments of which notice has not been given on the marshalled list or on a supplementary sheet. Occasionally a manuscript amendment is justified, even in the course of debate, for instance to correct an amendment already tabled or when an amendment under consideration is objected to and it is clear that with slight alteration of language it would become acceptable. However, manuscript amendments should rarely be moved, since other members

---

[1] But see paragraph 8.52.

of the House will not have had an opportunity to consider them and may be deprived of the opportunity of moving amendments to them.

8.63   When a manuscript amendment is moved, the text of the amendment is read out both by the mover and by the Lord on the Woolsack or in the Chair when putting the Question, unless the House or committee otherwise directs.

### Procedure on amendments

8.64   There is no selection of amendments. The clauses in the bill are proceeded with in sequence, unless an instruction varying the sequence has been agreed to. Each amendment on the marshalled list and each manuscript amendment is called in turn by the Lord on the Woolsack or in the Chair, subject only to pre-emption (see paragraph 8.68). An amendment which has been tabled need not be moved, but if none of the members named as supporters of the amendment moves it any other member may do so.[1]

8.65   After the member moving the amendment has spoken the Lord on the Woolsack or in the Chair puts the text of the amendment to the House or the committee. The debate on the amendment follows, at the end of which the member who has moved the amendment either begs leave to withdraw it or invites the House or committee to agree to it. The Lord on the Woolsack or in the Chair must put the Question that the amendment be agreed to if the member who has moved the amendment does not beg leave to withdraw, or if leave to withdraw is not unanimous.

8.66   Amendments to new clauses or amendments to other proposed amendments are taken after the new clause or original amendment has been moved and put for the first time to the House or committee. When any such amendments have been disposed of, the debate on the original amendment, or the original amendment as amended, may be resumed.

8.67   If a member whose amendment is called wishes to speak, other than to say "Not moved", he or she must move the amendment, and the Lord on the Woolsack or in the Chair must put it to the House or

---

[1]   HL Deb. 21 March 1984, col. 1325.

committee. This allows others to speak too. It is not in order to make a detailed speech and then to say "Not moved".

## Pre-emption

8.68 If an amendment has been pre-empted by one previously agreed to by the House, e.g. because the text proposed to be amended has been left out of the bill, the amendment will not be called. The Lord on the Woolsack or in the Chair alerts the House to this possibility, normally when putting the text of the pre-empting amendment after it has been moved, but sometimes (e.g. when the amendment is a key one which is expected to be divided on) when calling the pre-empting amendment.

## Grouping of amendments

8.69 In order to avoid repetition, related amendments are often grouped and debated together. Lists of such groupings are prepared by agreement between the members tabling the amendments and the Government Whips' Office, and are made available to the House. Groupings are informal and not binding. A member may speak to a group of amendments (not necessarily consecutive or in his own name) when the first amendment in the group is called. Usually only the first amendment in a group is moved and the rest are merely spoken to in the debate on the first amendment, even though it may be a minor or paving amendment. But each amendment in the group must be called, moved (if desired) and disposed of separately at its place in the marshalled list. Proceedings on later amendments in a group are often formal but further debate may take place and an amendment previously debated with others in a group may be moved at its place in the bill.[1] When proceedings on later amendments in a group are formal, the amendments are moved as follows:

*"My Lords, I have already spoken to this amendment. I beg to move."*

8.70 If the first amendment in a group is agreed to, it does not follow that the other amendments in the group will all be agreed to, unless they are directly consequential. It is a matter for the House or committee to judge in each case how the decision on the first amendment affects the others.

---

[1] Procedure 2nd Rpt 1976–77, 1st Rpt 1987–88.

*Effect of groupings on third reading amendments*

8.71  A member who believes that an amendment at committee or report stage has been wrongly grouped should make this clear in debate. Otherwise, under the rule against reopening at third reading an issue which has previously been decided, members may be precluded from retabling the same or very similar amendments at third reading, if another amendment in the group was voted on or negatived at committee or report stage (see paragraph 8.146).[1]

## Amendments moved *en bloc*

8.72  Amendments may be moved *en bloc* provided that:

- they are printed consecutively on the marshalled list;
- during committee stage, they all relate to the same clause or Schedule;
- they are consequential on an amendment or amendments already agreed to; and
- no member objects.

8.73  If any member objects to amendments being moved *en bloc* they must be moved separately to the extent desired. A vote cannot take place on amendments moved *en bloc*. Instead, the first amendment in each Group is moved and the Question on it resolved separately. If the first amendment is withdrawn or disagreed to, the other amendments are normally not moved. If the first amendment is agreed to, the other amendments may then be moved formally *en bloc*, without further debate.[2] Amendments may not be withdrawn *en bloc*.

# PROCEEDINGS IN COMMITTEE OF THE WHOLE HOUSE

8.74  A Committee of the whole House consists, as its name implies, of all the members of the House. It is, in fact, the House itself in a less formal guise, presided over by a Chairman[3], and conducting its business according to more flexible rules of procedure.

---

[1]  Procedure 2nd Rpt 1991–92.

[2]  Procedure 2nd Rpt 1982–83. Consecutive amendments which have been grouped separately may be moved *en bloc*, proving the criteria set out in paragraph 8.72 have been met.

[3]  Under SO 62 the Lord Speaker may preside over Committee of the whole House.

8.75   The Lord in charge of the bill moves, and the Question is put:

> "That the House do now resolve itself into a committee upon the bill."

8.76   This motion is sometimes used as an opportunity for a general discussion on the amendments or on the procedure to be followed in committee or on whether to go into committee at that time. The motion may be opposed by reasoned amendment or by an amendment to postpone the committee stage or to discharge the order of commitment and to commit the bill instead to another committee, though opposition to the motion seldom occurs. When the committee stage lasts more than one day, the motion moved on a subsequent day *"That the House do again resolve itself into a committee upon the bill"* may provide an opportunity to raise matters relating to the progress of the bill. The rejection of a motion to go into committee does not represent the rejection of the bill, but merely the rejection of the proposition that the bill be considered that day.

8.77   When the motion that the House go into committee has been agreed to, the Lord on the Woolsack leaves the Woolsack, takes the Chair at the Table of the House[1] and puts the formal Questions postponing the long title and any preamble (no motion being moved).

## Powers and duties of Chairman

8.78   The powers and duties of the Lord in the Chair are the same as those of the Lord Speaker or Deputy Speaker when the House is sitting (see paragraph 4.07). They are generally confined to the calling on of clauses, Schedules and amendments to bills referred to the committee, and putting the Question thereon. The Lord in the Chair also makes the formal report of the committee to the whole House. Like any other member, the Lord in the Chair may vote but does not (as in the Commons) have a casting vote.

## Powers of Committee of the whole House

8.79   A Committee of the whole House can only consider those matters which have been referred to it, including any instruction to the committee given by the House. Where a bill has been committed to a

---

[1] SO 62.

committee, the whole bill is the committee's order of reference. A Committee of the whole House has no power to adjourn the sitting or to adjourn its consideration of a bill to a future sitting (though Committees of the whole House may interrupt their consideration of a bill without Question put either in an emergency (such as a member being taken ill) or for a lunch or dinner break). If consideration of the bill is not completed, the House is resumed on motion and can again go into committee on a future day.

## Procedure in Committee of the whole House

8.80   SO 30, which forbids a member to speak more than once to any motion, does not apply when the House is in committee.[1] A Next Business motion (see paragraph 4.56) is not permitted.

## Clause stand part

8.81   As soon as the amendments to each clause have been disposed of, the Lord in the Chair puts the Question that the clause (or the clause as amended) stand part of the bill. On this Question a general debate on the clause may take place. Any member who wishes to leave out the clause speaks to this Question. Warning of such opposition will normally have been given by means of an italic notice on the marshalled list, and if there is no italic notice any member who wishes to speak on "clause stand part" should inform the Lord in the Chair. Once a clause has been disposed of, the committee cannot return to it and consider it further.

8.82   Where there are several consecutive clauses to which no amendment has been set down, the Question is put on all of them *en bloc*. If members wish to speak to one of these clauses or move a manuscript amendment they may do so when the clauses are called; but in this case they should warn the Lord in the Chair of their intention, and that clause or those clauses will then be dealt with separately.

## Postponement of clauses

8.83   Clauses or Parts may be postponed on a motion made to that effect of which notice has been given; they may also be postponed as the result of an instruction. A clause may be postponed without notice after

---

consideration of it has begun but it may not be postponed if it has already been amended.

## Schedules

8.84   The Schedules to the bill are considered in order after the clauses (unless there is an instruction to the committee to take them in a different order) and are dealt with in the same manner as clauses.

## Preamble and long title

8.85   As soon as the clauses and Schedules have been disposed of, the Lord in the Chair puts without any motion being moved the Questions on the preamble to the bill (if there is one) and on the long title. Amendments to the preamble and long title may be moved before each of these Questions is put.

8.86   Consequential or drafting amendments to the long title are frequently agreed to. Preambles may be omitted in committee and also amended, and it is in order to insert a preamble in a bill where none exists.

## House resumed during committee stage

8.87   If the committee stage is not completed at one sitting, it is necessary for a member (usually a government Whip) to move *"That the House be resumed"*. When this motion has been agreed to, the Lord in the Chair leaves the Chair and the Lord Speaker or a Deputy Speaker takes the Woolsack. The House goes into committee again either later on the same day (on occasions when the House has been resumed in order to take other business) or on a future day.

8.88   When it is agreed that there should be a break during a committee stage, and there is no other business to be taken, the House is not resumed and adjourned formally but the committee simply adjourns without question put until a time announced by a government Whip.

8.89   When the committee stage is resumed, the committee proceeds from the point in the bill where it left off.

## Conclusion of proceedings in committee

8.90   When the committee stage is completed the Lord in the Chair, without any motions being moved, puts the Questions that the bill be reported to the House with or without amendment, and that the House be resumed. The Lord in the Chair then goes to the Woolsack to report the bill to the House.[1] If the bill has been amended, an order is made for the bill to be reprinted as amended, and the report stage takes place ("the report is received") on a later date.

## Report received immediately

8.91   If the bill is reported without amendment, the member in charge of the bill may immediately move *"That this report be now received"*. If this is agreed to, the next stage is third reading. It is, however, common for a separate report stage to be taken on a later date even when the bill has not been amended in committee.[2] This ensures that there is an opportunity to amend the bill before third reading.

## Committee negatived or discharged

*Committee negatived*

8.92   See paragraph 8.47.

*Order of commitment discharged*

8.93   If no amendments have been set down to a bill and it appears that no member wishes to move a manuscript amendment or to speak to any clause or Schedule, the member in charge of the bill may move that the order of commitment (or recommitment) be discharged.[3] This motion may be moved only on the day the committee stage is set down for and notice must be given on the order paper.

8.94   The member in charge of the bill says:

*"My Lords,*
*I understand that no amendments have been set down to this bill, and that no noble Lord has indicated a wish to move a manuscript amendment or to speak in committee.*

---

[1]   Or, if the Lord Speaker or another Deputy Speaker takes over the Woolsack, the Lord who was in the Chair may report the bill from the Government front bench.

[2]   Procedure 1st Rpt 1956–57.

[3]   SO 47(2).

*Unless, therefore, any noble Lord objects, I beg to move that the order of commitment [or recommitment] be discharged."*

8.95   The Question is then put *"That the order of commitment [or recommitment] be discharged."* If this Question is agreed to, the next stage of the bill is third reading.

8.96   If any member objects, however, this Question cannot be completed and the member in charge of the bill must at once move *"That the House do now resolve itself into a committee [or a committee on recommitment] upon the bill."* If this is agreed to, the House goes into committee in the usual way.

8.97   For the purposes of SOs 40(5) and 46, the discharge of the order of commitment constitutes a stage of a bill. Unless SO 46 has been suspended or dispensed with, third reading may not be taken on the same day as that on which the order of commitment has been discharged.

### Bill reported forthwith

8.98   Where no amendment has been set down to a bill and no member of the House has indicated a wish to speak, but the order of commitment has not been discharged, the House goes into committee. The Lord in the Chair then says:

*"[Short title] – My Lords, I understand that no amendments have been set down to the bill, and that no noble Lord has indicated a wish to move a manuscript amendment or to speak in committee. With the agreement of the committee, I will now put the Question that I report the bill to the House without amendment."*

8.99   Members who wish to speak to any of the clauses or Schedules or to move a manuscript amendment should indicate their intentions on this Question, in which case the Lord in the Chair must postpone the title and put the clauses and Schedules in the usual way.

## PROCEEDINGS IN GRAND COMMITTEE

8.100  If a public bill is not committed to a Committee of the whole House, it is usually committed to a Grand Committee. As described above this is done on motion moved after Second Reading. Any bill may be committed to a Grand Committee, but bills which are unlikely to attract amendments and which would have their committee stage discharged on the day of the committee stage are not committed to Grand Committees.

8.101 The proceedings and forms of words in Grand Committees are identical to those in a Committee of the whole House save that no votes may take place. Only one bill per day may be considered in Grand Committee. Amendments, which may be tabled and spoken to by any member, are printed and circulated as for Committee of the whole House.

8.102 As divisions are not permitted in Grand Committee, decisions to alter the bill may only be made by unanimity. Thus when the Question is put, a single voice against an amendment causes the amendment to be negatived.[1] If there is opposition to an amendment, it should be withdrawn, to enable the House to decide the matter on report. For the same reason the Question that a clause or Schedule stand part cannot be disagreed to unless there is unanimity; provided there is a single voice in favour, the clause or Schedule must be agreed to.

8.103 Unless the House orders otherwise, the next stage of a bill reported from a Grand Committee is report.

## OTHER COMMITTEE PROCEDURES FOR PUBLIC BILLS

8.104 Certain other procedures have been developed to scrutinise public bills, either instead of or additional to proceedings in Committee of the whole House or Grand Committee. These are:

- public bill committee;
- special public bill committee;
- select or joint committee.

8.105 The purpose of these procedures is either to save the time of the House itself by taking the committee stage off the floor or to enable more detailed examination of bills to take place, involving the hearing of evidence. Public bill committees (like Grand Committees) fall into the first category[2] and the other procedures fall into the second.

---

[1] See paragraph 7.02

[2] Public bill committees have been largely superseded by Grand Committees. The last appointment of a public bill committee was in 1994.

8.106 Unless the House orders otherwise, the next stage of a bill reported from a special public bill committee or public bill committee is report; but a bill reported from a select or joint committee is recommitted to a Committee of the whole House, unless the committee has recommended that the bill should not proceed.

8.107 Bills may be considered under these procedures only if the House has agreed to a particular order of commitment. It is usual for such a motion to be moved immediately after the second reading has been agreed to. However, a motion to commit a bill to a select or joint committee may be moved at any time before third reading; and a motion that the order of commitment to a Committee of the whole House (or to a Grand Committee) be discharged and that an alternative order be made may be moved any day before the committee stage begins. Notice is required of any such motion.

8.108 The members of a public bill committee, special public bill committee, select or joint committee are subsequently appointed by the House on the recommendation of the Committee of Selection.

## Public bill committee

8.109 A public bill committee is a select committee to which mainly technical and non-controversial government bills may be committed in order to save time on the floor of the House.[1] The committees have consisted of between twelve and sixteen named members together with the Chairman of Committees. A member of the House not appointed to the committee is nevertheless free to speak and move amendments,[2] but not to vote.[3]

8.110 The programme of sittings is decided by the committee, on motion, at the outset, and should not be subject to alteration thereafter. The committee may sit whether the House is sitting or not.[4]

8.111 When there is a vote in the committee, the doors are locked eight minutes after the Question has been put and challenged, unless all members are present within that time. After the Question has been put

---

[1] Procedure 1st Rpt 1987–88; 1st Rpt 1992–93.

[2] LJ (1986–87) 392–395.

[3] SO 65.

[4] Procedure 3rd Rpt 1970–71; 2nd Rpt 1987–88.

the second time, the Clerk reads out the names of the members of the committee. Each member when his or her name is called replies "Content", "Not-content" or "Abstain".

## Special public bill committee

8.112 Special public bill committees are public bill committees that are empowered to take written and oral evidence on bills before considering them clause by clause in the usual way. Law Commission bills are normally committed to a special public bill committee,[1] but the procedure may also be used for any bill irrespective of the House of introduction.[2]

8.113 A bill is committed to a special public bill committee by a motion moved after second reading by the member in charge of the bill. The membership of the committee is proposed by the Committee of Selection, and the government have a majority over the other parties, with remaining places held by the Crossbench members. It has been the practice for the relevant minister and frontbench spokesmen from the other parties to be members. Any member of the House may attend any public meeting of the committee. Unlike select committees empowered to take evidence, a special public bill committee is not given powers such as those to appoint advisers or to travel. The committee may sit whether the House is sitting or not.[3]

8.114 The relevant government department produces with the bill a summary of the consultation undertaken, with an indication of representations received and changes made. The evidence taking usually begins with the minister giving evidence, following which the minister rejoins the committee on the other side of the table. Special public bill committees must conclude their taking of evidence within a 28-day period beginning with the date on which they are appointed, excluding any adjournment of the House for more than three days.

8.115 There is an interval after the conclusion of the evidence taking, to enable members of the committee to table amendments.[4] The

---

[1] Procedure 1st Rpt 2007–08.

[2] Procedure 1st Rpt 1994–95.

[3] Procedure 3rd Rpt 1970–71; 2nd Rpt 1987–88.

[4] Amendments may be tabled in the usual way at any time after second reading.

committee then meets to consider any amendments tabled. Proceedings are the same as for a public bill committee, and are not time-limited.

8.116 The committee does not produce any report on the bill other than the bill as amended, which is published in the usual way. The written and oral evidence are published, together with the verbatim report of the special public bill committee proceedings.[1]

## Procedures common to public bill committees and special public bill committees

8.117 Public bill committees and special public bill committees, when considering amendments, follow the procedure of a committee stage in the Chamber as closely as possible. Members speak standing and, so far as they can, observe the same degree of formality as in the Chamber. The committee adjourns for 10 minutes for a division in the House. Notice of the proceedings is given on the order paper and amendments for consideration in such proceedings, which may be tabled and spoken to by any member, are printed and circulated as for Committee of the whole House. The verbatim report of this part of a committee's proceedings is published. The committee's report to the House is recorded formally by entry in the Minutes of Proceedings.

## Bill committed to select or joint committee

8.118 A public bill (other than a consolidation bill which is referred automatically after second reading to the Joint Committee on Consolidation Bills under SO 51) may be committed to a select committee or a joint committee when detailed investigation is considered desirable or when the hearing of evidence is considered necessary. To achieve this a motion is moved that a bill be committed to a select committee or that a joint committee be appointed to consider the bill. Such a motion is usually moved immediately after second reading but is admissible at any stage before third reading. If the bill has previously been committed to a Committee of the whole House or Grand Committee, the order may be discharged and an order made to commit the bill instead to a joint or to a select committee. A motion may be tabled to commit a part of a bill to a select committee. If the bill is referred to a joint committee a message is sent to the House of Commons informing

---

[1] LJ (1992–93) 161, 163; ibid (1993–94) 586, 682; HL Deb. 13 December 1995, cols 1279–88.

them and desiring their agreement.[1] A bill may be committed to a select committee on another bill.

8.119 The method of appointment and powers of the committee are the same as for an *ad hoc* committee on a general subject (see paragraph 11.03); but the bill forms the committee's order of reference and defines the scope of the inquiry.

8.120 When the committee has completed its deliberations, it makes a report to the House on the provisions of the bill, recommending whether or not it should proceed. The committee usually gives reasons in a report similar to a report on a general subject. The committee has no power to put an end to the bill. If it considers that the bill should proceed, the committee reports it with such amendments as it thinks fit, and the bill is then recommitted to a Committee of the whole House in the form in which it has been reported. When a committee makes amendments, formal minutes of proceedings are required to record the amendments made. The minutes of proceedings serve as the authority for the making of the amendments and the reprinting of the bill as reported. If the committee considers that it should not proceed, it reports the bill accordingly, without amendment.

8.121 When a select committee reports that a bill should not proceed, the bill is not recommitted to a Committee of the whole House. The bill remains in the list of Bills in Progress until the end of the session under the heading *"Reported from the select committee that the bill should not proceed"*. The House normally acquiesces in a report from a select committee recommending that a bill should not proceed, and no further proceedings on the bill take place. If a bill is to proceed, a motion, of which notice is required, has to be agreed that the bill be recommitted to a Committee of the whole House. A bill may also be recommitted to a committee after the latter has reported that it should not proceed.[2]

8.122 If a committee is unable to complete its consideration of the bill, it makes a special report to that effect and reports the bill without amendment.

---

[1] LJ (1958–59) 97.
[2] LJ (1854–55) 277, 334.

## Recommitment

8.123 A bill which has been referred to a select or joint committee is, after being reported by that committee, recommitted to a Committee of the whole House unless the select or joint committee has reported that the bill should not proceed. Consolidation bills and hybrid bills are the most common examples of bills which are recommitted.

8.124 Other bills may, on motion (which is debatable and of which notice is required) moved at any time between committee and third reading, be recommitted to a Committee of the whole House or Grand Committee in their entirety, or in respect of certain clauses or Schedules.

8.125 This course is adopted when it is desirable to give further detailed consideration to the bill or certain parts of it without the constraints on speaking which apply on report and third reading; for instance:

- when substantial amendments are tabled too late in the committee stage to enable them to be properly considered;
- where there is extensive redrafting; or
- where amendments are tabled at a later stage on subjects which have not been considered in committee.

This procedure reserves to the report stage its proper function as an opportunity to review and perfect the bill as amended in committee.

8.126 A motion that the House resolve itself into a committee on recommitment on a bill may be debated and opposed in the same way as the motion to go into committee. Procedure on recommitment is the same as in Committee of the whole House. The next stage of any bill or part of a bill subject to recommitment is report stage. However, the minimum interval between committee and report does not apply between recommitment and report.

8.127 SO 47(2) provides for the order of recommitment to be discharged on the same conditions as apply to the order of commitment.

## Consideration in Committee of the whole House at later stages of bills

8.128 In exceptional circumstances the member in charge of the bill may, with notice, move that the House consider particular amendments (including Commons amendments) in Committee of the whole House without formally recommitting the bill.[1] The effect, in accordance with SO 62, is to give greater "freedom of debate" with regard to those amendments. When consideration of the specific amendments is concluded the House is resumed, and proceedings continue without further interruption; the bill is not formally reported to the House, and no report or third reading stage follows. The decisions of the committee in respect of the amendments have the same effect as decisions taken by the House itself.

## REPORT STAGE

8.129 If a bill has been amended in Committee of the whole House, the report stage cannot be taken until a later day, unless SO 46 has been suspended or dispensed with.

8.130 The motion *"That this report be now received"* may be objected to and debated and voted on; an amendment may be moved to postpone the report until a specified time; or a reasoned amendment[2] may be moved in opposition to the motion or to record a particular point of view in assenting to the motion.

### Amendments on report

8.131 When the Question that the report be now received has been agreed to, any amendments are called in the usual way. Notice of these is given in the same way as for committee, and the same practices apply for marshalling and grouping. The proceedings are confined to dealing with amendments, either in the order in which they relate to the bill or in a particular sequence agreed to in advance by order of the House.

### Repeat amendments[3]

8.132 Amendments identical (or of identical effect) to amendments pressed to a vote by the mover and defeated in committee may not be retabled on report. However, an issue which has been debated and voted on in committee can be reopened, provided that the relevant amendment is more than cosmetically different from that moved in committee.

---

[1] LJ (2008–09) 868.

[2] See paragraphs 8.38–8.41.

[3] Procedure 1st Rpt 1998–99.

8.133 An amendment agreed to on a vote in committee may not be reversed on report except with the unanimous agreement of the House. A clause or Schedule stood part on a vote in committee may not be removed on report except with the unanimous agreement of the House.

## Amendments grouped and *en bloc*

8.134 As in committee, amendments may be grouped, and a member may ask leave to speak to a number of related amendments. Likewise consecutive amendments may be moved *en bloc* but without any need to confine each bloc within a clause or Schedule.

## Opposition to clause or Schedule

8.135 The Question that the clauses and Schedules stand part is not put on report, so a proposal to leave out a clause or Schedule appears as an amendment. Such an amendment should not be tabled if the purpose underlying the amendment is to initiate a general debate, rather than a genuine desire to leave out the clause or Schedule: it may, however, be appropriate when, for instance, a member wishes to learn the outcome of an undertaking given in committee.[1]

## Manuscript amendments

8.136 Manuscript amendments are not out of order on report, but the disadvantages and inconvenience attaching to the moving of manuscript amendments on report are even greater than at committee stage. The rule requiring the text of such amendments to be read out to the House applies on report as in committee.

## Rules of debate on report

8.137 On report no member may speak more than once to an amendment, except the mover of the amendment in reply or a member who has obtained leave of the House, which may only be granted to:

- a member to explain himself in some material point of his speech, no new matter being introduced;
- the member in charge of the bill; and

---

[1] Procedure 9th Rpt 1970–71.

- a minister of the Crown.[1]

8.138 Only the mover of an amendment or the member in charge of the bill speaks after the minister on report except for short questions of elucidation to the minister or where the minister speaks early to assist the House in debate.[2]

8.139 Arguments fully deployed either in Committee of the whole House or in Grand Committee should not be repeated at length on report.[3]

## Conclusion of proceedings on report

8.140 When the amendments have been disposed of, the bill is reprinted if amended, and awaits its third reading on a day to be fixed.

# THIRD READING AND PASSING

8.141 The third reading of a bill is normally confined to the formal motion *"That this bill be now read a third time".* In exceptional circumstances a non-fatal amendment to the motion for third reading may be tabled, for instance to delay third reading so as to allow more time for amendments to be tabled. Notice of such an amendment is required. In all other circumstances, the motion for third reading is taken formally, without debate. General debate on or opposition to the bill normally now takes place on the subsequent motion *"That this bill do now pass".*

## Procedure on third reading

8.142 Amendments may be moved after the third reading has been agreed to and before the motion that this bill do now pass.[4]

## Notice of amendments

8.143 Except for privilege amendments (see paragraph 8.150), which are moved without notice, notice of amendments must be given in sufficient

---

[1] SO 30.

[2] Procedure 1st Rpt 1987–88.

[3] Procedure 2nd Rpt 1976–77.

[4] Procedure 1st Rpt 1980–81.

time to enable them to be printed and circulated in the form in which it is proposed to move them.[1] Manuscript amendments are not in order. Marshalled lists of amendments are published on the day of third reading itself, rather than the day before as for other stages. When third reading is on a Thursday, the marshalled list may be published the previous day.[2]

## Admissibility of amendments

8.144 The practice of the House is normally to resolve major points of difference by the end of report stage, and to use third reading for tidying up the bill.[3]

8.145 The principal purposes of amendments on third reading are:

- to clarify any remaining uncertainties;
- to improve the drafting; and
- to enable the government to fulfil undertakings given at earlier stages of the bill.

8.146 An issue which has been fully debated and voted on or negatived[4] at a previous stage of a bill may not be reopened by an amendment on third reading.[5]

8.147 Where the Legislation Office considers that amendments fall clearly outside the guidance, including, for example, amendments which are identical, or very similar, to ones tabled and withdrawn at committee and report (unless tabled to give effect to government undertakings), or amendments raising completely new major issues, it will advise the member concerned. If the member tables the amendments notwithstanding this advice, the Legislation Office sends notification of these amendments to all members of the Usual Channels and to the Convenor of the Crossbench Peers. They may then draw the matter to

---

[1] SO 48.

[2] Procedure 3rd Rpt 2003–04.

[3] Procedure 2nd Rpt 2005–06.

[4] See paragraph 7.02

[5] Procedure 2nd Rpt 1976–77. The term "issue" is wider than a specific amendment. Thus where amendments have been grouped and debated together at an earlier stage of the bill it is assumed that all amendments in the group relate to the same "issue".

the attention of the House; it is for the House itself to decide what action to take.[1]

8.148 In all other respects the procedure on third reading is the same as that on report.

## Further proceedings after third reading

8.149 If the amendments are not disposed of on the same day as third reading, further proceedings after third reading are taken on a later day.

## Privilege amendment

8.150 On third reading of a bill originating in the House of Lords whose provisions may infringe the privileges of the House of Commons with regard to the control of public money, a "privilege amendment" is made formally after all the other amendments have been disposed of. The privilege amendment is moved without notice, without the amendment being circulated and without stating its nature. The amendment consists of a new subsection, inserted at the end of the final clause of the bill, in the following form:

"( ) Nothing in this Act shall impose any charge on the people or on public funds, or vary the amount or incidence of or otherwise alter any such charge in any manner, or affect the assessment, levying, administration or application of any money raised by any such charge."

8.151 When the bill is printed for the Commons these words are printed in bold type. The Commons leave out the subsection by amendment and thus make the imposition of the charge their own act.

## Passing

8.152 The motion "*That this bill do now pass*" is moved immediately after third reading has been agreed to or, if amendments have been tabled, as soon as the last amendment has been disposed of. The motion is usually moved formally. It may be opposed, and reasoned or delaying amendments, of which notice must be given, may be moved to it, but in other circumstances it is not normally debated.[2]

---

[1] Procedure 1st Rpt 2006–07.

[2] Procedure 1st Rpt 1998–99.

### House bills

8.153 When a bill is passed by the House in which it has been introduced, a fair print of the bill, incorporating all the amendments made by that House, is made. This is called the House bill and it is then sent to the other House accompanied by a message seeking that House's agreement to it. Any amendments made in either House in the subsequent passage of the Bill are marked into the House bill, which is then returned to the other House with a further message. The House bill constitutes the formal record of what each House has done in respect of a bill and is the authority on which each House prints the text of a bill or any amendments brought from or made by the other. The House bill also provides the authority for the text of a bill when it is published as an Act.

8.154 Each time a bill is sent from one House to the other the House bill is endorsed by the Clerk of that House. The appropriate formulae, in Norman French, are given in Appendix H.

### Bill sent or returned to Commons

8.155 When a bill originates in the Lords, the House bill is endorsed and signed by the Clerk of the Parliaments after third reading and sent to the Commons with a message seeking their agreement to it. The Commons publish the bill in the form in which it appears in the House bill.

8.156 If the Lords agree to a Commons bill without amendment, proceedings on the bill are at an end. A message is sent to the Commons so informing them and the bill awaits the Royal Assent. The bill itself is only returned to the Commons if it is a supply bill and the Royal Assent is to be signified by Commission (see appendix F page 259).

8.157 Where a Commons bill is amended in the Lords, the amendments are marked into the House bill which is then endorsed by the Clerk of the Parliaments and sent back to the Commons with a message seeking the Commons' agreement to the Lords amendments. The Commons then publish the Lords amendments.

## PROCEEDINGS ON BILLS RETURNED FROM THE COMMONS

8.158 If the Commons pass a Lords bill without amendment, or if the only amendment made by the Commons is to remove the privilege amendment made by the Lords, the bill then awaits the Royal Assent. In the latter case the Commons amendment is deemed to be considered and agreed to without any proceedings taking place on it in the Chamber, and a message is sent to the Commons informing them of the Lords' agreement.

8.159 If the Commons amend the bill in any other respect, the amendments (including any privilege amendment) are printed and circulated. If the bill is returned when the House is not sitting, the amendments are printed pursuant to SO 50(2).

## Consideration of Commons amendments

8.160 When possible, reasonable notice should be given for the consideration of Commons amendments; but, if necessary, they may be considered forthwith on the day they are received if a motion for that purpose is agreed to.[1] In such circumstances it is usual to give notice by means of an italic note on the order paper.

## Amendments to Commons amendments

8.161 When a bill is returned from the Commons with amendments, it is only those amendments which are before the House. The other parts of the bill are no longer at issue, having been agreed to by both Houses, and cannot be amended except by a "consequential amendment", that is, an amendment immediately consequent upon the acceptance or rejection of a Commons amendment. So further amendments proposed at this stage are only admissible if they are relevant to a Commons amendment.

8.162 In dealing with a Commons amendment the following options are open to the Lords:

- to agree to the Commons amendment, either (a) without amendment, or (b) with a consequential amendment or an amendment in lieu of the words left out of the bill by the Commons, or (c) an amendment to the words restored to the bill by the Commons;

- to amend the Commons amendment;

- to disagree to the Commons amendment but to propose an alternative to it (an amendment "in lieu");

---

[1] Procedure 1st Rpt 1987–88. SO 41(4).

- to disagree to the Commons amendment.

8.163 Amendments to Commons amendments are handed in to the Legislation Office and published in the usual way. An amendment to a Commons amendment takes the same form as any other amendment to an amendment (see paragraph 8.66). But a proposal to disagree to a Commons amendment or to put forward an amendment in lieu takes the form of an amendment to the motion that the House do agree with the Commons in their amendment.[1]

8.164 A marshalled list of amendments and motions to be moved on consideration of Commons amendments is published on the day on which the amendments are to be taken. In some cases, where it is of assistance to the House, the text of the Commons amendments, or of the relevant ones, is printed on the marshalled list. Manuscript amendments to Commons amendments are not out of order but the disadvantages and inconveniences of such amendments are as great as on report.[2]

## Procedure on consideration of Commons amendments

8.165 Each Commons amendment is called from the Woolsack in the order in which it relates to the bill, unless the House orders differently. The member in charge of the bill moves that the House do agree with the Commons in their amendment, and the debate and decision follow as usual (see paragraph 8.64). An amendment to a Commons amendment is moved as soon as the Question on the Commons amendment has been put for the first time (see paragraph 8.66). A motion to disagree to a Commons amendment or to propose an amendment in lieu is moved as an amendment to the motion to agree with the Commons amendment. If the motion to disagree is agreed to, there are no further proceedings on the original motion. If the motion to disagree is withdrawn or disagreed to, the Question is put on the original motion that the House do agree with the Commons in their amendment.

8.166 If the member in charge of the bill wishes to move that the House disagree with a Commons amendment, the procedure above does not

---

[1] Procedure 2nd Rpt 1999–2000.
[2] Procedure 1st Rpt 1989–90.

apply and the motion to disagree is moved as a motion in its own right and not as an amendment to a motion to agree.

8.167 If the member in charge of the bill wishes to move that the House do agree or disagree to some or all of the Commons amendments *en bloc*, and there is no other motion or amendment tabled to those amendments, they explain their intentions and ask leave of the House to do so when the first of the bloc is called. If there is no objection the Question is put accordingly. If there is objection the Question must be put separately on each amendment to the extent desired.

8.168 The Legislation Office provides a brief for all movers of amendments and motions at these stages.

## Commons amendments agreed to

8.169 If all the Commons amendments are agreed to without amendment, the bill awaits the Royal Assent.

## Commons amendments agreed to with amendments

8.170 When the Lords agree to a Commons amendment with an amendment, the bill is returned to the Commons with a message to that effect. In dealing with the bill the Commons can agree to the Lords amendments, or agree to them with amendments, or disagree to them with or without proposing an alternative.

8.171 If the Commons amend the Lords amendments and send the bill back accordingly, it then becomes the turn of the Lords to agree or disagree to, or amend, such Commons amendments, and the communications proceed in the same way as on the original Commons amendments. At this and subsequent stages related amendments and reasons are printed together on the marshalled list and may, if appropriate, be debated and decided together. A set of amendments treated in this way is referred to as a "package". Packaging should be distinguished from the grouping of amendments at earlier stages, whereby amendments are debated together but may be decided separately.[1]

---

[1] Procedure 1st Rpt 2004–05.

## Commons amendments disagreed to

### Amendment in lieu of Commons amendment

8.172 The Lords can disagree to a Commons amendment but propose an amendment in lieu of it. When the bill goes back to the Commons they can agree to the Lords amendment in lieu, or propose an amendment to the amendment in lieu, or disagree to the amendment in lieu with or without proposing an alternative.

8.173 If the Commons amend the Lords amendment in lieu, or propose an alternative to it, the Lords can agree to or amend the Commons amendment, propose a new alternative or insist on their original amendment.

### Disagreement to Commons amendment with a reason

8.174 If the Lords disagree to a Commons amendment without proposing an alternative they have to give a reason for their disagreement. A "reasons committee", usually of three members, is appointed to do this. The committee consists of the proposer of the disagreement and one supporter, together with the member in charge of the bill or, in the case of a government bill, some other minister, if desired. The committee meets in the Prince's Chamber immediately after proceedings on Commons amendments have been concluded and agrees upon the reason, which is reported to the House by means of an entry in the Minutes of Proceedings.

8.175 In considering a Lords reason the Commons may insist on their amendments with a reason; or not insist on their amendments; or not insist on their amendments, but propose others in lieu. The reason, or new amendments, are then considered by the Lords in the same way as the original Commons amendments, except that where the reason given by the Commons is on grounds of privilege (see paragraph 8.183) the Lords do not insist on their amendment.

8.176 If the Commons insist, it is still open to the Lords not to insist on their disagreement, and thus to accept the Commons amendments, or not to insist on their disagreement but to amend the Commons amendments or propose alternatives. If the Lords simply insist on their disagreement without offering amendments or alternatives, the bill is lost.

### Further communications between the two Houses

8.177 Communications between the two Houses may be carried on until the end of the session,[1] subject to these limitations:

- the parts of the bill which both Houses have agreed on cannot be amended except by a "consequential amendment" (see paragraph 8.161);
- if the reason given by the Commons for their disagreement is on the ground of privilege, the Lords do not insist on their amendment.

8.178 In addition, if one House insists on an amendment to which the other has disagreed, and the other insists on its disagreement, and neither has offered alternatives, the bill is lost. However, there is no binding rule of order which governs these proceedings in either House, and, if there is a desire to save a bill, some variation in the proceedings may be devised in order to effect this object.[2]

8.179 If any communications are still continuing at the end of a session, the bill is lost.

## LORDS AMENDMENTS TO COMMONS BILLS

8.180 When any Lords amendments have been considered by the Commons, the bill is sent back to the Lords:

- with the Lords amendments agreed to, in which case the bill is ready for Royal Assent; or
- with the Lords amendments amended, or with amendments in lieu; or
- with the Lords amendments disagreed to, with reasons for such disagreement;

and communications, similar to those described for bills originating in the Lords, take place between the two Houses.

---

[1] Exchanges between the Houses at this stage are governed by provisions set out in Procedure 1st Rpt 2004–05.

[2] *Erskine May,* p. 636. For an example see the proceedings on the Planning and Compulsory Purchase Bill 2003–04: LJ (2003–04) 427.

# LORDS AMENDMENTS AND COMMONS FINANCIAL PRIVILEGE

8.181 Each House of Parliament is guardian of its own privileges. It alone may invoke them. Until it does so, the other House is free to act as it thinks fit. It follows that, with regard to Commons financial privilege, the Lords may properly make amendments to Commons bills (other than supply bills) which, when they come to be considered by the Commons, are deemed by them to infringe their financial privileges. It also follows that the Lords need not anticipate what view the Commons may take of any Lords amendments with respect to Commons financial privilege. The only exceptions are amendments which *prima facie* are material and intolerable infringements of privilege, in that they either offend Commons SO 78(3)[1] or impose a charge not authorised by a Ways and Means resolution, and which will be summarily rejected by the Commons unless they have previously passed a supplementary financial resolution. Unless there is reason to believe that the necessary supplementary financial resolution will be made by the Commons, it is unprofitable for the Lords to make amendments of this kind. When such Lords amendments are considered by the Commons:

> (a) in the case of an infringement of Commons SO 78(3), the amendment is deemed to have been disagreed to without debate and without Question put;
>
> (b) in the case of a Lords amendment imposing a charge upon the people which has not been authorised by a Ways and Means resolution, the Speaker calls upon the member of the Commons in charge of the bill to move to disagree with the Lords amendment forthwith.

8.182 With these exceptions, the Commons may either invoke their financial privileges in respect of Lords amendments or waive them; and the Commons regularly accept Lords amendments which have financial

---

[1] "If the Speaker is satisfied that a Lords amendment imposes a charge upon the public revenue such as is required to be authorised by resolution of the House under Standing Order No. 49 (Certain proceedings relating to public money) and that such charge has not been so authorised, on reaching that amendment, the Speaker shall declare that he is so satisfied and the amendment shall be deemed to have been disagreed to and shall be so recorded in the Journal."

implications. The Speaker of the Commons directs that a "special entry" be made in their Journals implicitly asserting their general rights but stating that the Commons accept the Lords amendment, "the Commons being willing to waive their privileges".

## Privilege reasons

8.183 If the Commons disagree to a Lords amendment that infringes their financial privileges, the disagreement is made on the ground of privilege alone, and not on the merits of the amendment, even though the Commons may have debated the merits. The Commons communicate in their message to the Lords that the amendment involves a charge upon public funds or a charge by way of national or local taxation or that it in some other way deals with financial arrangements made by the Commons; and they add words to the effect that the Commons do not offer any further reason, trusting that the reason given may be deemed sufficient. In such cases the Lords do not insist on their amendment. But they may offer amendments in lieu of amendments which have been disagreed to by the Commons on the ground of privilege.

8.184 If the Commons disagree to a Lords amendment which appears to have financial implications but offer an amendment in lieu or an amendment to the words restored to the bill, financial privilege is not at that stage invoked by the Commons and the question whether the Lords amendment infringes privilege does not arise. It is therefore open to the Lords to disagree to the Commons amendment in lieu and to insist on the original Lords amendment, which is then returned with the bill to the Commons for further consideration by them.

# CONSENT OF THE CROWN

8.185 Where a bill affects the prerogative or interest of the Crown, the Consent of the Crown is required and in respect of public bills must, after it has obtained by Her Majesty's Government, be signified to the House by a minister who is a Privy Counsellor. This Consent places the Crown's prerogative and interest at the disposal of Parliament for the purposes of the bill, but does not imply that the Crown approves the provisions that require its Consent.

8.186 A bill affecting the interests of the Duchy of Cornwall or the Duchy of Lancaster requires Consent, unless the Crown's Consent has been obtained and the effect on the Duchy is not distinct from that on the Crown. In such a case Consent is given by the Crown on behalf of each Duchy or, when the Prince of Wales is of age, by Him as Duke of Cornwall.

8.187 In the case of a bill affecting the prerogative of the Crown, Consent is normally signified before the motion for second reading. If a bill affects the interests of the Crown but not the prerogative, the normal practice is to signify Consent on third reading in order to take account of any amendments made to the bill.

8.188 The Consent of the Crown may also be signified on consideration of Commons amendments if it has not been previously signified and one of the Commons amendments makes it necessary.

*Measures and private bills*

8.189 Consent of the Crown may also be required in respect of a Measure or a private bill (see paragraphs 8.224 and 9.53).

## ROYAL ASSENT

8.190 Letters Patent are issued from time to time to signify the Royal Assent to bills and Measures passed by both Houses of Parliament.

8.191 Royal Assent is usually notified to each House sitting separately in accordance with the provisions of the Royal Assent Act 1967. Once Royal Assent has been notified to both Houses, the bills become Acts of Parliament. If notification is given on different days to each House, the date of Royal Assent is the date of notification in the second House.

8.192 Notification is frequently given before oral questions, but it may take place at any break between two items of business, or at the end of business, if necessary after an adjournment. The order in which notification is given is as follows: supply bills, other public bills, provisional order confirmation bills, private bills, personal bills, Measures.

8.193 Royal Assent may also be signified by Commission, as described in appendix F (page 259).

*Refusal of Royal Assent*

8.194 The power to refuse Royal Assent was last exercised in 1708, when Queen Anne refused Her Assent to a bill for settling the Militia in Scotland.[1]

### Record copies of Acts

8.195 Two record copies of each Act are printed, Public Acts on vellum and Private Acts on durable paper. One copy is signed and endorsed by the Clerk of the Parliaments. This copy is preserved in the Parliamentary Archives, the other in the National Archives.

# PROCEDURES WHICH APPLY ONLY TO CERTAIN TYPES OF BILL

### Parliament Acts 1911 and 1949

8.196 Under the Parliament Acts 1911 and 1949 certain public bills may be presented for Royal Assent without the consent of the Lords. The Acts do not apply to bills originating in the Lords, bills to extend the life of a Parliament beyond five years, provisional order confirmation bills, private bills or delegated legislation. The conditions which must be fulfilled before a bill can be presented for Royal Assent under the Acts vary according to whether or not the bill is certified by the Speaker of the House of Commons as a money bill.

*Money bills*

8.197 A money bill is a bill endorsed with the signed certificate of the Speaker of the House of Commons that it is a money bill because in the Speaker's opinion it contains only provisions dealing with national, but not local, taxation, public money or loans or their management. The certificate of the Speaker is conclusive for all purposes. If a money bill, which has been passed by the Commons and sent up to the Lords at least one month before the end of a session, is not passed by the Lords without amendment within a month after it is sent to them, the bill shall, unless the Commons direct to the contrary, be presented for Royal Assent without the consent of the Lords. This does not debar the Lords

---

[1] LJ (1705–09) 506.

from amending such bills provided they are passed within the month, but the Commons are not obliged to consider the amendments. On a few occasions minor amendments have been made by the Lords to such bills and have been accepted by the Commons.

### Other public bills

8.198 If the Lords reject any other public bill to which the Acts apply which has been sent up from the Commons in two successive sessions, whether of the same Parliament or not, then that bill shall, unless the Commons direct to the contrary, be presented for Royal Assent without the consent of the Lords. The bill must be sent up to the Lords at least one calendar month before the end of each session; and one year must elapse between second reading in the Commons in the first session and the passing of the bill by the Commons in the second. The Lords are deemed to have rejected a bill if they do not pass it, either without amendment or with such amendments only as are acceptable to the Commons. The effect of the Parliament Acts is that the Lords have power to delay enactment of a public bill until the session after that in which it was first introduced and until at least 13 months have elapsed from the date of second reading in the Commons in the first session.

## Supply bills

8.199 Supply bills, or bills of aids and supplies, such as Consolidated Fund Bills and Finance Bills, may be passed or rejected by the Lords but, since the supply is granted by the House of Commons, the Lords are debarred from offering any amendment. Consequently the committee stage is negatived.[1] Proceedings on Consolidated Fund Bills are always taken formally;[2] Finance Bills are usually debated on second reading and their subsequent stages taken formally.

8.200 When these bills have been passed by the Lords, they are returned to the Commons if Royal Assent is to be signified by Commission, and are brought up by the Speaker and receive Royal Assent before, and in a different form from, all other bills.[3]

---

[1] See paragraph 8.47

[2] Procedure 3rd Rpt 1992–93.

[3] See appendix F, page 244.

8.201 A supply bill may, or may not, be certified as a "money bill" within the meaning of s. 1(2) of the Parliament Act 1911. Finance Bills, which are supply bills, are frequently not certified as money bills.

## Separate subjects

8.202 The right of the Lords to reject a supply bill includes the right to omit supply provisions from a bill when such provisions form a "separate subject" from the general object of the bill, which the Lords are otherwise entitled to amend.

8.203 For example the Lords amended Part III of the Land Commission Bill 1966–67 (which provided for a betterment levy). The Lords amended the part in committee although it concerned supply, but then left it out in its entirety on third reading, since it would have been an infringement of Commons financial privilege to return the bill with that part concerning supply amended. This gave the Commons the opportunity to restore the entire separate subject to the bill with amendments, including some of the Lords amendments made in committee.

## Tacking

8.204 Commons financial privilege debars the Lords from amending supply bills. In order that the Commons should not abuse their financial privilege by including in such bills provisions unconnected with supply, the Lords passed a resolution in 1702 condemning the abuse of "tacking". It is now embodied in SO 52.[1]

## Consolidation bills

8.205 Consolidation bills are invariably introduced in the House of Lords, and are subject to scrutiny by the Joint Committee on Consolidation Bills (see paragraph 8.209). Such bills fall into the following categories:

(a) bills, whether public or private, which are limited to re-enacting existing law;

(b) bills to consolidate any enactments with amendments to give effect to recommendations made by the Law Commissions;

---

[1] LJ (1701–05) 185.

(c) statute law repeals bills, prepared by the Law Commissions to promote the reform of the statute law by the repeal of enactments which are no longer of practical utility;

(d) statute law revision bills, which are limited to the repeal of obsolete, spent, unnecessary or superseded enactments;

(e) bills prepared under the Consolidation of Enactments (Procedure) Act 1949, which include corrections and minor improvements to the existing law.

8.206 Almost all such bills now fall within categories (a) to (c).

8.207 Bills which re-enact in the form in which they apply to Scotland the provisions of United Kingdom Acts,[1] and consequential provisions bills which, although not consolidation bills, contain ancillary provisions normally found in a consolidation bill and form part of a consolidation,[2] have also on occasion been specifically referred to the Joint Committee on Consolidation Bills on motion. If the motion is agreed to, a message is sent to the Commons to ask for their agreement.

8.208 On second reading the Lord in charge of the bill may indicate to the House the category into which each bill falls. The bill is then automatically referred to the Joint Committee on Consolidation Bills.[3]

## Joint Committee on Consolidation Bills

8.209 The committee consists of 12 members of each House, the Lords members being nominated by the Committee of Selection.[4] It is normally chaired by a former holder of high judicial office. The function of the committee is to assure itself that all the provisions of a bill fall properly within one of the categories previously indicated, and to report thereon to each House. After taking evidence from the draftsmen responsible and any departmental or other witnesses, the committee reports the bill to the House of Lords with or without amendment. Where amendments are made by the committee, bills are usually reprinted as amended. Whether or not amended, they are then recommitted to a Committee

---

[1] LJ (1972–73) 383.

[2] Joint Committee on Consolidation Bills 4th Rpt 1987–88.

[3] SO 51.

[4] Report of the Select Committee on the Speakership of the House of Lords, HL Paper 92 2005–06.

of the whole House. Thereafter consolidation bills follow the same course as other public bills.

8.210 Amendments may be moved in the House to bills that have been referred to the joint committee, provided that they are restricted to the class of amendment that could have been moved in the joint committee.

## Moving of stages of consolidation bills en bloc

8.211 Where the same stage of several linked consolidation bills is to be considered by the House, the Lord in charge may, with notice (given by means of an italic note in *House of Lords Business*), move the bills *en bloc*. In the case of an amending stage, this is only possible if no amendments have been tabled. Any member may, however, propose that the bills be taken separately to the extent desired. The House can also resolve itself into a committee on recommitment in respect of several consolidation bills at once in order to debate any amendments tabled; the committee reports only when all the bills have been considered. In this case the procedure is applied by business of the House motion.[1]

## Hybrid bills

8.212 Hybrid bills are public bills which are considered to affect specific private or local interests, in a manner different from the private or local interests of other persons or bodies of the same class, thus attracting the provisions of the standing orders applicable to private business (see paragraph 9.07).

## Reference of bills to Examiners

8.213 Each bill introduced in the Lords is examined by the Legislation Office to see whether it may affect any private interests to which protection is given by the Standing Orders. If, *prima facie*, this is found to be so, an order is made referring the bill to the Examiners, and the second reading of the bill cannot be moved until the report of the Examiners has been received, although notice of second reading of the bill may be entered in the order paper. In the case of a Commons bill, an

---

[1] Procedure 2nd Rpt 1991–92.

order is made for it to be referred to the Examiners if it was so referred by that House.

8.214 It is open to any member who considers that a public bill may be hybrid, or has become hybrid as a result of any amendment made to it (see below), to move that the bill be referred to the Examiners. Such a motion is usually moved immediately before second reading, but may be moved with notice between stages at any time before third reading.

## Report from Examiners

8.215 If the Examiners report that no standing orders are applicable, the bill may proceed on its ordinary course.

8.216 However, if the Examiners find that the standing orders relating to private business are applicable, the bill is a hybrid bill, and (unless the House orders otherwise) an order of the House is made providing for petitions against the bill to be deposited by a given date.

## Petitions

8.217 If no petitions are deposited against the bill, the bill proceeds as a public bill in the usual way. If petitions are deposited, the bill is committed after second reading to a select committee.

## Commitment

8.218 Since the bill is a public bill, and has been affirmed in principle on second reading, the preamble does not have to be proved before the select committee; but in other respects the committee broadly follows the procedure of a select committee on an opposed private bill (see paragraph 9.38). When the bill is reported from the select committee it is recommitted to a Committee of the whole House and thereafter follows the usual course of a public bill. The bill is reprinted as amended by the select committee and the amendments are also printed separately.

## Hybridising amendments

8.219 A bill may become *prima facie* hybrid as a result of an amendment made to it (and a hybrid bill may be amended in such a way as to affect private or local interests not previously affected). If an amendment is agreed to which, in the opinion of the Legislation Office, has such an effect, the bill may be referred to the Examiners before its next stage, on a motion moved by the Chairman of Committees.

## MEASURES

8.220 A Measure passed by the General Synod of the Church of England is, under the provisions of the Church of England Assembly (Powers) Act 1919, as amended by the Synodical Government Measure 1969, submitted to Parliament for a resolution directing that it be presented to Her Majesty for Royal Assent.

8.221 The Measure is submitted first to the Ecclesiastical Committee, which is appointed pursuant to the 1919 Act for the duration of a Parliament and which consists of 15 members of the House of Lords, nominated by the Lord Speaker, and 15 members of the House of Commons, nominated by the Commons Speaker. The committee appoints its own chairman; by practice, this is a former holder of high judicial office. Being a statutory committee the committee is not formally a joint committee, nor are its proceedings "proceedings in Parliament";[1] but it has resolved to adopt the procedure of a joint committee.

8.222 The committee reports on the nature and legal effect of the Measure, and gives its views on whether the Measure should proceed ("is expedient"), especially with relation to the constitutional rights of all Her Majesty's subjects. During its consideration of a Measure the Ecclesiastical Committee may, either of its own motion or at the request of the Legislative Committee of the General Synod, invite the Legislative Committee to discuss its provisions at a conference.

8.223 The committee communicates its report in draft to the Legislative Committee, and may not present its report to Parliament until the Legislative Committee asks it to do so. The Legislative Committee may, at any time before the presentation of the Ecclesiastical Committee's report to Parliament, withdraw a Measure from the consideration of that committee, and has invariably done so in the face of an unfavourable draft report.

8.224 If the Legislative Committee decides to proceed with the Measure, the text of the Measure and the report of the Ecclesiastical Committee are laid before Parliament. If the Chairman of Committees and the Chairman of Ways and Means in the Commons think that a Measure deals with two or more subjects which might more properly be divided, they can divide a Measure at this point and it is printed as separate

---

[1] See paragraph 12.03.

Measures. A resolution for presenting the Measure to Her Majesty for Royal Assent may then be moved. Where a Measure affects the interests or prerogative of the Crown, Consent is required as for a bill. It is signified before the motion is moved in the House. If both Houses agree to such a motion, the Measure is ready for Royal Assent.

8.225 Neither the Ecclesiastical Committee nor either House has power to amend a Measure, but either House can reject it by disagreeing to the motion for a resolution.

# CHAPTER 9
# PRIVATE LEGISLATION

## Role of the Chairman of Committees

9.01   In addition to his duties in the House, the Chairman of Committees exercises a general supervision and control over private bills, personal bills, Scottish provisional order confirmation bills and hybrid instruments. References in any private business standing order or in the Statutory Orders (Special Procedure) Act 1945 to the Chairman of Committees are construed as including references to the Principal Deputy Chairman of Committees and to any other Deputy Chairman.[1]

9.02   The Chairman of Committees has the duty to name the Lords to form the following committees:

(a) select committees on private bills;

(b) select committees on opposed personal bills;

(c) select committees on opposed provisional order confirmation bills;

(d) joint committees under the Private Legislation Procedure (Scotland) Act 1936 (House of Lords members);

(e) joint committees under the Statutory Orders (Special Procedure) Act 1945 (House of Lords members);

unless he is of the opinion that any such committee should be selected and proposed to the House by the Committee of Selection or unless at least two members of that committee request a meeting for that purpose.[2] The Chairman of Committees also has the duty to name the chairman of any select committee on a private bill appointed by him.[3]

---

[1]   Private Business SOs 94A, 204.

[2]   SO 63(2).

[3]   Private Business SO 95(2).

# Private Bills

## Origination of private bills

9.03   Private bills originate outside Parliament and are promoted by bodies seeking special powers not available under the general law. They should not be confused with private members' bills, which are public bills (see paragraph 8.29). Each private bill starts with a petition to Parliament from the promoter for leave to bring in a bill.[1] The petition, with a copy of the proposed bill annexed to it, is deposited on or before 27 November in the House of Commons[2] and a copy of the proposed bill is deposited in the office of the Clerk of the Parliaments.

9.04   The government cannot promote a private bill. When a government department wants to promote a bill which would, if promoted by another person or body, be a private bill the bill is introduced as a public bill and is subsequently treated as a hybrid bill (see paragraph 8.212).

9.05   Where a bill deals exclusively with the personal affairs of an individual it may be certified by the Chairman of Committees and the Chairman of Ways and Means in the Commons ("the two Chairmen" or "the Chairmen") as a "personal bill", though such bills are rare. Personal bills can be presented at any time during the session.

9.06   Scottish private legislation on matters not wholly within the legislative competence of the Scottish Parliament (other than personal bills) is governed by a statutory procedure contained in the Private Legislation Procedure (Scotland) Act 1936 (see paragraph 9.91).

## Examination for compliance with standing orders

9.07   Each House normally appoints at least one official as an Examiner of Petitions for Private Bills.[3] Each Examiner may act on behalf of either House. On occasion Examiners from both Houses may sit to examine a particular bill. In the Lords, appointments are made by the House, and in the Commons by the Speaker. Beginning on 18 December, each petition for a

---

[1]   PBSO 2. In this chapter any reference to standing orders is, unless otherwise stated, a reference to the standing orders relating to private business and the abbreviation PBSO is used.

[2]   PBSO 38.

[3]   PBSO 69.

bill is examined by one of the Examiners, who certifies whether the standing orders applicable contained in the Private Business Standing Orders and similar standing orders of the House of Commons have been complied with.[1] These standing orders require notices and advertisements and the deposit of bills and other documents at various public offices.

9.08 Complaints of non-compliance with the standing orders ("memorials") may be presented, and memorialists are entitled to be heard before the Examiner.[2]

9.09 The Examiner certifies to both Houses whether the standing orders applicable have, or have not, been complied with. If they have not been complied with, the Examiner reports the facts and any special circumstances. Should the Examiner be in doubt as to the construction of any standing order in its application to a particular case, he or she makes a special report of the facts, without deciding whether the standing order has or has not been complied with.[3]

9.10 In a case of non-compliance or doubt the Examiner's certificate or report is referred by each House to its Standing Orders (Private Bills) Committee.[4] Both Committees must agree to suspend or dispense with the relevant Standing Orders in order for the bill to progress further.

## European Convention on Human Rights

9.11 The memorandum which accompanies each Private Bill when it is deposited on 27 November includes a statement by or on behalf of the promoters of the bill as to the compatibility of the provisions of the bill with the Convention Rights (as defined in the Human Rights Act 1998).[5] In the case of every private bill, whether introduced in the Lords or the Commons, a report from a minister of the Crown on the promoter's statement of opinion required by Private Business SO 38(3) is to be presented no later than the second sitting day after first reading in each House.[6]

---

[1] PBSOs 70, 3.

[2] PBSOs 76–79.

[3] PBSOs 72, 81.

[4] PBSO 87.

[5] PBSO 38(3).

[6] PBSO 98A.

## Late bills

9.12 A promoter who wishes to introduce a bill late (after 27 November) submits to the two Chairmen a statement of the objects of the bill, the reasons for the need to proceed during the current session, and the reasons why it was impracticable to deposit the bill by 27 November.

9.13 The Chairmen consider:

(a) whether the explanation justifies the delay in depositing the bill; and

(b) whether the proposals are so urgent that postponement of the bill to the following November would be contrary to the public interest.

9.14 If the Chairmen are satisfied on these points, or if they consider that the public interest so requires, the appropriate Chairman gives leave for the petition and the bill to be deposited in the House in which they decide the bill is to originate.[1]

9.15 After the petition together with the proposed bill has been presented to the House, it is referred to the Examiners. The Examiners certify to both Houses non-compliance with standing orders. The Certificate is referred to the Standing Orders Committee of each House. If both committees report that the standing orders ought to be dispensed with, the bill is presented and read a first time.

9.16 The bill, as presented, should not contain any non-urgent provisions nor any other than those outlined in the original statement of the promoters in support of their application.

## Lords bills: introduction and first reading

9.17 The allocation of private bills between the two Houses is determined between the two Chairmen or, more usually, their Counsel, on or before 8 January.[2] The private bills proposed to be introduced are divided as equally as possible between the two Houses with a view to general convenience. Where a bill has been rejected previously in one

---

[1] PBSO 97.

[2] PBSO 90.

House, a subsequent bill with similar objects normally originates in that House. Personal bills usually originate in the Lords.

9.18 It is usual, before any allocation is made, for Counsel to the two Chairmen to invite representations from each promoter.

9.19 First reading is "formal", that is to say, by way of an entry in the Minutes of Proceedings. No proceedings take place in the House itself. In the case of bills originating in the House of Lords, it takes place on 22 January or, if later, the day on which:

    (a) the Examiner has certified that standing orders have been complied with; or

    (b) the Standing Orders Committee has reported that standing orders have been complied with; or

    (c) the House, on report from the Standing Orders Committee that the standing orders ought to be dispensed with, has agreed that the bill should be allowed to proceed.[1]

## Subsequent stages

9.20 The Chairman of Committees normally moves subsequent stages of private bills in the House (but see paragraph 9.26 below). His Deputies may act for him for all purposes connected with private legislation.[2]

## Petitions against private bills

9.21 Parties affected by a bill may present a petition against it, which must state clearly the grounds of their objection to the bill.[3]

9.22 Petitions against Lords bills must usually be presented on or before 6 February. Petitions against a Commons bill, or a late bill originating in the House of Lords, may be deposited up to 10 days after first reading, subject to private business SOs 201 and 201A. Petitions against Commons bills are admissible whether or not the petitioner also petitioned against the bill in the Commons.

9.23 Petitions against proposed amendments must be lodged in time for the committee to consider them.

---

[1] PBSO 98.

[2] Procedure 2nd Rpt 1967–68; PBSO 94A.

[3] PBSO 111.

## Petitions for additional provision

9.24 After the introduction of a bill, the promoters may wish to make additional provision in the bill in respect of matters which require the service of new notices and advertisements. A petition for that purpose, after approval by the Chairman of Committees, who acts for this purpose in close accord with the Chairman of Ways and Means, is deposited in the office of the Clerk of the Parliaments with a copy of the provisions proposed to be added. The petition is referred to the Examiners, and may not proceed unless any standing orders applicable have been complied with or dispensed with. A petition for additional provision may not be presented in the case of a bill brought from the Commons.[1]

## Second reading

9.25 The second reading of a private bill is usually taken before public business and is usually brief. It does not, as in the case of public bills, affirm the principle of the bill, which may therefore be called in question before a committee, or at a later stage. The second reading is normally moved by the Chairman of Committees, and provides an opportunity for him to direct the attention of the House to any special circumstances connected with the bill.[2]

9.26 A member of the Lords who intends to debate the second reading of a bill is expected to notify the Chairman of Committees, the Public and Private Bill Office[3] or the Government Whips' Office; a member who intends to oppose it should always do so. The Chairman of Committees then usually asks the promoters to arrange for someone other than himself to move the second reading, and he may enter it at a lower place on the order paper.

9.27 The second reading of a bill originating in the House of Lords may not be taken earlier than the second sitting day after first reading[4] and it is customary to wait until the petitioning period has expired before taking second reading.

---

[1] PBSO 74.

[2] PBSO 91.

[3] Now part of the Legislation Office.

[4] PBSO 99.

9.28　Lords bills affected by the standing orders originally devised by Lord Wharncliffe, which govern the consents of proprietors, members and directors of companies,[1] are referred again to the Examiners after second reading.[2] Such bills are not committed unless those orders have been complied with or dispensed with.[3]

## Instructions

9.29　Instructions to committees on private bills may be moved at any time between the second reading and committee stage of the bill, but are usually put down for the same day as the second reading. The Chairman of Committees should be informed before an instruction is tabled.[4]

9.30　Permissive instructions enable the committee to do what it could not do without such an instruction. However, any enlargement of the scope of a bill should be effected by a petition for additional provision rather than such an instruction. Mandatory instructions compel the committee to do something which it already has discretion to do. However, the House has been reluctant to agree to any instruction which will restrict the decisions of the committee.

9.31　The most usual type of instruction on a private bill is of a cautionary nature. For example, the committee is sometimes instructed to have regard to certain matters or to ensure that various objections have been considered. An instruction of this nature is often accepted by the House, as it ensures that the committee considers matters which might not be raised by the parties appearing before it or in a departmental report.

9.32　To assist them in carrying out an instruction, committees have on occasion been given power by the House to hear evidence other than that tendered by the parties entitled to be heard. This procedure, however, is open to criticism: it may enable a person to oppose a bill without having petitioned against it, and there is no fund out of which the fees of any expert witness may be paid.

---

[1]　These are often referred to as the "Wharncliffe Orders".

[2]　PBSOs 62–68.

[3]　PBSO 100.

[4]　PBSO 93.

9.33   Instructions have occasionally been given to an unopposed bill committee.

9.34   It is customary for the committee to make a special report to the House upon matters referred to in an instruction.

9.35   Private business SOs 124A and 131–146 amount to "standing instructions" to committees on certain types of bill.

## Commitment

9.36   After second reading every unopposed bill is normally committed to an unopposed bill committee.[1] Every bill opposed by petitions is committed to a select committee.[2]

9.37   The Chairman of Committees may report to the House that, in his opinion, an unopposed bill should be proceeded with as an opposed bill and committed to a select committee.[3] In such a case the committee might be authorised to hear evidence tendered by parties other than the promoters, but this procedure has rarely been used.

## Committees on opposed bills

9.38   Select committees on opposed bills consist of five members, normally named by the Chairman of Committees, who also nominates the chairman, and reports his appointments to the House. Members of the House with an interest in the bill may not serve on the committee.[4] If the chairman is absent, the committee may appoint a substitute.[5]

9.39   In principle every member of the committee must attend the whole proceedings, but the committee may sit with only four members if all the parties agree. In this case a report is made to the House. If the consent of any party is withheld, the committee adjourns and may not resume in the absence of a member without leave of the House. No

---

[1] PBSO 121.

[2] PBSO 104.

[3] PBSO 92.

[4] PBSO 96.

[5] PBSO 95.

member who is not a member of the committee may take any part in its proceedings.[1]

9.40   If the committee adjourns over a day on which the House sits, it must report the reason to the House.[2] Promoters and petitioners may be represented by counsel or agents. The committee hears arguments and evidence from the parties and the representations of government departments, which may include opposition to all or part of the bill. The committee is not allowed to hear other evidence without an order of the House. The committee may decide that the bill should be allowed to proceed, with or without amendments, or "that it is not expedient to proceed further with the bill".[3]

*Locus standi*

9.41   In general, and subject to private business SOs 115–120, a petitioner has a right to be heard if his or her interests are specially and directly affected by the bill. If another party challenges a petitioner's *locus standi*, the question is heard and decided by the committee at the beginning of their proceedings.[4]

## Bill rejected

9.42   If the select committee rejects the bill, an entry to this effect is made in the Minutes of Proceedings. The bill does not then proceed further and is removed from the list of Bills in Progress in *House of Lords Business*.

## Recommitment

9.43   If the committee reports that the bill should be allowed to proceed, the bill is recommitted to an unopposed bill committee, which then considers the unopposed clauses. It may not vary any decision made by the select committee.[5]

---

[1]   PBSOs 105, 106.

[2]   PBSO 108.

[3]   PBSOs 110, 127, 124.

[4]   PBSO 114.

[5]   PBSO 121.

9.44 If no petitioner appears, or if all petitions are withdrawn before proceedings commence, or if the *locus standi* of all petitioners is disallowed, then the select committee reports accordingly; the bill becomes unopposed, and, unless there is an instruction, the Bill is recommitted to an unopposed bill committee.[1] However, if an instruction has been given to a select committee on a private bill, the committee must consider the bill and instruction.

## Special report

9.45 In certain circumstances, when it is thought that the House should be informed of the findings of a committee, and its reasons for reaching them, a special report is made and printed. It is usual, for instance, to make a special report in response to an instruction. An order for the special report to be considered can be made, to allow the House to debate and review the decisions of the committee; but third reading provides the normal opportunity for such a debate.

## Unopposed bill committees

9.46 Each unopposed bill committee normally consists of the Chairman of Committees assisted by his Counsel.[2] The Chairman of Committees may select further members from the panel of Deputy Chairmen.[3] No member who is not a member of the committee may take any part in the proceedings. The promoters may be represented by their agents (rather than by counsel) and may call witnesses; evidence called is not tendered on oath. Representatives of the government departments which have reported on the bill attend and may be questioned by the committee.[4]

9.47 The promoter's agent is called upon to justify any clauses on which the Chairman of Committees has asked for further information or which are the subject of a departmental report. The committee may then amend the bill as it thinks fit.

---

[1] PBSO 113.

[2] PBSO 121.

[3] PBSO 121, 122.

[4] PBSO 127.

9.48   When the committee is prepared to accept the bill, witnesses are called, on oath, to prove the preamble to the bill and to produce copies of any Private Acts, and the originals of any documents, referred to in the preamble.

## Report

9.49   The proceedings of committees on both unopposed and opposed bills are concluded by an entry in the Minutes of Proceedings reporting the bill from the committee. Amendments made in committee are available for inspection in the Private Bill Office; the bill as amended must be deposited by the promoter at certain public offices. No Report stage is held in the House. However, after the bill has been reported by the committee, drafting or consequential amendments can be inserted in the bill by Counsel to the Chairman of Committees on the authority of the Chairman, and endorsed "Amendments made on Report". No entry in the Minutes of Proceedings is made when this is done.[1]

## Third reading and passing

9.50   In the majority of cases the third reading of a private bill is formal. Any amendments proposed to be moved on third reading must be submitted to the Chairman of Committees at least "one clear day", that is, two days, in advance.[2] All amendments which have the approval of the Chairman of Committees are moved by him; the House usually accepts them without question. These are usually amendments asked for by the promoters to correct errors or to carry out agreements made during the committee stage. Occasionally an amendment contrary to the wishes of the promoters is submitted and moved by a member of the House. In such cases a debate would ordinarily arise.

9.51   Any member of the House who wishes to speak without proposing amendments is expected to notify the Chairman of Committees of his intention in advance. Such remarks should be made on the motion that the bill do now pass, not on the motion for third reading.

---

[1] PBSO 147.

[2] PBSO 148.

## Commons bills

9.52   A private bill brought from the Commons is read a first time forthwith by means of an entry in the Minutes of Proceedings, and referred to the Examiners in respect of the standing orders relating to such bills.[1] It may not be read a second time until the standing orders have been complied with or dispensed with.[2] Petitions against it may be deposited up to 10 days after first reading,[3] whether or not the petitioner also petitioned the House of Commons.[4] If it is amended in the House of Lords, it may be referred to the Examiners again in respect of the amendments.[5]

## Queen's Consent

9.53   When the Queen's or Prince of Wales' Consent (see paragraphs 8.185–8.188) is required for a private bill it is usually signified on third reading by a minister who is a Privy Counsellor.

## Commons amendments

9.54   Amendments made by the Commons to Lords bills, or to Lords amendments to Commons bills, and amendments to such amendments which the promoters wish to make in the House of Lords, are submitted to the Chairman of Committees for approval.[6] Commons amendments are usually agreed formally by an entry in the Minutes of Proceedings, without notice, and not taken in the House.

9.55   If there is disagreement between the Houses on amendments to private bills, the same procedure is followed as for public bills. However, decisions on private legislation are coordinated between the two Houses, so that the need for this procedure seldom arises. Neither House reinserts a provision struck out by the other House unless by agreement in advance between the two Houses.

---

[1]   PBSOs 98, 74, 60–61, 65–68.

[2]   PBSO 99.

[3]   PBSO 101.

[4]   PBSO 112.

[5]   PBSO 75.

[6]   PBSO 150.

### Royal Assent

9.56 Private bills other than personal bills receive Royal Assent in the same form as public bills, *"La Reyne le veult"* (see appendix H).

### Personal bills

9.57 Petitions for bills relating to the "estate, property, status, or style, or otherwise relating to the personal affairs, of an individual"[1] are presented to the House of Lords rather than the House of Commons. The petition must be signed by one or more of the parties principally concerned in the consequences of the bill, and may be deposited at any time during the session.[2] The petition and draft bill which must accompany it are considered by the Chairman of Committees and the Chairman of Ways and Means, who may certify that the proposed bill is of such a nature and that private business SOs 4–68 should not be applicable to it. Bills so certified are termed personal bills and are subject to private business SOs 151–153, 157–170 and 173–174. These bills are now rare, partly in consequence of the passing of the Marriage (Prohibited Degrees of Relationship) Act 1986, which relaxed the prohibitions on many previously prohibited relationships for which parliamentary approval was sought.

9.58 Every petition for a personal bill is referred to the Chairman of Committees for preliminary scrutiny, aided by Counsel. The procedure for first reading is the same as for other private bills. The Chairman of Committees may require the appointment by the Lord Chancellor of a guardian to represent the interests of any infant who should be protected.[3] In the case of personal bills affecting entailed estates and wills, private business SOs 162–165 and 168–172 govern the giving of notices, appointment of new trustees, consents and other matters.

### Proceedings after first reading for personal bills

9.59 Between first and second reading, copies of the bill as introduced are delivered to all persons affected by the bill by the promoter. The

---

[1] PBSO 3.

[2] PBSO 153.

[3] PBSO 167.

second reading is normally moved by the Chairman of Committees who also fixes a date by which petitions against the bill must be presented.[1]

9.60 If the bill is unopposed, it is committed to an unopposed bill committee.[2] At this stage the persons concerned in the bill give their consent by attending and signing a copy of the bill. In certain cases, such as absence abroad, illness or old age, the Chairman of Committees may admit affidavits in proof of signatures in lieu of attendance.

9.61 If the bill is opposed, it is referred to a select committee of five members named by the Chairman of Committees and proceeded with in the same manner as any other opposed private bill.[3] The Chairman of Committees may propose that an unopposed bill be treated as opposed.

9.62 No committee may consider a personal bill until 10 days after the second reading.[4]

9.63 The proceedings on third reading and passing of a personal bill are the same as for an ordinary private bill, but Royal Assent is given in the form *"Soit fait comme il est désiré."*

### Marriage enabling bills

9.64 Bills to enable persons to marry within the prohibited degrees of affinity are subject to a special procedure, intended to avoid discussion of personal details on the floor of the House.[5] The bill is granted a second reading without debate and is then committed to a select committee consisting of the Chairman of Committees, a bishop and two other members, which examines the promoters of the bill on oath in private before deciding whether the bill should proceed.

### Hybrid Instruments

9.65 The House of Lords alone has a procedure for considering hybrid instruments.

---

[1] PBSOs 157–158.

[2] PBSO 160.

[3] PBSO 161.

[4] PBSO 159.

[5] Procedure 2nd Rpt 1985–86.

9.66   When the Chairman of Committees is of the opinion that an affirmative instrument[1] is such that, apart from the provisions of the Act authorising it to be made, it would require to be enacted by a private or hybrid bill, he reports his opinion to the House and to the minister or other person responsible for the instrument. An instrument upon which such a Chairman's report has been made is known as a hybrid instrument. Such instruments can be opposed in the House of Lords by petitioning against them.[2]

9.67   Any petition asking the House not to affirm a hybrid instrument must be deposited with the Clerk of the Parliaments within 14 days following the day on which the Chairman's report is laid before the House. If no petition is received within this period the Chairman reports accordingly to the House. Any petition received during the period is referred to the Hybrid Instruments Committee (see paragraph 11.61) together with the instrument petitioned against.

9.68   The Hybrid Instruments Committee, after considering any representations made in writing by the parties to the proceedings and after hearing, if it thinks fit, the parties in person or by counsel or agents, decides whether any petitioner has a *locus standi*. If so, the committee reports to the House, in accordance with the criteria specified in private business SO 216, whether there ought to be a further inquiry by a select committee into all or any of the matters specified by the petitioner. In such a case, the House may refer all or any of the matters on which the committee has reported to a select committee consisting of five members, appointed by the House on the proposal of the Committee of Selection, with terms of reference specified by the House.

9.69   No motion to approve a hybrid instrument may be moved until the proceedings under private business SO 216 have been completed,[3] that is until either:

   (a) the Chairman of Committees has reported to the House that no petitions have been received, or that all petitions have been withdrawn; or

---

[1]  For this purpose, an affirmative instrument is as defined in SO 72, but excludes orders under s. 1 of the Manoeuvres Act 1958 and certain instruments exempted from this procedure by their parent Act.

[2]  PBSO 216.

[3]  SO 72.

(b) the Hybrid Instruments Committee has reported that no petitioner has a *locus standi*, or that there ought not to be an inquiry by a select committee; or

(c) the House has decided not to refer any matter to a select committee; or

(d) the select committee has reported to the House.

9.70    Where proceedings under private business SO 216 have not been completed in respect of an instrument which has expired or lapsed, a further instrument to substantially the same effect may be substituted for the purposes of those proceedings.

*Expedited hybrid instruments*

9.71    A hybrid instrument which, by virtue of the Act authorising it to be made, is, after the expiry of a period prescribed by that Act, to proceed in Parliament as if its provisions would, apart from that Act, require to be enacted by a public bill that is not hybrid, is known as an expedited hybrid instrument.[1] The procedure for such an instrument differs from that applicable to other hybrid instruments in several respects. A petition not to affirm an expedited hybrid instrument must be deposited within ten days following the day on which the instrument is laid. If the Hybrid Instruments Committee is of the opinion that there ought to be a further inquiry, it conducts that inquiry itself forthwith.

9.72    No motion to approve an expedited hybrid instrument may be moved until the proceedings under private business SO 216A have been completed, that is until the Chairman of Committees or the Hybrid Instruments Committee has reported, or the period prescribed by the parent Act has expired.

## Special Procedure Orders

9.73    The procedure for special procedure orders is laid down by the Statutory Orders (Special Procedure) Act 1945, as amended by the Statutory Orders (Special Procedure) Act 1965, supplemented by the private business standing orders of both Houses. That Act applies:

---

[1]    PBSO 216A.

- to orders made under Acts passed before the Act of 1945 which are specified in that Act, or to orders made under it;[1] and

- to orders made under Acts passed since the Act of 1945 which are expressed in those Acts to be "subject to special parliamentary procedure".[2]

## Laying of orders

9.74   An order subject to special parliamentary procedure must be laid before Parliament.[3] No order may be laid until the requirements[4] of the enabling Act, or of Schedule 1 to the 1945 Act, as to notices, consideration of objections and holding of inquiries have been complied with; and notice must be published in The London Gazette not less than three days before the order is laid. There must be laid with it a certificate by the minister specifying the requirements of the enabling Act and certifying that they have been complied with or (so far as the 1945 Act permits) dispensed with.

## Petitions

9.75   Petitions[5] may be presented against a special procedure order within a period of 21 days, known as the "petitioning period", beginning with the day on which the order is laid before Parliament or, if the order is laid before the two Houses on different days, with the later of the two days. If the petitioning period expires on a Sunday, it is extended to the following Monday; if it expires during a dissolution, prorogation or any period of 10 or more consecutive days on which the House does not sit for public business, it is extended to the day on which the House resumes.

9.76   There are two kinds of petition against a special procedure order:

- a petition calling for amendments to the order, which must specify the proposed amendments (a "petition for amendment");

- a general petition against the order, which must be presented separately (a "petition of general objection.").

---

[1] s. 8.

[2] s. 1.

[3] s. 1.

[4] s. 2.

[5] s. 3; PBSOs 206, 201, 201A.

9.77 Memorials[1] stating technical objections to petitions may be deposited in the office of the Clerk of the Parliaments within seven days beginning with the day on which the petition was presented.

9.78 After the petitioning period has expired, the Chairman of Committees and the Chairman of Ways and Means in the House of Commons consider all petitions and report to both Houses. If a petition complies with the Act and standing orders, and if the Chairmen consider the petitioner has *locus standi*, they certify that it is proper to be received and whether it is a petition for amendment or a petition of general objection. If a petition for amendment[2] involves amendments which would alter the scope of the order or affect the interests of persons other than the petitioner, the Chairmen may make a special report to that effect. If a petition for amendment involves amendments "which would constitute a negative of the main purpose of the order", the Chairmen certify it as a petition of general objection. But if only some of the amendments would defeat the main purpose of the order, the Chairmen may delete those amendments and certify the rest of the petition as a petition for amendment. In certain cases the Chairmen may find it necessary to hear the parties, and they must do so if memorials are deposited.

9.79 Within 14 days,[3] beginning with the day on which the Chairmen's report is laid before the House of Lords, counter-petitions may be presented against petitions for amendment.

*Resolution for annulment*

9.80 If either House within 21 days[4] beginning with the day on which the Chairmen's report on an order is laid before it (the "resolution period") resolves that the order be annulled, the order lapses. In reckoning the resolution period, time during which Parliament is dissolved or prorogued, or both Houses are adjourned for more than four days, is not counted.

---

[1] PBSO 207.

[2] PBSO 207A.

[3] PBSO 210.

[4] s. 4.

9.81   If there is an equality of votes on a resolution for annulment, the resolution is defeated and the order proceeds.

9.82   If no resolution for annulment is passed, any certified petition is referred to a joint committee, except that a petition of general objection is not referred if either House has resolved within the resolution period that it should not be. Any special report of the two Chairmen, and any counter-petitions, are also referred to the committee.

9.83   If no petition is referred to a joint committee at the end of the resolution period, and no resolution for annulment has been passed, the order may come into operation.

## Joint committee

9.84   Joint committees under the 1945 Act consist of three members of each House, and private business SO 209 governs their proceedings. Where a petition is for amendment,[1] the committee may report the order with or without amendments to give effect to the petition in whole or in part. Where the petition is of general objection, the committee may report the order with or without amendments, or report that the order be not approved. The report of the joint committee is laid before both Houses. Where the order is reported without amendment,[2] it may come into operation from the date when the report of the committee is laid before Parliament.

9.85   Where the order is reported with amendments,[3] the minister may bring the order as amended into operation on a date of his choice, or withdraw the order, or bring it to Parliament for further consideration by means of a bill for its confirmation.

9.86   Where the committee reports that the order be not approved, the order does not take effect unless confirmed by Act of Parliament.

## Confirming bills

9.87   A confirming bill presented in respect of an order reported with amendments is a public bill and sets out the order as amended.[4] It is

---

[1]  s. 5.

[2]  s. 6.

[3]  PBSO 214.

[4]  s. 6(4).

treated as if the amendments had been made in committee in the House in which it is presented, and in the second House likewise it proceeds straight to consideration on report.[1] A bill presented in respect of an order which the committee has reported be not approved goes through the same procedure, unless a petition for amendment was certified but was not dealt with by the joint committee. In that case the confirming bill has a first and second reading, and is referred to that committee for the purpose of considering that petition. Report and third reading follow. In the second House the bill proceeds straight to consideration on report.

### Orders relating to Scotland[2]

9.88    In the case of orders which do not deal with matters within the legislative competence of the Scottish Parliament but which relate exclusively to Scotland, a preliminary inquiry into objections is held in Scotland by Commissioners in accordance with the Private Legislation Procedure (Scotland) Act 1936. If the minister concerned accepts the Commissioners' recommendations, the order is laid before Parliament and the subsequent proceedings are as already described, except that no petition, whether for amendment or of general objection, is referred to a joint committee unless either House so orders within the resolution period. If the minister is not prepared to accept the Commissioners' recommendations, he or she may, instead of laying the order before Parliament, introduce a bill for the confirmation of the order. The procedure on such a bill is the same as for a bill under section 9 of the 1936 Act.

## Provisional Order Confirmation Bills

9.89    Procedure by way of a provisional order confirmation bill is simpler than private bill procedure. It is available only where a statute so provides, and has now been largely superseded by procedure outside Parliament. No such bills have been introduced since 1980.

---

[1]  s. 6(5).
[2]  s. 10.

## Scottish Private Legislation

9.90    Private legislation on matters affecting interests in Scotland, and not wholly within the legislative competence of the Scottish Parliament, is governed by the Private Legislation Procedure (Scotland) Act 1936.[1] A person seeking such legislation does not present a petition for a private bill to Parliament but submits a draft order to the Secretary of State for Scotland; and petitions him to issue a provisional order in the terms of the draft or with such modifications as may be necessary.[2] Legislation for purposes which would require a personal bill, as defined by private business SO 3(2), is exempted from this provision.

9.91    In this Part "s." refers to sections of the Private Legislation Procedure (Scotland) Act 1936; and "GO" refers to General Orders made under s.15(1).

### Legislation not confined to Scotland

9.92    A person who seeks powers "to be operative in Scotland and elsewhere" may make representations to the Secretary of State that the powers should be conferred by a single enactment.[3] The Secretary of State, the Chairman of Committees and the Chairman of Ways and Means in the House of Commons consider such a representation. If they are of the opinion that the powers would be more properly obtained by a private bill than by the duplicated process of a provisional order for Scotland and a private bill for the areas affected beyond Scotland, they publish their decision and report it to Parliament. The promoter then proceeds by private bill.[4] A petition for such a bill may not be presented sooner than four weeks after the representation has been made to the Secretary of State.

---

[1] s. 1(1).
[2] s. 1(1).
[3] s. 1(4).
[4] PBSO 193.

## Draft orders

9.93   Application for provisional orders may be made twice a year, on 27 March and 27 November. A printed copy of every draft order must be deposited in the appropriate offices of both Houses of Parliament.[1]

9.94   Promoters are required to comply with General Orders made under the 1936 Act, which correspond with the standing orders that have to be complied with prior to the introduction of a private bill. These require them to deposit copies of draft orders at certain public offices, and to give notice by public advertisement to owners and occupiers of land or houses affected. The Secretary of State refers all draft orders to the Examiners, who report to the Secretary of State and the two Chairmen whether these General Orders have been complied with. If they have not, the promoters may apply for dispensation to the two Chairmen, whose decision is final.[2]

9.95   The last date for advertisements is 11 April or 11 December, as the case may be, and for six weeks from the last date of advertisement persons may petition against any draft order to the Secretary of State, who notifies the two Chairmen.[3] When this period has expired, the two Chairmen examine all the draft orders and any petitions, and report to the Secretary of State, who lays each report before Parliament.[4]

## Order refused

9.96   If the two Chairmen report that the provisions, or some of the provisions, of any draft order relate to matters outside Scotland to such an extent, or raise questions of public policy of such novelty and importance, that they ought to be dealt with by private bill and not by provisional order, the Secretary of State must, without further inquiry, refuse to issue a provisional order, to the extent objected to by the Chairmen.[5]

---

[1]  GO 2, s. 1(2).

[2]  s. 13, GO 4–56, 58–60, 65–67, 69–72, s. 3(2).

[3]  GO 75.

[4]  s. 2, PBSO 189.

[5]  s. 2(2).

## Substituted bill

9.97 The promoters of a draft order which the two Chairmen consider should not be issued by the Secretary of State, may, if they wish, introduce a private bill known as a "substituted bill". They must, within 14 days after the Secretary of State has notified them of his or her refusal to make the provisional order, deposit a copy of the bill in every public office where a copy of the draft order was deposited, and they must notify their intention to the opponents of the draft order and prove to the Examiner that they have done so. They must satisfy the Examiner that the bill does not contain any provision which was not contained in the draft order, though it is not required to contain all the provisions which were in the order. Subject to these conditions, the notices which were given for the draft order are deemed to have been given for the substituted bill, and the petition to the Secretary of State for the provisional order is taken to be the petition for the bill. Petitions deposited against the draft order are received from the Scotland Office by the House in which the bill originates as petitions presented against the substituted bill. In the House of Lords no other petition may be received.[1]

## Unopposed orders

9.98 If the two Chairmen raise no objection to the draft order and if there is no opposition outstanding, the Secretary of State issues the provisional order, with such modifications as may be necessary to meet recommendations made by the two Chairmen or any public department affected. The Secretary of State has power to send an unopposed order to an inquiry by Commissioners before issuing it, but this is seldom done.[2]

## Opposed orders

9.99 Opposed orders are referred to Commissioners, who hear parties in Scotland. There are four Commissioners, normally two members of each House, selected by the two Chairmen from parliamentary panels appointed by the Chairman of Committees in the House of Lords and the Committee of Selection in the House of Commons. One of the Commissioners is appointed as Chairman and, by custom, is chosen alternately from each House. There is an extra-parliamentary panel for

---

[1] PBSO 194, 195, 196, s. 2(4), PBSO 197.
[2] s. 7, s. 3(1).

emergencies, which consists of twenty persons "qualified by experience of affairs to act as Commissioners" under the Act. This panel is revised every five years.[1]

9.100 The proceedings of the Commissioners follow closely those of select committees on private bills. After inquiry the Commissioners report on the order to the Secretary of State. They either report that the order should not be made, in which case the order is rejected; or they approve it, with or without modification.[2]

9.101 The Secretary of State then issues the provisional order. He or she is entitled to make further amendments after the inquiry, and is required at this stage to have regard to any recommendations made by the Chairmen or by departments. It is an essential feature of the procedure, however, that the fullest respect is paid to the views of the Commissioners. With the rarest exception, further amendments are limited to matters of drafting.

### Confirmation bills

9.102 No provisional order issued by the Secretary of State for Scotland has any validity until it has been confirmed by public Act of Parliament. A bill to confirm any such order or orders is usually introduced by the Secretary of State in the House of Commons. A bill to confirm an order into which no inquiry has been held is deemed to have passed through all its stages up to and including Committee in each House.[3] In the House of Lords, after first reading, it is put down for consideration on report. The Lord in charge of the bill moves:

*"That this bill be now considered on Report."*

9.103 The third reading and passing of the bill are usually taken on the next convenient day. Proceedings on such a bill are usually formal. Such bills are not printed in the Lords unless amended on consideration on report.

9.104 A bill to confirm an order into which an inquiry has been held may be petitioned against within seven days of introduction in the House of origin.[4] If a petition is presented, a member may, with notice, move

---

[1] s. 5, PBSO 190, s. 4.

[2] s. 6, 10–12, 14, 17, GO 73–115, s. 8.

[3] s. 7(2).

[4] s. 9.

immediately after second reading to refer the bill to a joint committee, which broadly follows the procedure of a select committee on an opposed private bill.[1] Such a motion is rare. If such a motion is agreed to in the House of Commons and the bill is passed by that House, then in the House of Lords the bill proceeds straight from second reading to third reading.[2] If no such motion is agreed to, then, if the bill was introduced in the Lords, it proceeds from second reading to consideration on report; if the bill was introduced in the Commons, it proceeds in the Lords straight from first reading to consideration on report.

9.105 Because Scottish provisional order confirmation bills are not printed in the House of Lords, the ministerial statement of compatibility with the Convention rights under section 19 of the Human Rights Act 1998 is made by means of a written statement.

## Transport and Works Act 1992

9.106 Under the Transport and Works Act 1992, projects such as railways, tramways, harbours and barrages no longer come before Parliament for approval by way of private bill, but are dealt with by ministerial orders, in most cases following local public inquiries. Such orders are not normally subject to parliamentary proceedings, but may be deposited in the libraries of both Houses for information. However, section 9 of the Act provides that schemes which are adjudged by the Secretary of State to be of national significance must be approved by each House on a motion moved by a minister before an order is made to give effect to the scheme. In practice such a motion precedes any local public inquiry.

9.107 Motions take the following form:

> *"The Lord X to move that, pursuant to section 9 of the Transport and Works Act 1992, this House approves the following proposals which in the opinion of the Secretary of State are of national significance, namely, ....".*

---

[1] PBSO 191.

[2] PBSO 192.

# CHAPTER 10

# DELEGATED LEGISLATION AND OTHER MATTERS

## DELEGATED LEGISLATION

10.01 Acts of Parliament do not make detailed provision for many of the subsidiary and procedural matters necessary to give effect to the policy embodied in the Act. So Acts often confer legislative power upon the government. This legislative power is exercised by means of "delegated" (or "secondary") legislation. Delegated legislation is made most often by ministers but may also be made by other persons and bodies. The statutory basis for delegated legislation is usually a provision in an Act of Parliament, often referred to as the "parent Act".

### General powers of the House over delegated legislation

10.02 The Parliament Acts do not apply to delegated legislation. So delegated legislation rejected by the Lords cannot have effect even if the Commons have approved it. Neither House of Parliament has the power to amend delegated legislation.[1] The House of Lords has only occasionally rejected delegated legislation.[2] The House has resolved "That this House affirms its unfettered freedom to vote on any subordinate legislation submitted for its consideration".[3] Delegated legislation may be debated in Grand Committee, but must return to the floor of the House if a formal decision is required.[4]

---

[1] Except in the very small number of cases where the parent act specifically provides for such amendment, e.g. Census Act 1920 s. 1(2), Civil Contingencies Act 2004 s. 27(3).

[2] The last three instances of the rejection of an affirmative instrument were 18 June 1968: Southern Rhodesia (United Nations Sanctions) Order 1968; 22 February 2000: Greater London Authority (Election Expenses) Order 2000; and 28 March 2007: Gambling (Geographical Distribution of Casino Premises Licences) Order 2007. A motion for an address praying against a negative instrument (Greater London Authority Elections Rules 2000) was agreed to on 22 February 2000.

[3] LJ (1993–94) 683, HL Deb. 20 October 1994 cols 356–83.

[4] Procedure 3rd Rpt 2003–04, 1st Rpt 2008–09.

## Types of delegated legislation

10.03 Delegated legislation that comes before the House consists mostly of statutory instruments.[1] The parent Act makes clear which procedures apply to the delegated legislation made under its various provisions.

10.04 The most common forms of delegated legislation are:

- affirmative instruments[2] which must be approved by resolutions of both Houses if they are to come into force, or remain in force having been made, or which may not be made except in response to an Address by each House to Her Majesty;

- negative instruments which are subject to annulment by a resolution of either House, i.e. have effect unless specifically rejected;

- "general instruments", which may be required to be laid before Parliament for information but are not subject either to approval or annulment or to any other kind of proceedings;

- instruments not laid before Parliament.[3]

10.05 There are also certain "super-affirmative" procedures, which give Parliament an opportunity to exercise a greater scrutiny role than it may exercise in respect of affirmative instruments. Examples include certain legislative reform orders (paragraphs 10.26–10.30) public bodies orders (paragraphs 10.31–10.33) and human rights remedial orders (paragraphs 10.22–10.25).

10.06 Other types of delegated legislation include:

- hybrid instruments (affirmative instruments which, if they were primary legislation, would be subject to private business standing orders: see paragraphs 9.65–9.72);

- special procedure orders (which are required where certain protected categories of land, such as open space land,[4] are subject to compulsory purchase. These orders are subject to private business procedures: see paragraphs 9.73–9.88).

---

[1] The Statutory Instruments Act 1946 defines the main categories of statutory instrument.

[2] SO 72.

[3] Codes of practice and protocols may also be delegated legislation, though in most cases they are not legally binding, and are described as "quasi-legislation".

[4] See Acquisition of Land Act 1981, s. 19(1).

## Scrutiny of delegated powers and delegated legislation

10.07 The Delegated Powers and Regulatory Reform Committee examines the way in which bills delegate legislative power, and also scrutinises legislative reform and similar orders (see paragraphs 11.49–11.51). The Secondary Legislation Scrutiny Committee scrutinises and reports on delegated legislation, including public bodies orders (see paragraph 11.58). The Joint Committee on Statutory Instruments considers and reports on technical and legal aspects of delegated legislation (see paragraph 11.59). The Joint Committee on Human Rights examines proposed remedial orders (see paragraphs 10.22–10.25).

## Negative instruments

10.08 Negative procedure is the most common form of parliamentary control over delegated legislation. Most negative instruments take effect on a specified future date, but some may come into effect on the date they are laid. Both negative instruments and draft negative instruments are subject to annulment in pursuance of a resolution of either House adopted within a specified time limit.

### Amendments and motions relating to negative instruments

10.09 Opposition to or concern about a negative instrument may be expressed in various ways; and a negative instrument may also be debated on a neutral motion.

- A resolution to reject a negative instrument takes the form of a motion that "an Humble Address" be presented to Her Majesty praying that the instrument be annulled.[1] The reason for seeking to annul the instrument may be given, by means of the addition of the words "on the grounds that" etc.[2] Since 1948 the period during which a negative resolution may be moved ("praying time") has been 40 days in respect of either the negative procedure for annulment or the negative procedure for preventing further proceedings in the case of a draft negative instrument. Swearing-in days in either House[3] are included in the reckoning of the 40 days, but periods of dissolution,

---

[1] The procedure is set out in the Statutory Instruments Act 1946.

[2] Procedure 6th Rpt 2010–12.

[3] See paragraph 2.01.

prorogation or adjournment of both Houses for more than four days are not. Praying time in respect of an instrument laid during the recess does not therefore begin to run until one of the Houses sits.

- Critical amendments or motions may be moved relating to negative instruments, inviting the House to call on the government to take action or record a particular point of view, without annulling the instrument itself.

- A negative instrument may be debated on a neutral "take note" motion, either in Grand Committee or in the House.

### Negative instruments in Grand Committee

10.10 Where a neutral motion is tabled in *House of Lords Business* to take note of the instrument, this may be debated in Grand Committee without a referral motion, and no further proceedings are required once the debate has taken place. If another member were to table a prayer or some other substantive motion on the same instrument, the motion inviting a decision of the House, which could not be taken in Grand Committee, would take precedence. A prayer or other substantive motion may also be tabled following the debate in Grand Committee.[1]

### Affirmative instruments

10.11 Affirmative instruments require the express approval of Parliament, or sometimes of the Commons only.[2] The affirmative procedure takes one of two forms, depending on the parent Act:

- A draft affirmative instrument is an instrument that is required to be laid in draft before both Houses and will not be made or have effect unless both Houses agree to resolutions approving the draft instrument (this is by far the most common form);[3]

---

[1] Procedure 1st Rpt 2008–09. While debates on neutral "take note" motions on negative instruments are deemed suitable for consideration in Grand Committee, they may also be debated in the Chamber.

[2] These are primarily financial instruments. The rest of this paragraph refers to both Houses but it must be remembered that some instruments need only be laid before and approved by the House of Commons.

[3] In some cases one or both Houses must present Addresses to the Crown praying that the Order be made.

- A made affirmative instrument is an instrument that is made before being laid before Parliament and which requires both Houses to agree to the appropriate resolutions approving the instrument either (a) before it may come into force, or (b) if already in force, to enable it to remain in force beyond a specified period.[1] The latter is less common.

10.12 Motions to approve most types of affirmative instrument may not be moved until a report on the instrument from the Joint Committee on Statutory Instruments has been laid before the House.[2] Special considerations apply to certain categories of affirmative instrument, such as those laid under section 17 of the Legislative and Regulatory Reform Act 2006 and hybrid instruments (see SO 72 and paragraphs 10.26–10.30 and 9.65–9.72).

10.13 A motion to approve an affirmative instrument must be moved by a minister of the Crown. If the responsible minister is unable to be in the Chamber, another minister may move the motion on his or her behalf.

*Amendments and motions relating to affirmative instruments*

10.14 Opposition to or concern about an affirmative instrument may be expressed in a number of ways (in addition to speaking in the debate in Grand Committee or on the approval motion):

- Members may give notice of direct opposition by means of an amendment to the approval motion, the effect of which would be to withhold the agreement of the House;

- Members may, by means of an amendment or a separate motion, call upon the government to take specified action (but which will not, even if agreed, prevent the approval of the instrument);

- Members may, by means of an amendment or a separate motion, invite the House to put on record a particular point of view relating to the instrument, but without calling on the government to take any specific action.

10.15 It is usual for all such amendments and motions to be debated at the same time as the substantive approval motion on the instrument.

---

[1] Stated in the parent Act and usually 28 or 40 days in duration.

[2] SO 72. The House has agreed from time to time to dispense with the standing order, e.g. 1 & 14 July 1999.

Notice should be given of any intention to divide on a motion or amendment concerning delegated legislation.[1]

## Moving affirmative instruments en bloc

10.16 If several affirmative instruments are closely enough related to justify being taken together, the motions for resolutions or Addresses on them may be moved *en bloc*.[2] It is for the minister in charge, in the first instance, and ultimately for the House, to decide whether groups of instruments qualify for this procedure. An *en bloc* motion may be moved only with the unanimous leave of the House; if any member objects, motions on the individual instruments must be moved separately to the extent desired.[3] Notice of a motion to take instruments *en bloc* is given by means of an italic note in *House of Lords Business* reminding members of their right to object to taking the instruments *en bloc*.

## Affirmative instruments in Grand Committee

10.17 Affirmative instruments may be considered in Grand Committee. No referral motion is required. After the debate has been held in Grand Committee each instrument is approved by the House on a separate motion.

10.18 Motions to approve affirmative instruments after they have been debated in Grand Committee are normally taken *en bloc* in the House. The requirement for the unanimous leave of the House applies as for other *en bloc* motions.[4]

## Orders subject to super-affirmative and other strengthened scrutiny procedures

10.19 Certain parent Acts contain provision for procedures that make orders subject to a form of parliamentary procedure more rigorous than that provided by the affirmative procedure. The most commonly used

---

[1] Procedure 1st Rpt 1990–91.

[2] Procedure 2nd Rpt 1970–71.

[3] Procedure 3rd Rpt 1971–72.

[4] Procedure 1st Rpt 2005–06.

are procedures under the Human Rights Act 1998, the Legislative and Regulatory Reform Act 2006 and the Public Bodies Act 2011.[1]

10.20 The parent Act sets out the precise scrutiny procedure, which varies in each case, though they share some or all of the following characteristics:

- A requirement for the government to consult before laying a draft order or draft proposal before Parliament;

- A requirement to lay supporting documents with the draft order;

- Power for a designated scrutiny committee in each House to determine the level of parliamentary scrutiny the draft order is subject to;

- Power for the designated scrutiny committee to recommend the draft order be not proceeded with;

- A requirement for the minister to consider or take account of recommendations made by the relevant committee, or resolutions made by either House.[2]

10.21 The scrutiny procedures that apply under the various Acts are described in more detail in the following paragraphs.

## Remedial orders

10.22 Under section 10 of the Human Rights Act 1998, if primary legislation is found by a higher United Kingdom court or by the European Court of Human Rights to be incompatible with the European Convention on Human Rights, then "If a minister of the Crown considers that there are compelling reasons for proceeding under this section, he may by order make such amendments to the legislation as he considers necessary to remove the incompatibility". Such an order is known as a remedial order, and is subject to special procedures set out in Schedule 2 to the Act.

10.23 For non-urgent orders, the minister must first lay a document containing a draft order and an explanation of why it is being made.

---

[1] Other similar procedures are found in the Northern Ireland Act 1998 (s 85), the Local Government Act 1999 (s 17), the Local Government Act 2000 (s 9), the Local Government Act 2003 (s 98), the Fire and Rescue Services Act 2006 (s 5E), the Local Transport Act 2008 (s 102), and the Localism Act 2011 (s 7 and s 19). See paragraphs 10.34–10.46.

[2] See Delegated Powers and Regulatory Reform Committee, 3rd Report, 2012–13 (HL Paper 19).

Parliament and the public have 60 days (not counting prorogation, dissolution, or any adjournment of both Houses for more than four days) to make representations; "representations" explicitly include "any relevant Parliamentary report or resolution". The minister may then lay a second draft order. If there have been representations, a summary of them must be laid; and if the second draft order is different from the first, the changes must be explained. After a second 60-day period, the order must be approved by both Houses, and may then be made.

10.24 If the order is declared to be urgent, it may be made before being laid. It is then laid, with an explanatory document. There follow 60 days for representations, counted from the date of making the order. If representations are made, the minister must lay a summary; and, if it is intended to amend the original order, a new order may be made and laid, with an explanation. Both Houses must then approve the original or replacement order within 120 days of the making of the original order; otherwise the orders lapse.

10.25 The Joint Committee on Human Rights is charged to consider remedial orders, and to perform for such orders the functions otherwise carried out by the Joint Committee on Statutory Instruments. Under Standing Order 72, no motion to approve such an order may be moved until the committee's report has been laid before the House. In the case of a draft order, the committee must report within 60 days of the laying of the draft. In the case of an urgent order, the committee must report within 119 days of the making of the original order.[1]

## Legislative reform orders

10.26 The Legislative and Regulatory Reform Act 2006 gives ministers wide-ranging powers to amend primary legislation by order so as to remove or reduce burdens (section 1) or to promote regulatory principles (section 2). The key components of the statutory scrutiny procedure are: (a) the minister recommends which scrutiny procedure should apply to the draft order (negative, affirmative or super-affirmative), though that recommendation is subject to a decision of either House to upgrade the scrutiny procedure; (b) either House may propose amendments to the draft order; and (c) either House may veto the instrument.

---

[1] Procedure 3rd Rpt 1999–2000.

10.27 In summary the procedure is as follows:

- A minister wishing to make an order under the Act must first consult on his or her proposals;

- The minister must lay a draft order before both Houses, with an explanatory document recommending which procedure should apply: negative resolution; affirmative resolution; or super-affirmative resolution (see paragraph 10.30);

- Within 30 days of the date the draft order is laid, either House may require that another procedure should apply—requiring either that that a draft order laid as a negative instrument be treated as an affirmative instrument or a super-affirmative instrument, or that a draft order laid as an affirmative instrument be treated as a super-affirmative instrument.

- The procedure to which the draft order is subject may be changed in one of two ways. Either (i) the designated scrutiny committee in one or other House recommends another procedure, and this becomes the requirement unless, within the 30-day period, a contrary resolution is passed by the relevant House; or (ii) one or other House resolves that another procedure should apply.

10.28 In addition to the statutory scrutiny requirements, in 2006 the government gave an undertaking that the legislative reform order (LRO) procedure would not be used for highly controversial changes, and that an LRO proposal would not be pursued in the face of opposition from the designated scrutiny committee in either House.[1]

10.29 In the House of Lords, the Delegated Powers and Regulatory Reform Committee is the designated scrutiny committee in respect of LROs.

10.30 The three procedures set out in the 2006 Act are as follows:

- Negative procedure (section 16): the minister may make the order unless, within 40 days from the date the draft order was laid, either House resolves otherwise, or the designated scrutiny committee of either House recommends otherwise (and that recommendation is not rejected by the relevant House in the same session);

---

[1] HC Deb. 9 February 2006 col. 1058–1059.

- Affirmative procedure (section 17): the minister may make the order if, after the expiry of 40 days from the date the draft order was laid, both Houses resolve to approve the draft. If, however, the designated scrutiny committee of either House recommends within the 40-day period that the order should not proceed, it may not proceed unless that recommendation is rejected by resolution in the same Session;

- Super-affirmative procedure (section 18): the draft order is laid before both Houses for 60 days, during which time either House may make resolutions, and the designated scrutiny committee of each House may make recommendations. The minister must have regard to any resolutions or recommendations, or any other representations made during the 60 days. After the 60-day period, the minister may decide either to proceed with the draft order without amendment or lay a revised draft which is subject to the normal affirmative procedure. In either case, the minister must lay before Parliament a statement about any representations received. Between the laying of the statement (or the revised draft and the statement) and the approval of the draft, the designated scrutiny committee of either House may recommend that the order should not proceed, in which case it may not then proceed unless the relevant House rejects the recommendation, by resolution, in the same session.

## Public bodies orders

10.31 Schedules 1 to 5 of the Public Bodies Act 2011 list a number of public bodies. Under the Act ministers may make orders, with a view to "improving the exercise of public services", and subject to certain conditions (section 8), to abolish listed bodies (section 1), merge them (section 2), modify their constitutional arrangements (section 3), modify their funding arrangements (section 4), or modify or transfer their functions (section 5).

10.32 Public bodies orders are subject to an enhanced scrutiny procedure, as follows:

- A minister wishing to make an order under the Act must first consult on his proposals;

- A draft order is laid before both Houses with an explanatory document setting out the reasons for the draft order and why the minister considers the section 8 requirements have been met;

- Unless either House, or a committee of either House, resolves otherwise, the draft order is subject to a 40-day scrutiny period from the date on which the draft order was laid, after which the draft order may be approved by a resolution of both Houses.

- Within 30 days from the date the draft order was laid, the designated scrutiny committee of either House can recommend that the order should be subject to an enhanced 60-day scrutiny period, and this recommendation applies unless the relevant House resolves to the contrary.

- The minister must have regard to any representations, resolutions of either House or recommendations of the designated scrutiny committee of either House made during the 60-day scrutiny period.

- After the expiry of the 60 days, the draft order may be approved by a resolution of both Houses; or the minister may make material changes and lay a revised draft order, together with a summary of the changes, before both Houses. Any revised draft order requires the approval by resolution of both Houses.

10.33 In the House of Lords, the Secondary Legislation Scrutiny Committee is the designated scrutiny committee for draft orders and revised draft orders laid under the Public Bodies Act 2011.

## Other strengthened scrutiny procedures[1]

*Local Government Act 1999*

10.34 Section 16 of the Local Government Act 1999 enables the Secretary of State, by order, to modify or exclude the application of any enactment which he or she thinks prevents or obstructs compliance by "best value authorities" with the principles of best value, in particular the duty "to secure continuous improvement" in the way they exercise their functions (section 3). Such orders may also confer new powers on authorities to permit or facilitate such compliance. In summary the procedure for the scrutiny of these orders is as follows:

- The Secretary of State must consult before making an order;

---

[1] A fuller account of these procedures is given in the Delegated Powers and Regulatory Reform Committee, 3rd Rpt, 2012–13.

- He or she must lay before Parliament a document explaining the proposals, and in particular setting out the proposed draft order and giving details of the consultation;
- There is a scrutiny period of 60 days from the date the document is laid, and the Secretary of State must consider any representations made during this period;
- At the expiry of the 60 days, the Secretary of State may lay before Parliament a draft order for approval, accompanied by a statement giving details of any representations received and any changes made to the original proposal laid before Parliament.

10.35 Orders under the Local Government Act 1999 are scrutinised by the Delegated Powers and Regulatory Reform Committee.

## Local Government Act 2000

10.36 Sections 5 and 6 of the Local Government Act 2000 enable the Secretary of State to amend, repeal, revoke or disapply any enactment which he or she thinks prevents or obstructs local authorities from exercising their power under section 2(1) to promote well-being, or which requires a local authority to prepare, produce or publish any plan or strategy relating to any particular matter. The procedure for the scrutiny of these orders, set out in section 9 of the Act, is similar to that for orders made under section 16 of the Local Government Act 1999 (paragraph 10.34). These orders are scrutinised by the Delegated Powers and Regulatory Reform Committee.

## Local Government Act 2003

10.37 Section 97 of the Local Government Act 2003 enables the Secretary of State to amend, repeal, revoke or disapply enactments which either (a) he or she considers prevent or obstruct "best value authorities" (see paragraph 10.34) charging for the provision of discretionary services, or doing for a commercial purpose anything which they are authorised to do as part of their ordinary functions, or (b) make provision for or in connection with such charging. The procedure for the scrutiny of these orders is similar to that for orders made under section 16 of the Local Government Act 1999 (paragraph 10.34). These orders are scrutinised by the Delegated Powers and Regulatory Reform Committee.

*Fire and Rescue Services Act 2006*

10.38 Section 5C(1) and (2) of the Fire and Rescue Services Act 2006 enable the Secretary of State to amend, repeal, revoke or disapply any provision which he or she thinks either (a) prevents or restricts fire and rescue authorities from exercising any power conferred by section 5A(1) to do, for a commercial purpose or otherwise, things that are incidental to or connected with their functions, or (b) overlaps any such power. The procedure for scrutiny of such orders is the same as for LROs (paragraphs 10.26–10.30), except that the ministerial undertakings given in respect of LROs do not extend to the use of these orders.

10.39 Orders under the Fire and Rescue Services Act 2006 are scrutinised by the Delegated Powers and Regulatory Reform Committee.

*Local Transport Act 2008*

10.40 Section 101 of the Local Transport Act 2008 enables the Secretary of State, by order, to amend, repeal, revoke or disapply any enactment he or she thinks prevents or obstructs "Integrated Transport Authorities" from exercising their power under section 99(1) to promote economic, social or environmental well-being in their areas. The procedure for the scrutiny of these orders is similar to that for orders made under section 16 of the Local Government Act 1999 (paragraph 10.34). These orders are scrutinised by the Delegated Powers and Regulatory Reform Committee.

*Northern Ireland Act 1998*

10.41 Section 85 of the Northern Ireland Act 1998 provides that Her Majesty may, by Order in Council, make provision about certain of the "reserved matters" specified in Schedule 3 to the Act. In summary, the procedure for the scrutiny of these orders is as follows:

- Before any recommendation can be made to Her Majesty to make an Order in Council under section 85, a draft order must be laid and approved by resolution of both Houses;

- Before any draft order is laid before Parliament, the Secretary of State must lay before Parliament a document containing a draft of the proposed order and refer the document to the Northern Ireland Assembly for consideration;

- There is a scrutiny period of 60 days from the date the document is laid before Parliament;

- After the expiry of the 60-day period the Secretary of State can lay a draft order together with a statement (i) summarising any representations made during the 60-day scrutiny period, (ii) containing any report made to the Secretary of State by the Northern Ireland Assembly, and (iii) giving details of any changes made to the proposed order as a result of representations made. The term "representations" includes resolutions of either House or the Assembly or a relevant report or resolution of any committee of either House or the Assembly.

10.42 This scrutiny procedure does not apply if, by reason of urgency, the order is required to be made without a draft having been considered and approved as set out above. In this case, the Order in Council is laid before Parliament after having been made and ceases to have effect after 40 days, unless within that period it has been approved by resolution of both Houses.

10.43 Orders under the Northern Ireland Act 1998 are scrutinised by the Delegated Powers and Regulatory Reform Committee.

*Localism Act 2011*

10.44 Under section 5 of the Localism Act 2011, the Secretary of State may by order amend, repeal, revoke or disapply a statutory provision which he or she thinks prevents a local authority from exercising its "general power of competence" (conferred by section 1 of the Act), or which he thinks overlaps that general power. The procedure for scrutiny of such orders is the same as for LROs (paragraph 10.26–10.30), except that the Ministerial undertakings given in respect of LROs do not extend to the use of these orders. Orders under section 5 of the Localism Act 2011 are scrutinised by the Delegated Powers and Regulatory Reform Committee.

10.45 Under section 15 of the Localism Act, the Secretary of State may by order apply, extend, disapply, amend, repeal or revoke any enactment in order either to transfer a local public function from the public authority whose function it is to a "permitted authority", or to make provision about the discharge of functions which have already been transferred. The procedure for scrutiny of such orders is based on that for LROs except that (a) the level of scrutiny is specified in section 19 of the Act, and there is no power for either House or the designated scrutiny committee in either House to change the scrutiny arrangements, and (b) the Ministerial undertakings given in respect of LROs do not extend to the use of these orders.

10.46 Orders under section 15 of the Localism Act 2011 are scrutinised by the Delegated Powers and Regulatory Reform Committee.

## NORTHERN IRELAND ASSEMBLY LEGISLATION[1]

10.47 The Northern Ireland Assembly legislates on transferred or devolved matters, and the United Kingdom Parliament has no part to play in the enactment of such legislation. However, certain matters such as taxation and international relations are excepted or reserved for legislation by the United Kingdom Parliament. The Northern Ireland Assembly can legislate on excepted and reserved matters with the consent of the Secretary of State.

10.48 In such circumstances, section 15 of the Northern Ireland Act 1998 provides that the Secretary of State may not submit for Royal Assent a bill of the Northern Ireland Assembly touching on an excepted or reserved matter unless he has laid the bill before the United Kingdom Parliament. In an urgent case, the Secretary of State may submit the bill for immediate Royal Assent; but he must then lay the Act before both Houses at Westminster. Either way, when such a bill or Act has been laid at Westminster, each House has 20 sitting days within which a motion to oppose the bill or Act may be tabled.

10.49 Under the Act, any such motion must be signed by at least 20 members of the House. The usual rules of the House on adding names to motions (see paragraph 6.50) are dispensed with for these motions on Northern Ireland Assembly legislation.

10.50 Procedure on these motions is as follows:

- When a Northern Ireland Assembly bill or Act is laid before the House, its arrival is recorded in the Minutes of Proceedings, and in a table in the legislation section of *House of Lords Business* entitled "Northern Ireland Assembly Legislation on Reserved/Excepted Matters in Progress". This table shows the expiry date of the 20-day statutory period. If 20 sitting days pass and no motion is put down, the House's involvement is at an end;

---

[1] Procedure 4th Rpt 1999–2000.

- If within the 20 days a member of the House tables a motion to oppose the bill or Act, the motion is printed in *House of Lords Business*;

- Signatures to the motion may be added in the Table Office or the Legislation Office;

- Signatories to the motion are listed in *House of Lords Business*. If further members of the House add their names, they are added to the list. Once 20 have signed, the list is replaced with a total number;

- A signature is required, either on a copy of the motion, or on a note clearly indicating the Lord's wish to be associated with the motion. Fax, e-mail and telephone are not acceptable;

- The master copy of the motion, with a consolidated list of signatures, is kept in the Table Office, and is open for inspection;

- Members may withdraw their signatures at any time, by giving written authority;

- If, on the 20th day, the number of signatories has not reached 20, the motion is ineffective. If it has reached 20, the motion may be put down for a day and debated in the usual way. When the motion is put down for a day, only the name of the person who originally tabled the motion appears on the order paper as the person who is to move the motion. The total number of signatures which the motion has attracted is indicated with the text of the motion.

# EUROPEAN UNION LEGISLATION[1]

*Challenging EU legislation on grounds of subsidiarity*

10.51 The work of the European Union Committee is summarised below (see paragraph 11.53). In addition to the normal scrutiny work of the committee, the House itself possesses certain powers in respect of proposed or recently adopted European legislation, by virtue of amendments to the Protocol on the application of the principles of subsidiarity and proportionality ("the Protocol") which came into force on 1 December 2009:

---

[1] Procedure 2nd Rpt 2009–10.

- The House may challenge draft European Union proposals on the grounds of subsidiarity, by adopting a "reasoned opinion" to that effect within eight weeks of the proposal's transmission to national parliaments. Any such reasoned opinion is then forwarded to the Presidents of the European Union institutions; if enough opinions are submitted by national parliaments or chambers of national parliaments, the institutions are required to respond in the terms set out in the Protocol.

- The House may, within two months and ten days of the adoption of a European Union legislative act, agree a resolution to the effect that the act breaches the principle of subsidiarity, and call upon the government to bring an action on these grounds before the European Court of Justice. The government have made a commitment, in the event of such a resolution being passed, to bring such an action on behalf of the House.

10.52 In either case, it is normal practice that the House's consideration of such a resolution would follow the publication of a report by the European Union Committee, and that the committee's report and the resolution would be debated together. However, it would remain open to any member to table a free-standing motion for resolution, containing a short, self-contained "reasoned opinion", as required by the Protocol.

10.53 The government have made a commitment that they will not support a proposal in the Council of Ministers which has been the subject of a reasoned opinion from either House without first communicating to Parliament their reasons for doing so.

*European Union Act 2011*

10.54 Under the European Union Act 2011, the United Kingdom will not agree any change to the European Union treaties without prior approval by Act of Parliament. Certain types of treaty change (broadly speaking, those which would move a power or area of policy from the UK to the EU level) would also require approval in a referendum. The European Union Act 2011 also specifies certain other categories of proposals which may be made under the EU treaties, which would require each House of Parliament to approve a motion agreeing the proposal; or which would require approval by Act of Parliament; or which would require approval by Act of Parliament and a referendum.

*Scrutiny of United Kingdom "opt-ins"*

10.55 During passage of the European Union (Amendment) Act 2008, the government gave an undertaking[1] that they would take account of the views of the EU Committees of the two Houses before exercising their right, under the Protocol on the position of the United Kingdom and Ireland in respect of the Area of Freedom, Security and Justice, to notify the Council of Ministers of their decision to take part in the adoption and application of proposals within that area. Without the exercise of such an "opt-in" such proposals are not binding upon the United Kingdom.

10.56 The government's undertaking applies only if the views of the EU Committee are forthcoming within eight weeks of publication of the proposal. If, within this time-limit, the EU Committee makes a report to the House on the proposal, recommending the report for debate, the government will seek to arrange a debate through the Usual Channels. The debate takes place on a motion, tabled in the name of either the Chairman or a member of the committee, that the House agrees the recommendation of the committee that the government should or, as the case may be, should not exercise their right to opt in to the proposal. The motion is amendable and may be divided upon.

## NATIONAL POLICY STATEMENTS

10.57 National policy statements (NPSs) set out national policy on particular types of development. Under section 9(2) of the Planning Act 2008, each proposal for a NPS must be laid before Parliament. In so doing, the Secretary of State specifies a relevant period for parliamentary scrutiny. If, during this scrutiny period, either House passes a resolution with regard to the proposal, or a committee of either House makes recommendations regarding the proposal, the Secretary of State must lay before Parliament a statement setting out his or her response to the resolution or recommendations. The proposal is then laid before Parliament again, and is subject to approval by resolution of the House of Commons before being formally designated as a NPS. The final NPS is also laid before Parliament.[2]

---

[1] 9 June 2008. See European Union Committee 2nd Report 2008–09, appendix 1.

[2] Planning Act 2008 s. 9 and s. 5, as amended by the Localism Act 2011, s. 130.

10.58 In the House of Lords, NPSs are normally debated in Grand Committee, for up to four hours. However, this does not restrict the freedom of committees of the House or of individual members to make use of the statutory procedures outlined above. In the event of a motion for resolution being tabled, the usual channels have undertaken to provide time for a debate in the Chamber within the scrutiny period.[1]

## SCRUTINY OF TREATIES[2]

10.59 No treaty[3] may be ratified unless the minister responsible has:

- laid a copy before Parliament;
- published it; and
- allowed a period of 21 sitting days (beginning with the day after that on which the treaty was laid) during which either House may resolve that the Treaty should not be ratified.

10.60 The minister may extend the scrutiny period by up to 21 sitting days by publishing and laying before Parliament a statement to that effect before the original period expires; this can be done more than once.

10.61 If the House of Lords pass a resolution within the 21 sitting days (or within the extended scrutiny period) that the treaty should not be ratified, the government can only proceed with ratification after they have laid a statement before Parliament explaining why the minister believes the treaty should nevertheless be ratified.

10.62 These requirements do not apply if the minister is of the opinion that, exceptionally, the treaty should be ratified without their being met. In such a case, either before or as soon as practicable after the treaty has been ratified, it must be published and laid before Parliament by the minister, along with a statement explaining why the treaty is being ratified outside this process.

---

[1] Procedure 2nd Rpt 2008–09. A similar procedure was applied to the Marine Policy Statement (Procedure 3rd Rpt 2010–12).

[2] See Constitutional Reform and Governance Act 2010, ss 20–25.

[3] This procedure does not apply to (i) treaties covered by the European Union Act 2011, or amendments to the Euratom Treaty; (ii) double taxation conventions and arrangements and international tax enforcement arrangements; and (iii) treaties concluded under authority given by the UK Government by any of the Channel Islands, the Isle of Man or any of the Overseas Territories.

10.63 In laying a treaty before Parliament, the minister shall accompany the treaty with an explanatory memorandum explaining the provisions of the treaty, the reasons for seeking its ratification, and such other matters as the minister considers appropriate.

10.64 For the purposes of these provisions, a sitting day is a day when both Houses are sitting.

# CHAPTER 11
# SELECT COMMITTEES

11.01 The House may appoint committees to perform functions on its behalf. All committees whose members are appointed ("named of the committee") by the House from among its members are select committees.[1]

11.02 A select committee is appointed by "orders of appointment" setting out the committee's remit ("orders of reference"), powers and membership. Typically, a committee fulfils its remit by making one or more reports to the House.

11.03 A committee may be appointed to perform a particular task, on completion of which the committee ceases to exist (an "*ad hoc* select committee"). Alternatively a new committee may be appointed for a specified period, such as the duration or remainder of a Parliament, or to a particular date. A committee may be given continuing existence by being reappointed session by session (a "sessional select committee"); but the continued existence of such committees may be reviewed, particularly at the start of a Parliament.[2] This chapter concludes with a list of the committees currently reappointed session by session, with notes on each.

## Motions of appointment

11.04 A committee being set up for the first time is usually appointed by means of two motions. The first, moved by the Leader of the House, sets the orders of reference. This gives the House an opportunity to discuss the desirability of setting up the new committee, and authorises the Committee of Selection to select members. A second motion is then moved, by the Chairman of Committees, to complete the orders of appointment. Both motions require notice, and may be debated and amended.

---

[1] The following committees are not select committees: Committees of the whole House, Grand Committees, second reading committees, unopposed private bill committees, and committees to prepare reasons for disagreeing to Commons amendments to bills. The Ecclesiastical Committee and the Intelligence and Security Committee are statutory bodies and not select committees.

[2] Liaison 3rd Rpt 2005–06.

11.05 The "sessional committees" are:

- Administration and Works Committee
- Consolidation Bills Committee (Joint)
- Constitution Committee
- Delegated Powers and Regulatory Reform Committee
- Economic Affairs Committee
- European Union Committee
- House Committee
- Human Rights Committee (Joint)
- Hybrid Instruments Committee
- Information Committee
- Liaison Committee
- National Security Strategy Committee (Joint)
- Committee for Privileges and Conduct
- Procedure Committee
- Refreshment Committee
- Science and Technology Committee
- Secondary Legislation Scrutiny Committee
- Standing Orders (Private Bills) Committee
- Statutory Instruments Committee (Joint)
- Works of Art Committee

11.06 For a sessional select committee, the orders of appointment are made on a single motion. The Chairman of Committees may, at the beginning of a new session, move *en bloc* the motions appointing select committees, deputy chairmen and other bodies nominated by the Committee of Selection. Notice is given by means of an italic note in *House of Lords Business* informing the House that, unless any Lord objects, the motions of appointment will be moved *en bloc*.[1]

---

[1] Procedure 1st Rpt 2000–01.

## Instructions

11.07 The House may amend, amplify or restrict a committee's orders of reference at any time by passing an instruction, e.g. to consider (or not to consider) a certain aspect of the matter, to give certain parties an opportunity to give evidence, or to report by a given date. An instruction may be mandatory or permissive.

## Membership

11.08 The Committee of Selection[1] selects and proposes to the House the membership of select committees, with the exception of the Committee of Selection itself and committees on private legislation.[2]

11.09 There is no formal rule on the political balance of committee membership,[3] and in most cases no fixed number of members.

11.10 The Chairman of Committees may propose to the House, without reference to the Committee of Selection, members of the House to fill casual vacancies on select committees.[4] Such motions may be moved *en bloc*, subject to the rules set out in paragraph 3.52.[5]

## Rotation rule

11.11 In order to secure a regular turnover of membership, a "rotation rule"[6] operates in the case of most committees, whereby members who have been appointed (or co-opted) for a given number of successive sessions (or parts of sessions) may not be reappointed in the following session. The House Committee is subject to a five-session rotation rule. All other committees of the House are subject to a four-session rotation rule; the four sessions may be extended to allow a member appointed as Chairman a three-session term as Chairman. The following committees, which meet only rarely, are exempt from any rotation rule—

---

[1] SO 63.

[2] Unless the Chairman of Committees or two or more members of the Committee of Selection think otherwise: SO 63(2).

[3] At the start of the 2010 Parliament the Committee of Selection concluded that the coalition government should not have a majority over the other parties and Crossbenchers on any committee or sub-committee (1st Rpt 2010–12).

[4] SO 63(7).

[5] Procedure 3rd Rpt 2010–12.

[6] Procedure 1st Rpt 2005–06.

- Joint Committee on Consolidation etc. Bills[1]
- Committee for Privileges and Conduct
- Standing Orders (Private Bills) Committee
- Hybrid Instruments Committee.

11.12 The Lord Speaker, Leaders, Chief Whips, Deputy Chief Whips, Convenor of the Crossbench peers, Chairman of Committees and Principal Deputy Chairman of Committees are exempt from the rotation rule.

11.13 Members who leave a committee under the rotation rule are eligible for reappointment after the lapse of one full session.[2] Select committees apply the rotation rule to their sub-committees.

### Chairman

11.14 The chairman of a committee may be appointed by the House on the proposal of the Committee of Selection. Otherwise the Chairman of Committees or, in his absence, a Deputy Chairman takes the chair.[3] In the absence of an appointed chairman, the committee may appoint a substitute. Alternatively, a committee may be given power to appoint its own chairman; this is usually done only in the case of a joint committee.

### Powers

11.15 A select committee may be appointed to report on a matter referred to it. When such a committee has reported, it ceases to exist. Alternatively, a committee may be given power to report "from time to time", i.e. more than once.

11.16 A committee cannot appoint sub-committees or delegate its powers to sub-committees without an order of the House. The maximum number of members on a sub-committee is 12, except for the European Union Committee, for which the maximum number is 14, or where exceptional circumstances apply.[4]

---

[1] Procedure 2nd Rpt 2006–07.

[2] Procedure 10th Rpt 1970–71.

[3] SO 61.

[4] Procedure 1st Rpt 1992–93; Liaison 3rd Rpt 2010–12.

11.17 A committee may be given power to co-opt other members of the House as members of the committee or of a sub-committee.

11.18 Committees are given the power to "send for persons, papers and records". Ordinarily witnesses attend and documents are produced voluntarily. However, the existence of this power means that, should it be necessary to issue a formal summons for the attendance of witnesses or the production of papers, the chairman may put a motion before the committee, that such a summons be issued. The issuing of a summons is to be used as a last resort, and only where a witness has refused repeated invitations, and his or her evidence is vital to an inquiry in progress. Refusal to attend in response to a formal summons would be reported to the House as a *prima facie* contempt.[1]

11.19 Members or staff of the House of Commons, and persons outside United Kingdom jurisdiction (such as foreign ambassadors), may give evidence by invitation, but cannot be compelled to do so. If a committee desires to examine an official of the House of Commons, a message is sent requesting the official's attendance, and the leave of the House of Commons must be obtained. No such messages are sent in respect of joint committees or committees on private bills, nor in respect of members of the House of Commons.[2]

11.20 Committees on private business have authority to hear parties by counsel or on oath but other committees do not have this authority unless authorised to do so by the House.[3]

11.21 An order "that the minutes of evidence taken from time to time shall, if the committee think fit, be published" gives the committee power to print evidence, or make it available online,[4] in advance of its report.

11.22 A committee may be given other powers including:

- power to appoint specialist advisers;
- power to "adjourn from place to place", i.e. to travel.

11.23 Select committees have the power to confer and meet concurrently with any committee or sub-committee of the Commons

---

[1] Procedure 1st Rpt 2008–09.

[2] Commons SO 138.

[3] SO 66.

[4] Procedure 2nd Rpt 2006–07.

appointed to consider a similar matter. Such meetings can be held to deliberate or to take evidence. Select committees may also give this power to sub-committees.[1]

11.24 The powers of committees of the House to inquire into matters relating to Scotland, Wales and Northern Ireland have not been limited formally by the devolution statutes.

## Proceedings in committee

11.25 The quorum of a committee is three, unless the House orders otherwise. The quorum of sub-committees of the European Union Committee and the Lords joining with the Commons as the Joint Committees on Human Rights and Statutory Instruments is two.

11.26 The chairman of a committee has a vote, but not a casting vote.

11.27 Proceedings are conducted in English. However, the use of the Welsh language is permitted for the purpose of committee proceedings held in Wales.[2]

## Participation by non-members

11.28 Members of the House who are not members of a select committee may attend and speak when evidence is being taken; but they may not attend any meeting while the committee deliberates, unless invited by the committee to do so, they do not count towards the quorum, and they may not vote.[3] Members of the House who are not members of a committee or sub-committee do not receive papers on a regular basis.[4]

11.29 For the composition of the Committee for Privileges and Conduct when hearing claims of peerage, see below, paragraph 11.68.

## Recess, prorogation and dissolution

11.30 A committee can sit at any time during a recess, but no committee may sit during prorogation or dissolution.

---

[1] SO 67.

[2] Procedure 2nd Rpt 2008–09.

[3] SO 65.

[4] Procedure 1st Rpt 1992–93.

11.31 Sessional committees, and their sub-committees, continue in the same form, notwithstanding prorogation, until they are reappointed in the next session.[1] Other committees cease to exist at prorogation. All committees cease to exist on the dissolution of Parliament.

11.32 If an *ad hoc* committee has not completed its inquiry in the session in which it is appointed, it may be appointed again in the following session. In this case an order may be made to refer the evidence taken before the original committee to its successor. In the case of a sessional committee this is unnecessary.

## Report

11.33 A report from a committee embodies the text agreed by the majority of the committee on the basis of a draft presented by the Chairman. Members of a committee may not make a minority report. However, members who wish to express dissent may move amendments to the chairman's draft report or propose an alternative draft report. Amendments moved or alternative drafts proposed are recorded in the minutes of proceedings of the committee, together with a record of any vote. The minutes of proceedings are published with the report whenever a difference of opinion has been recorded in a division.[2] Minutes of proceedings are also required to record the making of any amendments to a bill by a select committee on a bill, whether there is a division or not. The minutes of proceedings serve as the authority for the making of the amendments and the reprinting of the bill as reported.

11.34 Where a committee intends to make a personal criticism of a named individual (other than a minister) in its report, the committee is encouraged to consider whether to give notice to that individual.[3]

11.35 When a committee has agreed its report, an order is made for the report to be printed.[4]

11.36 A motion to debate the report of a committee requires notice. Reports of some committees are debated on a neutral motion to "take note" of the report. Other reports are debated on a motion to "agree

---

[1] SO 64.

[2] Procedure 3rd Rpt 1981–82, 1st Rpt 1982–83.

[3] Procedure 4th Rpt 2010–12.

[4] SO 68.

to" the report, to which amendments may be moved. A committee report may also be debated as the subject of a question for short debate.

11.37 The House has agreed that it is desirable that there should be regular debates on select committee reports in prime time.[1] Select committee reports may also be debated in Grand Committee with the concurrence of those concerned. Whether select committee reports are debated on the floor of the House or in Grand Committee, the debate may be time limited.[2]

11.38 The government have undertaken to respond in writing to the reports of select committees, if possible, within two months of publication.[3] Debate takes place after the government have responded, unless the committee wishes otherwise.[4]

11.39 There is no set time limit for government responses to reports from the Delegated Powers and Regulatory Reform Committee, as these need to be made in good time for amendments to be tabled to the bill in question. These responses are made available to the relevant frontbenchers, and placed in the Library of the House.[5]

11.40 A committee without leave to report from time to time may make a special report on incidental matters relating to its powers, functions or proceedings. Committees have used this procedure to invite evidence, or to review their own work over a period.

## Joint committees

11.41 Joint committees of both Houses of Parliament usually have an equal number of members from each House, but this is a matter for arrangement between the Houses.

11.42 The standard procedure for setting up a joint committee proposed by the Lords is as follows. A motion is moved that it is expedient that a joint committee of both Houses be appointed to consider some particular subject. If this is agreed to, it is communicated by message to the Commons, with a request for their concurrence. If the

---

[1] Procedure 5th Rpt 2001–02.

[2] Procedure 3rd Rpt 2003–04.

[3] Departmental evidence and response to Select Committees, Cabinet Office March 2009.

[4] Procedure 1st Rpt 1992–93, as amended 9 July 1992.

[5] Liaison 1st Rpt 1998–99.

Commons agrees then a message is returned which contains the Commons membership and orders of reference. The House then appoints a select committee, on a proposal from the Committee of Selection, and agrees the powers, orders of reference and time and place of the first meeting.

11.43 An addition to the number of members of a joint committee, or a change in its order of reference, is made in the same way.

11.44 Leave is always given to a joint committee to appoint its own chairman. Any power to be exercised by a joint committee must be granted by both Houses. Except where otherwise provided in the orders of reference, the procedure in a joint committee is that of select committees of the House of Lords.

## SESSIONAL COMMITTEES

11.45 The following committees are usually reappointed by the House in each new session. They fall into three categories: first, those on public matters; second, those on private business; finally, the "domestic" committees through which the House regulates its internal affairs.

### Committees on public matters

11.46 The chairman of these committees is nominated by the Committee of Selection, except for the joint committees which appoint their own chairman.

### Joint Committee on Consolidation Bills

11.47 This joint committee is described at paragraphs 8.209–8.210.

### Constitution Committee

11.48 The committee's terms of reference are to examine the constitutional implications of all public bills coming before the House; and to keep under review the operation of the constitution.

### Delegated Powers and Regulatory Reform Committee

11.49 The committee's terms of reference require it to report "whether the provisions of any bill inappropriately delegate legislative power, or whether they subject the exercise of delegated power to an inappropriate degree of parliamentary scrutiny. The committee also reports on "documents and draft orders laid before Parliament under or by virtue of (a) sections 14 and 18 of the Legislative and Regulatory Reform Act 2006, (b) section 7(2) or section 15 of the Localism Act 2011, or (c) section 5E(2) of the Fire and Rescue Services Act 2004; and to perform, in respect of such draft orders, and in respect of subordinate provisions orders made or proposed to be made under the Regulatory Reform Act 2001, the functions performed in respect of other instruments and draft instruments by the Joint Committee on Statutory Instruments." Finally, the committee reports on various other documents and draft orders subject to enhanced scrutiny procedures (see paragraphs 10.34–10.46).

11.50 The committee considers bills (except consolidation and supply bills) as soon as possible after introduction, on the basis of a memorandum from the relevant government department. The committee aims to issue its reports before the bills are considered at committee stage. If time allows, the committee also reports on government amendments if these involve delegated powers.[1] The committee has also reported on delegated powers in draft bills.[2]

11.51 The committee also scrutinises draft orders laid before Parliament under the Legislative and Regulatory Reform Act 2006 (see paragraph 10.26).

## Economic Affairs Committee

11.52 This committee is appointed "to consider economic affairs". The committee usually appoints a sub-committee to examine the Finance Bill each year.[3] The sub-committee examines tax administration, clarification and simplification, and not the incidence or rates of tax. The sub-committee conducts its activities with full regard to the traditional boundary between the two Houses on fiscal policy.[4]

---

[1]  Procedure 1st Rpt 1999–2000.

[2]  Liaison 1st Rpt 1998–99.

[3]  Procedure 5th Rpt 2001–02.

[4]  Procedure 3rd Rpt 2003–04.

### European Union Committee

11.53 This committee considers European Union documents and other matters relating to the European Union. The work of the committee is supported by the scrutiny reserve resolution passed by the House on 30 March 2010 (see appendix L page 271).

11.54 The chairman of the committee is the Principal Deputy Chairman of Committees, and the Second Counsel to the Chairman of Committees acts as its legal adviser. The chairman of the committee is authorised in urgent cases to present the report of a sub-committee to the House on behalf of the committee.[1]

### Joint Committee on Human Rights

11.55 The Joint Committee on Human Rights is empowered to consider matters relating to human rights in the United Kingdom, excluding individual cases. It also has functions in connection with remedial orders (see paragraphs 10.22–10.25).

### Joint Committee on the National Security Strategy

11.56 This committee is appointed to consider the National Security Strategy. It has 10 Lords members and 12 Commons members.

### Science and Technology Committee

11.57 This committee reports on subjects of its own choosing within the fields of science and technology.

### Secondary Legislation Scrutiny Committee

11.58 The Secondary Legislation Scrutiny Committee scrutinises all instruments laid before each House of Parliament and subject to parliamentary proceedings (with certain exceptions). In particular, it is required to draw to the special attention of the House those instruments which are politically or legally important or give rise to issues of public policy likely to be of interest to the House; those which may be inappropriate in view of the changed circumstances since the enactment of the parent Act; those which may inappropriately implement European Union legislation; and those which may imperfectly achieve their policy

---

[1] Procedure 1st Rpt 1973–74.

objectives. The committee may conduct broader inquiries from time to time.[1]

## Joint Committee on Statutory Instruments

11.59 This joint committee scrutinises delegated legislation in certain technical and legal respects. Its terms of reference are embodied in SO 73 and its powers in a resolution of 16 December 1997. It does not consider the merits or policy of delegated legislation. Under SO 72 a motion to approve an affirmative instrument may not be moved in the House of Lords until the joint committee has reported on the instrument.[2] The chairman is, by practice, a member of the House of Commons.

## Committees on private business

11.60 The Chairman of Committees chairs these committees.

## Hybrid Instruments Committee

11.61 This committee considers hybrid instruments in accordance with private business SOs 216 and 216A. The committee rarely meets, reflecting the fact that many bills now include provisions exempting delegated legislation from hybrid instrument procedure.

## Standing Orders (Private Bills) Committee

11.62 This committee considers cases referred to it on a certificate of non-compliance, or on a special report, from the Examiners of Petitions for Private Bills, who certify whether in the case of a particular private bill the standing orders have been complied with. In a case of doubt, the committee decides whether the standing orders have been complied with. In case of non-compliance, it reports whether the standing orders ought to be dispensed with and, if so, on what conditions.

11.63 The parties either appear in person or are represented by their parliamentary agents. Counsel are not heard. In opposed cases, the

---

[1] Procedure 1st Rpt 2005–06.

[2] SO 72 sets out certain exceptions, including legislative reform orders, remedial orders and hybrid instruments.

quorum of the committee is three; but in unopposed cases, the Chairman of Committees normally acts alone.

## Domestic committees

### Administration and Works Committee

11.64 This committee is appointed to consider administrative services, security, works and accommodation, including works relating to security, within the strategic framework and financial limits approved by the House Committee. It decides on requests to make television programmes about the House. The chairman is the Chairman of Committees.

### House Committee

11.65 This committee is appointed to set the policy framework for the administration of the House and to provide non-executive guidance to the Management Board; to approve the House's strategic, business and financial plans; to agree the annual Estimates and Supplementary Estimates; to supervise the arrangements relating to financial support for members; and to approve the House of Lords Annual Report.[1] The Lord Speaker chairs the committee. The Chairman of Committees is a member, and speaks for the committee in the House when presenting its reports and answering questions on administrative matters.[2]

### Information Committee

11.66 This committee is appointed to consider information and communications services, including the Library and the Parliamentary Archives, within the strategic framework and financial limits approved by the House Committee. The chairman is nominated by the Committee of Selection.

### Liaison Committee

11.67 This committee advises the House on the resources required for committee work and on allocation of resources between committees. It reviews the committee work of the House; it considers requests for *ad*

---

[1] House Committee 1st Rpt 2007–08.

[2] Report of the Select Committee on the Speakership of the House of Lords, HL Paper 92 2005–06.

*hoc* committees for particular inquiries; it seeks to ensure effective co-ordination between the two Houses; and it considers the availability of members of the House to serve on committees. The committee consists of 11 members of the House, including the Leaders of the three main parties and the Convenor of the Crossbench Peers or their representatives, together with six backbenchers. The Chairman of Committees is chairman, and the chairmen of the main investigative committees are entitled to attend the meetings of the committee on agenda items which concern them.

## Committee for Privileges and Conduct

11.68 The House refers to this committee questions regarding its privileges and claims of peerage and of precedence. The House referred to the committee two questions of law arising from the House of Lords Bill in 1999.[1] The Committee for Privileges and Conduct also oversees the operation of the Code of Conduct and Register of Interests (see Chapter 5). The committee consists of 16 members of the House, two of whom are former holders of high judicial office.[2] In any claim of peerage, the committee sits with three current holders of high judicial office, who are granted the same speaking and voting rights as the members of the committee. The chairman is the Chairman of Committees.

11.69 The work of the Committee for Privileges and Conduct in respect of the Code of Conduct and the Register of Interests is normally delegated to a Sub-Committee on Lords' Conduct (paragraphs 5.03 and 5.32).

## Procedure Committee

11.70 This committee considers any proposals for alterations in the procedure of the House that may arise from time to time, and whether the standing orders require to be amended.

11.71 The committee is composed of the Chairman of Committees (in the chair), the Lord Speaker, the Party Leaders and Chief Whips, the Convenor of the Crossbench Peers, three Labour backbenchers, three

---

[1] LJ (1998–99) 653.
[2] SO 77; Procedure 1st Rpt 2009–10.

Conservative backbenchers, two Liberal Democrat backbenchers and two other Crossbenchers.[1]

11.72 The committee as named by the Committee of Selection is supplemented by one alternate for each party group of backbench members and one for the Crossbenchers, plus an alternate for the Convenor. The alternates are also named by the Committee of Selection. They receive papers, and are entitled to attend if any of the relevant members cannot, and if necessary to vote.

11.73 The committee appoints a Leave of Absence Sub-Committee, which advises the Clerk of the Parliaments on the operation of the leave of absence and voluntary retirement schemes. The Sub-Committee is chaired by the Chairman of Committees; the other members are the Chief Whips of the three main parties and the Convenor of the Crossbench Peers.[2]

### Refreshment Committee

11.74 This committee is appointed to consider the refreshment services provided for the House, within the strategic framework and financial limits approved by the House Committee. The chairman is the Chairman of Committees.

### Committee of Selection

11.75 In addition to proposing the names of members of the House to form, and to chair, select committees, this committee also proposes the panel of Deputy Chairmen of Committees for each session, as well as the members of any other bodies referred to it by the Chairman of Committees, such as the Lords members of the Board of the Parliamentary Office of Science and Technology (POST)).[3] The chairman is the Chairman of Committees.

### Works of Art Committee

11.76 This committee is appointed to administer the House of Lords Works of Art Collection Fund; and to consider matters relating to works

---

[1] Procedure 2nd Rpt 2005–06.

[2] Procedure 6th Rpt 2010–12.

[3] SO 63.

of art and the artistic heritage in the House of Lords, within the strategic framework and financial limits approved by the House Committee. The chairman is nominated by the Committee of Selection.

### Bodies analogous to select committees

*Audit Committee*

11.77 The Audit Committee consists of members of the House and an external element. The peers concerned hold no other office in the House, and do not sit on any other domestic committee.[1] Membership of the committee and its terms of reference are the responsibility of the House Committee.

*Ecclesiastical Committee*

11.78 The Ecclesiastical Committee is a statutory body, whose proceedings are not proceedings in Parliament; but by a committee resolution of 22 March 1921 it follows the procedure of a parliamentary joint committee. It consists of 30 members, 15 of whom are nominated by the Lord Speaker[2] from the House of Lords for the duration of a Parliament, to consider Measures: see paragraphs 8.220–8.225.

*Intelligence and Security Committee*

11.79 The Intelligence and Security Committee (ISC) is a statutory body, whose proceedings are not proceedings in Parliament, appointed by the Prime Minister in accordance with the Intelligence Services Act 1994. Before putting forward a name or names to the Prime Minister, the Leader of the House consults the usual channels and tables a motion inviting the House to approve the nomination.

11.80 The ISC is required to publish an annual report, and may also publish special reports. There is a presumption that annual reports will be debated in Grand Committee and that special reports will be debated either in Grand Committee or in the Chamber. Such debates are on a

---

[1] Offices 5th Rpt 2001–02.

[2] Under the Church of England Assembly (Powers) Act 1919, as amended by Schedule 6 to the Constitutional Reform Act 2005.

take-note motion (see paragraph 6.55) moved by a Lords member of the ISC. A minister winds up the debate, and the mover has a right of reply.[1]

## POST

11.81 The Parliamentary Office of Science and Technology (POST) provides members of both Houses with information on science and technology issues. It is controlled by a Board of members and officials of both Houses and non-parliamentarians. Four Lords members currently sit on the Board. By practice they include the chairman of the Science and Technology Committee and a member of the Information Committee.

# INTERNATIONAL DELEGATIONS

11.82 Members of the House serve on United Kingdom delegations to various international bodies:

- British-Irish Parliamentary Assembly;
- Commonwealth Parliamentary Association;
- Council of Europe Parliamentary Assembly;
- Inter-Parliamentary Union;
- NATO Parliamentary Assembly;
- Organisation for Security and Co-operation in Europe.

These delegations are appointed after consultations through the usual channels.[2]

---

[1] Procedure 3rd Rpt 2007–08.

[2] On 18 June 1992 the House confirmed this practice in respect of the Parliamentary Assembly of the Council of Europe: LJ (1992–93) 112.

# CHAPTER 12

# PARLIAMENTARY PRIVILEGE AND RELATED MATTERS

### Privilege of Parliament

12.01 In order to carry out its duties, Parliament and its members and staff need certain rights and immunities. These are known as parliamentary privilege. It is a basic principle that parliamentary privilege is the privilege of the House as a whole and not of the individual member[1] and that the protection afforded by privilege is no more than Parliament needs to carry out its functions effectively. Privilege extends to the staff of the House in carrying out their duties and to witnesses and parties attending the House or a committee. But parliamentary privilege does not protect the activities of individuals, whether members or non-members, simply because they take place within the precincts of Parliament. Privilege is intended to protect each *House* in respect of the conduct of *its* internal affairs.

12.02 In general, the House of Lords enjoys the same parliamentary privileges as the House of Commons. These privileges include:

- freedom of speech[2];
- control by the House of its affairs ("exclusive cognisance");
- power to discipline its own members for misconduct and punish anyone, whether a member or not, for contempt of Parliament;
- exemption from Acts of Parliament within the precincts of either House unless there is express provision that they should apply;
- freedom from interference in going to, attending at, and going away from Parliament;
- freedom from arrest in civil cases;
- exemption from subpoenas to attend court as a witness;

---

[1] For this reason privilege of Parliament does not extend to minors or the husbands, wives, widows or widowers of members of the House (SO 83).

[2] But see *sub judice* rule, paragraphs 4.63–4.67.

- freedom from service of court documents within the parliamentary precincts;
- absolute protection of all papers published by order of either House.[1]

## Freedom of speech

12.03 Members need to be able to speak freely in the House and in committee, uninhibited by possible defamation claims. Freedom of speech is guaranteed by article 9 of the Bill of Rights 1689: "freedom of speech and debates or proceedings in Parliament ought not to be impeached or questioned in any court or place out of Parliament". Article 9 affords legal immunity ("ought not to be questioned") to members for what they say or do in "proceedings in Parliament". The immunity applies in "any court or place out of Parliament". The meaning of "proceedings in Parliament" and "place out of Parliament" has not been defined in statute.[2]

12.04 The scope of article 9 has been the subject of two recent developments in the courts. In 1993 the House of Lords decided (in *Pepper v Hart*) that when interpreting ambiguous statutes the courts may look at ministerial statements made in Parliament during the passage of the bill through Parliament. The courts have also established a practice of examining ministerial statements made in Parliament in another circumstance, namely, when considering challenges by way of judicial review to the lawfulness of ministers' decisions.

12.05 In order to prevent abuse, freedom of speech is subject to self-regulation by Parliament. Thus, for example, by the *sub judice* rule[3] the two Houses ensure that court proceedings are not prejudiced by discussion in Parliament.

## Freedom to attend freely

12.06 SO 82 governs this privilege. Traditionally the privilege extends from forty days before until forty days after the session, and it may cover

---

[1] Parliamentary Papers Act 1840. SO 16 provides that the printing or publishing of anything relating to the proceedings of the House is subject to the privilege of the House.

[2] The registers of members' interests and related proceedings have been found by the court not to be "proceedings in Parliament": see *Rost v. Edwards* [1990] 2 QB 60.

[3] See paragraphs 4.63–4.67.

any form of molestation of, or interference with, a member while carrying out parliamentary duties. This privilege covers any form of arrest or detention, except on a criminal charge or for refusing to give security for the peace or for a criminal contempt of court. Notification of any order for the imprisonment or restraint of a member should be given to the House by the court or authority making the order. Such notification is read out in the Chamber and recorded in the Minutes of Proceedings.

12.07 The House has expressed the opinion that privilege would not protect a member of the House suffering from mental illness from detention under the Mental Health Act 1983.[1]

## Attendance as witnesses

12.08 Any member of the House of Lords requested by a committee appointed by the Commons to attend as a witness has the leave of the House to attend, if he thinks fit.[2]

12.09 Members of the House of Lords may give evidence to the Scottish Parliament, National Assembly for Wales or Northern Ireland Assembly if requested to do so.

## Jury service

12.10 Members of the House are liable for jury service.[3] Judges have discretion in relation to jurors with important public service commitments.[4]

## Control by Parliament of its affairs

12.11 Freedom of speech is one facet of a broader principle that what happens within Parliament is a matter for control by Parliament alone. This principle of control by Parliament of its affairs, free from interference by the courts, is often called "exclusive cognisance." It consists of a collection of related rights and immunities. Thus each House has the right to judge the lawfulness of its own proceedings. Unless there is express

---

[1] Privileges Rpt 1983–84.

[2] SO 24.

[3] Criminal Justice Act 2003 s. 321.

[4] Amendment 9 to the Consolidated Criminal Practice Direction, handed down on 22 March 2005.

provision to the contrary, each House is exempt from statute law, e.g. on employment, health and safety at work, and from the regulation of the sale of alcohol, although the two Houses apply many of the statutory provisions voluntarily. Each House has the right to institute inquiries and require the attendance of witnesses and the production of documents. Wilful failure to attend committee proceedings or answer questions or produce documents may be punished by the House.

## Disciplinary and penal powers

12.12 The House's disciplinary and penal powers are part of the control exercised by Parliament over its affairs. Conduct, whether of a member or non-member, which improperly interferes with the performance by either House of its functions, or the performance by members or staff of their duties, is a contempt of Parliament. The House of Lords has the power to punish contempts by imprisonment, fine and reprimand. Periods of imprisonment imposed by the House do not end with the prorogation of Parliament.

12.13 The House possesses an inherent power to discipline its members; the means by which it does so are described in Chapter 5.

12.14 A member can be disqualified temporarily either by statute or at common law, for reasons such as bankruptcy, or the holding of a disqualifying judicial office (see paragraph 1.02).

## Privilege of peerage

12.15 Privilege of peerage, which is distinct from parliamentary privilege, still exists although the occasions for its exercise have now diminished into obscurity. Privilege of peerage belongs to all peers, whether or not they are members of the House of Lords, and also to the wives of peers and widows of peers provided they do not marry commoners.[1] The extent of the privilege has long been ill-defined. Three of its features survived into the twentieth century. The first was the right of trial by peers which was abolished by statute in 1948. The second is the right of access to the Sovereign at any time. The third is freedom from arrest in civil matters; but the application of this aspect of the privilege appears to

---

[1] SO 83.

have arisen in only two cases in the courts since 1945.[1] All privilege of peerage is lost upon a disclaimer under the Peerage Act 1963.

## HUMAN RIGHTS

12.16 Section 6(1) of the Human Rights Act 1998, which provides that "It is unlawful for a public authority to act in a way which is incompatible with a Convention right", does not apply to the House or its committees, or to a person exercising functions in connection with a proceeding in parliament.[2] However, the United Kingdom as a whole is a signatory to the European Convention on Human Rights, and the House is therefore in certain circumstances subject to the jurisdiction of the European Court of Human Rights.[3]

## PARLIAMENTARY COPYRIGHT

12.17 Under sections 165–7 of the Copyright, Designs and Patents Act 1988 "parliamentary copyright" exists in:

- bills;
- select committee reports;
- any other work made by or under the direction or control of either House of Parliament.

12.18 Parliamentary copyright in a public bill belongs in the first instance to the House into which the bill was introduced, and once the bill has reached the second House, to both Houses jointly. It subsists from the time the bill is handed in to the House in which it is introduced, and ceases on Royal Assent, or the withdrawal or rejection of the bill, or the end of the session.

12.19 Parliamentary copyright in a private bill belongs to both Houses jointly from the time the bill is first deposited in either House. Parliamentary copyright in a personal bill belongs first to the House of Lords (since it is the practice to introduce such bills into that House first),

---

[1] Stourton v Stourton [1963] 1 All ER 366; Peden International Transport, Moss Bros, The Rowe Veterinary Group and Barclays Bank plc v Lord Mancroft (1989).

[2] Human Rights Act 1998 s. 6(3).

[3] Compare *Erskine May*, p 301.

and when the bill reaches the House of Commons to both Houses jointly. Acts and Measures once enacted are subject to Crown copyright.

12.20 Literary, dramatic, musical or artistic work made by or under the direction of either House is subject to parliamentary copyright for 50 years from the end of the year in which it was made. Such work includes works made by employees of either House in the course of their duties, and any sound recording, film, live broadcast or live cable programme of the proceedings of either House. The ownership of such copyright belongs to the House under whose direction or control the work was made (or, as appropriate, both Houses).

12.21 The functions of the House of Lords as owner of copyright are exercised by the Clerk of the Parliaments on behalf of the House, and legal proceedings relating to copyright are brought by or against the House of Lords in the name of the Clerk of the Parliaments. Any person may, without charge and subject to certain conditions, reproduce, adapt or commercially exploit parliamentary copyright material.[1]

## BROADCASTING

12.22 The sound broadcasting and televising of proceedings are governed by resolutions of the House of 28 July 1977 and 15 May 1986.[2] The Information Committee has responsibility for supervising the arrangements for, and dealing with any problems or complaints arising out of, the televising and sound broadcasting of the proceedings of the House and its committees. The House has given power to a committee to refuse to allow the televising of proceedings to which visitors are admitted.[3] The Administration and Works Committee considers requests for permission to make programmes about the House. Day-to-day monitoring of adherence to rules of coverage laid down by the Information Committee is delegated to the Director of Parliamentary Broadcasting.

---

[1] These terms are set out in full in the Open Parliament Licence, published online at http://www.parliament.uk/site-information/copyright/open-parliament-licence/.

[2] LJ (1976–77) 820, (1985–86) 331.

[3] Animals in Scientific Procedures Committee (HL Deb. 12 July 2001 col. 1181).

## DATA PROTECTION

12.23 The Data Protection Act 1998 applies to both Houses of Parliament[1]. The Act gives individuals (data subjects) a general right of access to personal information held about them, subject to certain exemptions. It also places a duty on all data controllers to comply with the eight Data Protection Principles (Schedule 1 to the Act). These relate to the collection, use, maintenance, accuracy and security of personal information. The Clerk of the Parliaments has the role of data controller in relation to the processing of personal data by or on behalf of the House of Lords. Under section 35A of the Act[2] personal data are exempt from certain provisions of the Act if the exemption is required for the purpose of avoiding an infringement of the privileges of either House of Parliament.

## FREEDOM OF INFORMATION

12.24 The Freedom of Information Act 2000 gives a general right of access to information held by public authorities, sets out exemptions from that right and places a number of obligations on public authorities. The House of Lords is a separate public authority under the Freedom of Information Act 2000 and therefore has a separate scheme and arrangements for implementing and complying with the Act. The Clerk of the Parliaments has entrusted day-to-day responsibility for House of Lords' arrangements to the Freedom of Information Officer. The Act requires every public authority to maintain a publication scheme setting out the classes of information which it publishes or intends to publish, the form in which it intends to publish the information, and details of any charges. The initial House of Lords' publication scheme was approved by the Information Commissioner and laid before the House by the Clerk of the Parliaments in November 2002; it was last updated in November 2011.

12.25 The Clerk of the Parliaments as the authorised officer of the House may refuse to disclose information on the ground of either parliamentary privilege (section 34) or prejudice to the effective conduct

---

[1] The Act is applied to both Houses by s. 63A (added by Schedule 6 to the Freedom of Information Act 2000).

[2] Schedule 6 to the Freedom of Information Act 2000.

of public affairs (section 36). A certificate signed by him is conclusive of the fact, and a dissatisfied applicant has no right of appeal to the Information Commissioner. Where the Clerk of the Parliaments is minded to refuse to disclose information he may refer the matter to a panel for advice. The panel, appointed by the House Committee, comprises one member from each of the three main parties and a Crossbencher, and is chaired by the Chairman of Committees.[1]

[1] House Committee 2nd Rpt 2003–04.

# APPENDIX A
## DIVISIONS: INSTRUCTIONS TO TELLERS

Within three minutes from the order "Clear the Bar", two Tellers for the Contents and two for the Not-contents must be appointed. Tellers must give their names to the Clerk at the Table, and state whether they are telling for the Contents or Not-contents and in return they receive a wand and a counter.

The Tellers take up their posts in the Lobbies and, once they and two Clerks are in place, may start to count members through the lobbies. The Tellers count the Lords as they pass through, the first Lord counted being number 3, so as to include automatically the two Tellers on each side.

After three minutes the Lord on the Woolsack or in the Chair repeats the Question and, if one or more voices from each side shouts "content" and "not content", says, *"The Contents will go to the right by the Throne, the Not-contents to the left by the Bar".*

If the Lord on the Woolsack or in the Chair does not direct the Contents and Not-contents into the Lobbies, the Division does not take place, regardless of whether or not the Tellers have started to count members through the lobbies. The Tellers should inform Lords waiting in the Lobbies accordingly and return their wands to the Table.

Eight minutes after the Bar is ordered to be cleared, the doors leading into the Chamber from outside are locked, and only those already in the Chamber or in the Lobbies can from that moment vote.

After eight minutes the Tellers must remain in the Lobbies until they are satisfied that all Lords who wish to vote in their Lobby have done so. The Tellers then walk the length of the Lobbies and return to the Chamber by the door furthest from their telling position in order to be able to collect last-minute votes. They inform the Clerk at the Table of the numbers who have voted in their Lobby. To this figure the Clerk adds any votes taken in the House.

One of the Tellers for the majority then receives from the Clerk a paper on which the numbers are recorded. The teller hands this, with a bow, to the Lord on the Woolsack or in the Chair, who announces the figures to the House. The Teller waits by the Woolsack or the Chair until the result is announced.

When the result is announced, the Teller rejoins the other three Tellers who meanwhile have remained at the Table. All four then hand back their wands to the Clerk and disperse.

# APPENDIX B
## RULES FOR THE ADMISSION OF VISITORS

(a) Pursuant to SO 13 and as Agent of the Administration and Works Committee, Black Rod is responsible for security in, and control of access to, the precincts of the House as defined in (b) below in respect both of persons and of vehicles, whether or not the House is sitting.

(b) For the purposes of the interpretation of SO 13 and these Rules, the "precincts of the House" comprise all that area of the Palace of Westminster control of which was vested by the Queen in the Speaker of the House of Lords, with effect from 26 April 1965, as well as all other areas under the control of the House.

(c) Before admission to the galleries of the House visitors may be required:

(i) to sign an undertaking to abstain from making interruption or disturbance and to obey the rules for the maintenance of good order in the galleries;

(ii) to deposit in the appropriate cloakroom all cameras, tape recorders, electronic devices, binoculars, umbrellas and walking sticks, parcels, packages, cases and bags other than ladies' handbags; and

(iii) to open for inspection at the request of Black Rod, or of the staff under his control, any parcel, package, case or bag, including ladies' handbags, which a visitor may bring into the precincts.

(d) In the galleries visitors are not permitted to read books or papers other than the papers of the House, draw or write (except in the south-west gallery), stand in or behind the galleries, or make use of cameras, tape recorders, electronic devices, or binoculars. Any offence against this rule may result in the confiscation of any offending material.

(e) Where committees of the House are sitting in public, the rules governing the admission of visitors to committee rooms are, so far as practicable, the same as those for admission to the galleries of the House. Members of the public are permitted to take notes during committee meetings, and to use electronic devices or tape recorders, as long as they do not cause any disturbance.

(f) Any visitor who is suspected by Black Rod of having committed a criminal offence within the precincts of the House shall be taken into custody and handed over by him to the police for such further action as may be appropriate under the law. Any such action shall be reported by Black Rod to the Lord Speaker or, in her absence, to the Chairman of Committees.

(g) Any visitor who is suspected by Black Rod of having committed contempt of the House, including the contravention of an order or rule of the House, may, at the discretion of Black Rod, either be ejected from the precincts forthwith, or be detained by him until not later than three hours after the rising of the House, or, on a day on which the House is not sitting, for a period not exceeding three hours, in order to enable inquiries to be made into the circumstances of the contempt. If the contempt is of such a nature that, in the opinion of Black Rod, the House may wish to consider it, he shall report it to the Lord Speaker or, in her absence, to the Chairman of Committees.

(h) Any visitor who is suspected by Black Rod of intending to commit a contempt of the House, including the contravention of an order or rule of the House, may be ejected from the precincts forthwith.

(i) The Lord Speaker or, in her absence, the Chairman of Committees shall communicate to the House any report by Black Rod made in pursuance of these Rules.

(j) A vehicle which is causing obstruction, or appears to Black Rod to be endangering security, within the precincts of the House may be removed by him, or by the servants of the House, or by the police on his instructions.

# APPENDIX C
# ROYAL COMMISSIONS

A Royal Commission consists of three or more (usually five) Commissioners, who are Privy Counsellors appointed by Letters Patent to perform certain functions on the Queen's behalf. These functions include:

- proceedings at the opening of a new Parliament in connection with the election of a Speaker by the Commons (see appendix D page 252);

- proceedings at the Opening of Parliament[1] when the Queen is not present (see appendix E page 256);

- proceedings in relation to the giving of Royal Assent to bills (see appendix F page 259);

- proceedings at the prorogation of Parliament (see appendix G page 261).

A minister of the Crown of cabinet rank normally presides. The Commissioners wear robes and (optionally for female Commissioners) hats.

Proceedings on Royal Commissions differ in their details but share common characteristics, which are described in this appendix. Appendices D–G describe the differences.

## Entry of Commissioners

The Lords Commissioners enter the Chamber by the door on the spiritual side near the Throne. They take their seats on a form placed between the Throne and the Woolsack. The presiding Commissioner sits in the centre; the senior in precedence of the other Lords Commissioners sits on his or her right and the next senior on his or her left, the remaining two in order of seniority on the right and left of these respectively.

---

[1] Either a new Parliament or a new session.

## Summoning the Commons

The presiding Commissioner commands Black Rod:

*"Let the Commons know that the Lords Commissioners desire their immediate attendance in this House [to hear the Commission read¹]."*

Black Rod summons the Commons.

The Commons proceed from their Chamber and advance to the Bar of the House of Lords, bowing three times, the first time at the step, the second time midway between the step and the Bar, the third time at the Bar. Each bow is acknowledged by the Lords Commissioners. Male Commissioners raise their hats; women Commissioners do not.

## Reading the Commission

The Commission is read by the Reading Clerk at the Table. He bows to each Lord Commissioner as he names them, and a male Commissioner responds by raising his hat. Women Commissioners keep their hats on.

## Departure of the Commons

The Commons withdraw, with three bows which are acknowledged as on their arrival.

## Departure of Commissioners

The Commissioners, led by the presiding Commissioner, leave the Chamber by the door on the spiritual side near the Throne, and disrobe.

---

¹ These words are added on the first day of a new Parliament, or if Parliament is to be prorogued.

# APPENDIX D

# OPENING OF A NEW PARLIAMENT AND ELECTION OF COMMONS SPEAKER

The election of a Speaker of the House of Commons takes place only at the beginning of a new Parliament and not at the beginning of subsequent sessions.

### First day

On the day appointed the Lord Speaker, in her black gown, preceded by the Mace, enters the House by the Bar and takes her seat on the Woolsack. No prayers are said at this stage. The Leader of the House or another government minister rises and says:

> "My Lords,
>
> It not being convenient for Her Majesty to be personally present here this day, She has been pleased to cause a Commission under the Great Seal to be prepared in order to the holding of this Parliament."

The Lord Speaker then leaves the Chamber by the door on the spiritual side near the Throne, the Mace remaining on the Woolsack. The Lords Commissioners enter, and the Commons are summoned (see appendix C page 250).

> Black Rod summons the Commons with the following words:
>
> "Members of the House of Commons,
>
> The Lords who are authorised by virtue of Her Majesty's Commission to declare the Opening of Parliament, desire the presence of this Honourable House in the House of Peers to hear the Commission read."

The presiding Commissioner says:

> "My Lords and Members of the House of Commons,
>
> We are commanded by Her Majesty to let you know that, it not being convenient for Her to be present here this day in Her Royal Person, she has thought fit by Letters Patent under the Great Seal to empower several Lords therein named to do all things in Her Majesty's Name which are to be done on Her Majesty's Part in this Parliament, as by the Letters Patent will more fully appear."

The Commission is read (see appendix C page 250).

Then the presiding Commissioner says:

*"My Lords and Members of the House of Commons,*

*We have it in command from Her Majesty to let you know that, as soon as the Members of both Houses shall be sworn, the causes of Her Majesty calling this Parliament will be declared to you: and, it being necessary that a Speaker of the House of Commons should be first chosen, it is Her Majesty's Pleasure that you, Members of the House of Commons, repair to the place where you are to sit, and there proceed to the choice of some proper person to be your Speaker; and that you present such person whom you shall so choose here [tomorrow] for Her Majesty's Royal Approbation."*

The Commons and the Commissioners depart (see appendix C page 250).

The House is adjourned during pleasure for the Lords Commissioners to disrobe. The House is resumed, and prayers are read.

The Lord Speaker first takes the oath.

After her, the Archbishops, the party leaders, the Chairman of Committees and the occupants of the front benches, including those used by ex-ministers nearest the Bar, may take the oath, followed by the remaining Lords present.

## Second day

On the second day of the Parliament, the sitting opens with prayers.

The first business is the confirmation, by the Lords Commissioners, of the election of the Speaker of the House of Commons.

After prayers the House adjourns during pleasure to allow the Commissioners to robe.

The Lords Commissioners enter, and the Commons are summoned.

Black Rod summons the Commons with these words:

*"Mr/Madam Speaker-Elect and Members of the House of Commons, the Lords who are authorised by virtue of Her Majesty's Commission to declare Her Royal Approval to the election of a Speaker, desire the presence of this Honourable House in the House of Peers to hear the Commission read."*

The Commons arrive preceded by their Speaker-elect. The Speaker-elect makes a speech to this effect:

"My Lords,

I have to acquaint your Lordships that in obedience to the Royal Command, Her Majesty's most faithful Commons have, in the exercise of their undoubted rights and privileges, proceeded to the election of a Speaker; and that their choice has fallen upon me. I now present myself at your Lordships' Bar, and submit myself with all humility for Her Majesty's gracious Approbation."

The presiding Commissioner then says:

"Mr/Mrs/Miss [and then surname of Speaker-elect]

We are commanded to assure you that Her Majesty is so fully sensible of your zeal in the public service, and of your ample sufficiency to execute the arduous duties which Her faithful Commons have selected you to discharge, that Her Majesty does most readily approve and confirm you as their Speaker."

The Speaker then addresses the Lords Commissioners to the following effect:

"My Lords,

I submit myself with all humility and gratitude to Her Majesty's gracious Commands. It is now my duty, in the name and on behalf of the Commons of the United Kingdom, to lay claim, by humble petition to Her Majesty, to all their ancient and undoubted rights and privileges, especially to freedom of speech in debate, to freedom from arrest, and to free access to Her Majesty whenever occasion shall require, and that the most favourable construction shall be put upon all their proceedings. With regard to myself I pray that, if in the discharge of my duties I shall inadvertently fall into any error, it may be imputed to myself alone and not to Her Majesty's most faithful Commons."

The presiding Commissioner then says:

"Mr [Madam] Speaker,

We have it further in command to inform you that Her Majesty does most readily confirm all the rights and privileges which have ever been granted to or conferred upon the Commons by Her Majesty or any of Her Royal Predecessors.

With respect to yourself, Sir [Madam], though Her Majesty is sensible that you stand in no need of such assurance, Her Majesty will ever *place the most favourable construction upon your words and actions."*

Upon this the Commons and the Commissioners depart (see appendix C page 250). The House adjourns for the Commissioners to disrobe, and afterwards resumes to enable Lords to be introduced or to take the oath.

## New Speaker in mid-Parliament

If during the course of a Parliament there is a vacancy in the office of Speaker, the Commons receive a direction from the Sovereign, signified by a minister of the Crown. A Commission is then issued, and the Lords Commissioners assemble in the House of Lords in the usual way, and summon the Commons, who come with their Speaker-elect. The Speaker-elect makes the usual speech, and the presiding Commissioner declares the approbation of Her Majesty as follows, but the further exchanges claiming the confirming privileges, made at the commencement of a Parliament, are omitted:

*"Mr/Mrs/Miss [and then surname of Speaker-elect]*

*We have it in command from her Majesty to declare Her Majesty's entire confidence in your talents, diligence and sufficiency to fulfil the important duties of the high office of Speaker of the House of Commons to which you have been chosen by that House, and in obedience to the Commission which has been read and by virtue of the authority therein contained, we do declare Her Majesty's royal allowance and confirmation of you, Sir [Madam], as Speaker of the House of Commons."*

# APPENDIX E
# THE QUEEN'S SPEECH

## FIRST SESSION OF A NEW PARLIAMENT

**By the Queen in Person**[1]

The State Opening of Parliament usually takes place in the morning. The Lords are attired in their Parliament robes or such other dress as may be approved by the Earl Marshal on behalf of the Queen. Certain members of the royal family and spouses of members of the House who are successful in the ballot for places are seated on the floor of the House. An enclosure is reserved for the Diplomatic Corps. Judges are seated on the Woolsacks in their robes.

The Queen is met at the Sovereign's Entrance by the Lord Great Chamberlain and moves up the stairs preceded by the Earl Marshal, Lord Great Chamberlain, Lord Chancellor (with the Purse containing the Queen's Speech), Lord Speaker and Lord Privy Seal. They proceed to the Robing Room where the Queen robes and puts on the Crown and regalia. A procession is formed, marshalled by the Earl Marshal, and proceeds through the Royal Gallery and the Prince's Chamber to the Chamber of the House of Lords. When Her Majesty has taken Her seat on the Throne, the Lord Speaker and Lord Chancellor stand on Her right at the foot of the steps of the Throne. The Queen is attended by the Officers of State. The Queen then commands Black Rod, through the Lord Great Chamberlain, to summon the Commons, which he does in these words:

*"Mr/Madam Speaker,*

*The Queen commands this honourable House to attend Her Majesty immediately in the House of Peers."*

The Commons come from their Chamber and advance to the Bar with their Speaker, bowing once only at the Bar.

Her Majesty then delivers Her Speech from the Throne.

---

[1] SO 1.

It is also possible for the Queen's Speech to be read by the Lord Chancellor, standing on one of the lower steps of the Throne in the presence of the Sovereign. This was done during the reign of George I and in the later years of Queen Victoria.

The Queen then retires. The Commons withdraw, bowing once.

### By Royal Commission

If the Queen is not present, there is no State Opening. The Queen's Speech is delivered by the Lord Chancellor, or by one of the other Lords Commissioners, by virtue of the Royal Commission for opening Parliament.

At the hour appointed, usually in the morning, the Lords Commissioners enter the Chamber, and the Commons are summoned (see appendix C pages 250–251).

The Lord Chancellor says:

*"My Lords and Members of the House of Commons,*
*We are commanded to deliver to you Her Majesty's Speech in Her Majesty's own words."*

The Lord Chancellor, remaining seated and with his hat on, then delivers the Speech.

Then the Commons and the Commissioners depart (see appendix C page 250).

A further opportunity may then be given for Lords to take the oath. The Lord Speaker, in this case, takes her seat on the Woolsack and prayers are read. After the Lords present have taken the oath, or at a time previously fixed, the House is adjourned during pleasure until the time fixed for the meeting in the afternoon.

## SUBSEQUENT SESSIONS

### By the Queen in Person

If the Queen opens subsequent sessions in person, the ceremony is similar to that described above for the delivery of the Queen's Speech at the beginning of a new Parliament.

## By Royal Commission

When the Queen is not present, her functions are performed by Lords Commissioners.

The Lords Commissioners enter the Chamber, and the Commons are summoned (see appendix C pages 250–251).

The Lord Chancellor says:

*"My Lords and Members of the House of Commons,*

*We are commanded by Her Majesty to let you know that, it not being convenient for Her to be present here this day in Her Royal Person, She has thought fit by Letters Patent under the Great Seal to empower several Lords therein named to do all things in Her Majesty's Name which are to be done on Her Majesty's part in this Parliament, as by the Letters Patent will more fully appear."*

The Commission is read (see appendix C page 250).

The Lord Chancellor then says:

*"My Lords and Members of the House of Commons,*

*We are commanded to deliver to you Her Majesty's Speech in Her Majesty's own words."*

The Lord Chancellor, remaining seated and covered, then delivers the Speech.

Then the Commons and the Lords Commissioners depart (see appendix C page 250). The Lord Speaker then takes her seat on the Woolsack, and the House adjourns during pleasure until the meeting of the House in the afternoon.

# APPENDIX F
# ROYAL ASSENT BY COMMISSION

At the time appointed for the Royal Assent, if the House is sitting, the House adjourns during pleasure to enable the Lords Commissioners to robe. The Lords Commissioners enter the Chamber, and the Commons are summoned (see appendix C pages 250–251). They arrive with their Speaker. Any supply bills that may be ready for Royal Assent are brought up by the Clerk of the House of Commons, to whom they have been previously returned. The Clerk of the Parliaments receives them from the Speaker at the Bar, and brings them to the Table, bowing to the Lords Commissioners. The Lord Chancellor, remaining seated and covered, then says:

> *"My Lords and Members of the House of Commons,*
>
> *Her Majesty, not thinking fit to be personally present here at this time, has been pleased to cause a Commission to be issued under the Great Seal, and thereby given Her Royal Assent to certain Acts [and Measures] which have been agreed upon by both Houses of Parliament, the Titles whereof are particularly mentioned, and by the said Commission has commanded us to declare and notify Her Royal Assent to the said Acts [and Measures] in the presence of you, the Lords and Commons assembled for that purpose, which Commission you will now hear read."*

The Commission is read (see appendix C page 250).

When this has been done, the Lord Chancellor says:

> *"In obedience to Her Majesty's Commands, and by virtue of the Commission which has been now read, we do declare and notify to you, the Lords Spiritual and Temporal and Commons, in Parliament assembled, that Her Majesty has given Her Royal Assent to the Acts [and Measures] in the Commission mentioned, and the Clerks are required to pass the same in the usual form and words."*

The Clerk of the Parliaments and the Clerk of the Crown then rise and stand at the Despatch Boxes on either side of the Table, bowing to the Lords Commissioners as they reach their places. From the temporal side the Clerk of the Crown reads out the short title of each bill in turn. As soon as each title has been read, both Clerks bow to the Lords Commissioners. The Clerk of the Parliaments then turns towards the Bar,

259

where the Commons are assembled, and pronounces the appropriate formula in Norman French, namely, for a supply bill:

> *"La Reyne remercie ses bons sujets, accepte leur benevolence, et ainsi le veult."*

For each other public or private bill and Measure:

> *"La Reyne le veult."*

For a personal bill:

> *"Soit fait comme il est désiré."*

When all the bills have been thus disposed of, the Clerk of the Parliaments and the Clerk of the Crown bow to the Lords Commissioners and return to their places at the Table. The Commons and the Lords Commissioners then retire (see appendix C page 250).

# APPENDIX G
## PROROGATION BY COMMISSION

### Without Royal Assent

At the time appointed, the Lords Commissioners enter the Chamber, and the Commons are summoned (see appendix C pages 250–251), as follows:

*"Mr Speaker, the Lords who are authorised by virtue of Her Majesty's commission to declare Her Royal Assent to Acts [and Measures] passed by both Houses [and to an Act passed in accordance with the provisions of the Parliament Acts 1911 and 1949], and also to declare the prorogation of Parliament, desire the presence of this honourable House in the House of Peers."*

The presiding Commissioner says:

*"My Lords and Members of the House of Commons,*

*Her Majesty, not thinking fit to be personally present here at this time, has been pleased to cause a Commission to be issued under the Great Seal, for proroguing this present Parliament; and we are commanded to deliver to you Her Majesty's Speech in Her Majesty's own words."*

The presiding Commissioner then reads the Queen's Speech.

The Commission for proroguing Parliament is then read (see appendix C page 250), after which the presiding Commissioner, still seated and covered, says:

*"My Lords and Members of the House of Commons,*

*By virtue of Her Majesty's Commission under the Great Seal to us and other Lords directed and now read, we do in Her Majesty's Name, and in obedience to Her Majesty's Commands, prorogue this Parliament to ... the ... day of ... to be then here holden, and this Parliament is accordingly prorogued to ... the ... day of ...."*

The Commons then withdraw (see appendix C page 250).

As soon as the Commons have withdrawn, the Commissioners rise and bow to the House. The Lord Speaker, if she is a member of the Commission, moves to stand in front of the Woolsack. The Deputy Serjeant-at-Arms (the Yeoman Usher) takes up the Mace from the Woolsack, and the Lord Speaker leaves the House by the Bar. As soon as she has left the House the remaining Commissioners turn right and are led by the presiding Commissioner out of the House through the door on the spiritual side near the Throne.

## With Royal Assent

If at the time of prorogation there are bills ready for Royal Assent, they must be dealt with before Parliament can be prorogued. One Commission is issued for both Royal Assent and prorogation. When the Commons have arrived, the presiding Commissioner, remaining seated and covered, says:

> *"My Lords and Members of the House of Commons,*
>
> *Her Majesty, not thinking fit to be personally present here at this time, has been pleased to cause a Commission to be issued under the Great Seal, and thereby given Her Royal Assent to divers Acts which have been agreed upon by both Houses of Parliament, the Titles whereof are particularly mentioned, and by the said Commission has commanded us to declare and notify Her Royal Assent to the said several Acts, in the presence of you the Lords and Commons assembled for that purpose; and has also assigned to us and other Lords directed full power and authority in Her Majesty's Name to prorogue this present Parliament. Which Commission you will now hear read."*

The Commission is read (see appendix C page 250) and Royal Assent signified (see appendix F page 259).

> Then the presiding Commissioner says:
>
> *"My Lords and Members of the House of Commons,*
>
> *We are commanded to deliver to you Her Majesty's Speech in Her Majesty's own words."*

The presiding Commissioner reads the speech and then says:

> *"My Lords and Members of the House of Commons,*
>
> *By virtue of Her Majesty's Commission which has been now read, we do, in Her Majesty's Name, and in obedience to Her Majesty's Commands, prorogue this Parliament to ... the... day of ... to be then here holden, and this Parliament is accordingly prorogued to ... the ... day of ...."*

The Commons then withdraw, and the Commissioners leave the House, in the manner described for prorogation by Commission without Royal Assent.

## APPENDIX H
## ENDORSEMENTS TO BILLS

### Lords bill sent to Commons

The Clerk of the Parliaments[1] signs the bill and writes on it *"Soit baillé aux Communes."*

### Lords bill agreed to by Commons without amendment

The Clerk of the House of Commons writes on the bill *"A ceste Bille les Communes sont assentus."*

### Lords bill agreed to by Commons with amendments

The Clerk of the House of Commons writes on the bill *"A ceste Bille avecque des Amendemens* (or *avecque une Amendement*) *les Communes sont assentus."*

### Commons amendments to Lords bill agreed to with amendments

The Clerk of the Parliaments writes on the bill *"A ceste Amendement* (or *ces Amendemens) avecque une Amendement* (or *des Amendemens) les Seigneurs sont assentus."*

### Disagreement with the Commons

The Clerk of the Parliaments writes on the bill *"Ceste Bille est remise aux Communes avecque des Raisons* (or *une Raison)."*

### Commons bill sent to Lords

The Clerk of the House of Commons signs the bill and writes on it *"Soit baillé aux Seigneurs."*

### Commons bill returned with amendments

The Clerk of the Parliaments writes on the bill *"A ceste Bille avecque des Amendemens* (or *une Amendement) les Seigneurs sont assentus."*

---

[1] In the absence of the Clerk of the Parliaments, the Clerk Assistant may sign or endorse a bill on his behalf. In the absence of both Clerk of the Parliaments and Clerk Assistant they may authorise any other Table Clerk to endorse or sign a bill on their behalf.

## Supply bill returned to Commons agreed pending Royal Assent by Commission

The Clerk of the Parliaments writes on the bill *"A ceste Bille les Seigneurs sont assentus."*

# APPENDIX J
## PRAYERS FOR THE PARLIAMENT

One of the following:[1]

Psalms 1, 15, 24, 34 (vv. 1–8), 46, 66 (vv. 1–14, 18), 67, 93, 95 (vv. 1–7), 100, 111, 112 (vv. 1–6), 119 (vv. 33–40), 121, 145 (vv. 1–6 and 21).

The Lord be with you.
*And with thy Spirit.*
Let us pray.
Lord, have mercy upon us.
*Christ, have mercy upon us.*
Lord, have mercy upon us.

Our Father, which art in Heaven, Hallowed be Thy Name. Thy Kingdom come. Thy will be done, in earth as it is in Heaven. Give us this day our daily bread. And forgive us our trespasses, as we forgive them that trespass against us. And lead us not into temptation; but deliver us from evil. For thine is the kingdom, the power, and the glory, for ever and ever. *Amen.*

O Lord our heavenly Father, high and mighty, King of kings, Lord of lords, the only Ruler of princes, who dost from thy throne behold all the dwellers upon earth; most heartily we beseech thee with thy favour to behold our most Gracious Sovereign Lady Queen Elizabeth; and so replenish her with the grace of thy Holy Spirit, that she may always incline to thy will, and walk in thy way: Endue her plenteously with heavenly gifts; grant her in health and wealth long to live; strengthen her that she may vanquish and overcome all her enemies; and finally after this life she may attain everlasting joy and felicity, through Jesus Christ our Lord. *Amen.*

Almighty God, the Fountain of all Goodness, We humbly beseech thee to bless Philip Duke of Edinburgh, Charles Prince of Wales and all the Royal Family: Endue them with thy Holy Spirit; enrich them with thy Heavenly Grace; prosper them with all happiness; and bring them to thine everlasting kingdom, through Jesus Christ our Lord. *Amen.*

Almighty God, by whom alone Kings reign, and Princes decree justice; and from whom alone cometh all counsel, wisdom, and understanding;

---

[1] Offices 3rd Rpt 1979–80.

we thine unworthy servants, here gathered together in thy Name, do most humbly beseech thee to send down thy Heavenly Wisdom from above, to direct and guide us in all our consultations; and grant that, we having thy fear always before our eyes, and laying aside all private interests, prejudices, and partial affections, the result of all our counsels may be to the glory of thy blessed Name, the maintenance of true Religion and Justice, the safety, honour, and happiness of the Queen, the publick wealth, peace and tranquillity of the Realm, and the uniting and knitting together of the hearts of all persons and estates within the same, in true Christian Love and Charity one towards another, through Jesus Christ our Lord and Saviour. *Amen.*

One of the following:[1]

Almighty God, give us grace that we may cast away the works of darkness, and put upon us the armour of light, now in the time of this mortal life, in which thy Son Jesus Christ came to visit us in great humility; that in the last day, when he shall come again in his glorious Majesty, to judge both the quick and the dead, we may rise to the life immortal; through him who liveth and reigneth with thee and the Holy Ghost, now and ever. *Amen.* (*Advent*)

Almighty God, who hast given us thy only-begotten Son to take our nature upon him, and as at this time to be born of a pure Virgin: Grant that we being regenerate, and made thy children by adoption and grace, may daily be renewed by thy Holy Spirit; through the same our Lord Jesus Christ, who liveth and reigneth with thee and the same Spirit, ever one God, world without end. *Amen.* (*Christmas*)

Almighty and everlasting God, who hatest nothing that thou hast made, and dost forgive the sins of all them that are penitent: Create and make in us new and contrite hearts, that we worthily lamenting our sins, and acknowledging our wretchedness, may obtain of thee, the God of all mercy, perfect remission and forgiveness; through Jesus Christ our Lord. *Amen.* (*Lent*)

Almighty God, who through thine only-begotten Son Jesus Christ hast overcome death, and opened unto us the gate of everlasting life: We humbly beseech thee, that as by thy special grace preventing us thou dost put into our minds good desires, so by thy continual help we may bring

---

[1] Procedure 3rd Rpt 2012–13.

the same to good effect; through Jesus Christ our Lord, who liveth and reigneth with thee and the Holy Ghost, ever one God, world without end. *Amen. (Easter)*

God, who of old time didst teach the hearts of thy faithful people, by the sending to them the light of thy Holy Spirit; Grant us by the same Spirit to have a right judgement in all things, and evermore to rejoice in his holy comfort; through the merits of Christ Jesus our Saviour, who liveth and reigneth with thee, in the unity of the same Spirit, one God, world without end. *Amen. (Pentecost and general)*

Prevent us, O Lord, in all our doings, with thy most gracious favour, and further us with thy continual help, that in all our works begun, continued, and ended in thee, we may glorify thy Holy Name, and finally by thy mercy obtain everlasting Life, through Jesus Christ our Lord. *Amen.* *(General)*


*The Grace of our Lord Jesus Christ, and the love of God, and the fellowship of the Holy Ghost, be with us all evermore. Amen.*

# APPENDIX K
# INTRODUCTIONS

The Lord Speaker sits on the Woolsack, wearing court dress and a black gown. In the absence of the Lord Speaker, a Deputy Speaker wearing a parliamentary robe occupies the Woolsack.

The newly created peer and two supporters, all in their Parliament robes,[1] with Garter Principal King of Arms[2] and Black Rod, assemble in the Peers' Lobby. Garter and Black Rod are sometimes represented by deputies. A procession is formed, which enters the Chamber in the following order:

1. Black Rod
2. Garter, carrying the peer's Letters Patent
3. junior supporter
4. new peer, carrying his or her writ of summons
5. senior supporter.

At the Bar each member of the procession bows in turn to the Cloth of Estate. They enter the House on the temporal side and proceed towards the Table.

Black Rod passes in front of the Cross Benches, goes behind the Clerks' seats and stands on the spiritual side. Garter hands the new peer's Letters Patent to the Reading Clerk who has taken up a position by the first gangway on the temporal side. Garter then proceeds behind the Clerks' seats and stands next to Black Rod.

The junior supporter moves down the temporal side to a position beyond the Table by the second gangway. The Reading Clerk, the new peer and the senior supporter follow the junior supporter. On arrival at the Table, when the Reading Clerk has reached the Despatch Box, the procession halts and turns inwards. The new peer hands his or her writ of summons to the Reading Clerk.

---

[1] Knights of Orders also wear their Collars.

[2] Under SO 4, the Heralds may not charge a Lord any fee upon his introduction into the House.

The Reading Clerk reads the Letters Patent and administers the oath of allegiance or the solemn affirmation to the new peer, who then signs the Test Roll upon the Table. The new peer then signs an undertaking to abide by the House of Lords Code of Conduct.

The new peer and the supporters then process in front of the Cross Benches and turn to face the Woolsack: the senior supporter on the spiritual side, the new peer in the centre and the junior supporter on the temporal side. Meanwhile, Black Rod and Garter have moved to the spiritual side of the House between the Table and the government front bench, facing the three peers. Together, the new peer and the supporters bow to the Cloth of Estate.

The procession then moves up the spiritual side of the House towards the Woolsack, with Black Rod leading, followed by Garter, the senior supporter, the new peer and the junior supporter. On reaching the Woolsack, the new peer shakes hands with the Lord Speaker. The procession passes into the Prince's Chamber through the door on the spiritual side of the House.

The new peer and the two supporters, without robes, then return to the Chamber, and the new peer sits for the first time in that part of the House where he or she intends to sit in the future.

## Lords Spiritual

The ceremony of introduction of an archbishop or bishop is broadly the same as for Lords Temporal, but Lords Spiritual are not preceded by Garter or Black Rod and have no Letters Patent to present.

The new bishop, in his episcopal robes (white rochet with black bands, black chimere and scarf) and carrying his writ of summons, enters the Chamber, preceded and followed by a supporting bishop, the junior in front and the senior behind, likewise in their robes.

At the Bar the three bishops bow in turn to the Cloth of Estate. They then enter the House, on the temporal side, and proceed towards the Table. The junior bishop moves to a position beyond the Table by the second gangway. The new bishop hands his writ to the Reading Clerk who has moved from the first gangway to the Table. The senior bishop halts by the first gangway.

The Reading Clerk reads the writ and administers the oath of allegiance to the bishop, who then signs the Test Roll upon the Table.

The bishop then signs an undertaking to abide by the House of Lords Code of Conduct.

The new bishop and his supporters then process in front of the Cross Benches and turn to face the Woolsack: the senior bishop on the spiritual side, the new bishop in the centre and the junior bishop on the temporal side. Together, they bow to the Cloth of Estate.

The three bishops then move up the spiritual side of the House towards the Woolsack. On reaching the Woolsack, the new bishop shakes hands with the Lord Speaker. The three bishops then immediately[1] take their seats on the appropriate bench, led by the junior bishop.

---

[1] Unlike new Lords temporal, who exit the Chamber, disrobe and then return to take their seat upon the appropriate bench.

# APPENDIX L
## SCRUTINY RESERVE RESOLUTION RELATING TO THE WORK OF THE EUROPEAN UNION COMMITTEE

(30 March 2010)

The House has resolved:

That—

(1) Subject to paragraph (5) below, no Minister of the Crown shall give agreement in the Council or the European Council in relation to any document subject to the scrutiny of the European Union Committee in accordance with its terms of reference, while the document remains subject to scrutiny.

(2) A document remains subject to scrutiny if—

(a) the European Union Committee has made a report in relation to the document to the House for debate, but the debate has not yet taken place; or

(b) in any case, the Committee has not indicated that it has completed its scrutiny.

(3) Agreement in relation to a document means agreement whether or not a formal vote is taken, and includes in particular—

(a) agreement to a programme, plan or recommendation for European Union legislation;

(b) political agreement;

(c) agreement to a general approach;

(d) in the case of a proposal on which the Council acts in accordance with the procedure referred to in Article 289(1) of the Treaty on the Functioning of the European Union (the ordinary legislative procedure), agreement to the Council's position at first reading, to its position at second reading, or to a joint text; and

(e) in the case of a proposal on which the Council acts in accordance with Article 289(2) of the Treaty on the Functioning of the European Union (a special legislative procedure), agreement to a Council position.

(4) Where the Council acts by unanimity, abstention shall be treated as giving agreement.

(5) The Minister concerned may give agreement in relation to a document which remains subject to scrutiny—

    (a) if he considers that it is confidential, routine or trivial, or is substantially the same as a proposal on which scrutiny has been completed;

    (b) if the European Union Committee has indicated that agreement need not be withheld pending completion of scrutiny; or

    (c) if the Minister decides that, for special reasons, agreement should be given; but he must explain his reasons—

        i. in every such case, to the European Union Committee at the first opportunity after reaching his decision; and

        ii. if that Committee has made a report for debate in the House, to the House at the opening of the debate on the report.

# INDEX

ISBN 978-0-10-855030-0

PEFC
PEFC/16-33-622

Printed in the United Kingdom by The Stationery Office Limited
1/2013   26556   19585